Advance Prai_

"You hold in your hand a work of practical wisdom that will open the door to the empowered life. No gimmicks, no tricks, no shortcuts to a better and more prosperous life and ministry will be found in this book. Rather, what you will find is a solidly Biblical work from a man that seeks to live out what he preaches as a forgiven and transformed son that longs to live, love and lead like Jesus in the fullness, power and joy of the Holy Spirit. Hansen invites you to join him in this journey to live as an empowered son or daughter. He wants us to know that there is so much more to this life in Christ. Hansen provides the key to the victorious life as daily surrender that is "filled to flow". He writes: "If you're filled with the Spirit, the flesh gets defeated, and the fruit of the Spirit grows!" You will find this book to be a river of hope and refreshing, providing you with renewed energy, resolving the dryness of your soul, bringing healing to the broken places as the refreshing and empowering presence of the person of the Holy Spirit energizes you and fills you to flow in Him and with Him for the glory and expansion of the Kingdom of God."

-Mike Chong Perkinson
Pastor / Author / Consultant/ Life Coach Superintendent of the PCJC Network of the Free Methodist Church, USA
Co-Founder and Senior Developer of The Praxis Center for Church Development; President and Dean of Church & Ministry at Trivium Institute of Leader Development

"Filled to Flow is a desperately needed and masterful gift that effectively addresses the power deficiency in the church. On the subject of the person, work, and ministry of the Holy Spirit, there is no one I know more trustworthy, insightful, balanced, and biblical than Pastor John Hansen. His life and ministry dynamically exemplify all he writes here. With compelling clarity, engaging style, and deep insights, John leads us on a journey to greater fullness and overflowing impact. *Filled to Flow* demystifies and makes accessible what often seems ethereal and out of reach. Every Christian, and especially every leader, needs to make this "a must-read many times." Our spiritual landscape is a desert, and the church must indeed be *filled to flow."*

-Dr. Larry Walkemeyer
Director of Equipping and Spiritual Engagement - Exponential Strategic Catalyst for Multiplication Free Methodist Church USA

From the moment I started reading this book, I could feel the passion and authenticity behind John Hansen's words. His journey of leading a church and discovering what it truly means to live 'filled to flow' resonated deeply with me. It's not just a story of growth; it's a testimony of surrender, obedience, and the transformative power of the Holy Spirit. John's ability to weave his personal experiences with practical teaching makes this book both inspiring and accessible. Through clear insights and Spirit-led activations, he invites us to embrace the gifts of the Spirit and step into a life of purpose and power. This isn't just another book about the Holy Spirit—it's an invitation to experience revival personally and see it ripple into every area of life.

If you're longing to encounter God in a fresh way and to live a life of Spirit-filled impact, this book will guide you every step of the way. I'm so grateful for the way it's challenged and equipped me, and I know it will do the same for you.

-Jeff T. Osborne
Speaker, Author, and CEO of God Morning LLC
https://www.jefftosborne.com/

"John Hansen is a true authority on integrating the Spirit into one's life. He has been a spiritual mentor not only to me personally but also to our organization, Rise Up Kings. His work has played a pivotal role in transforming thousands of lives through spiritual development. This book is a powerful resource for understanding the Holy Spirit and includes practical tools and prompts to facilitate spiritual transformation. Game-changing!"

-Skylar Lewis
*Founder and President of RISE UP KINGS - **www.riseupkings.com***
Author of The 2-Day-CEO

"Jesus said that those who believe in Him would do the works He did (see John 14:12), and having a coach to show you the way can make all the difference. That's exactly what John Hansen offers in his new book, Filled to Flow. As I read, I was deeply inspired by John's pastoral gift, through which he tenderly guides readers into a deeper understanding of walking with the Spirit and flowing in His gifts. This book is rich with theology, inspiring illustrations, and powerful activations that are sure to jump-start your journey in the flow! If you're looking for a guide to lead you into the deeper waters of the Spirit, look no further. I'm confident that as you read this book, you'll be equipped, empowered, and activated to live like Jesus and flow with the Holy Spirit."

-**Andrew Hopkins**
Revivalist, Prophetic Worship Leader, Author
Breaker Ministries, San Diego, CA
www.breakerministries.com

"The book of Revelation repeats seven times in two chapters: "Let anyone who has an ear listen to what the Spirit is saying to the churches." Pastor John Hansen has that ear, and *Filled to Flow* is what the Spirit says to the Church. Having worked for and been mentored by John Hansen for the last fifteen years, I have often mentioned his need to write the recipe for his secret sauce. *Filled to Flow* is that recipe. This book invites everyday Christians and Church leaders to "Say hello to the Holy Spirit" (Hansen 14) and move beyond passivity into a life of bold, Spirit-led responding. I love this book and believe in its author!"

-**Mike Wilson**
Lead Pastor Sage Hills Church - sagehillschurch.com
Superintendent of Reach Conference - reachfmc.com

"If there is one challenge that has consistently plagued the church throughout history, it's the gap between learning and doing. In "Filled to Flow," John Hansen, a visionary leader whose pastoral heart and authentic faith have inspired countless lives, bridges this gap in regards to the Holy Spirit. I have seen firsthand how John's leadership transforms into action, and this book captures that same spirit. This is an invitation to not just learn about the Holy Spirit but to also experience the Holy Spirit. Whether you are a church leader looking to guide your congregation or an individual curious about the Holy Spirit and spiritual gifts, have daily encounters with the Holy Spirit, or have only heard about the Holy Spirit and never had an experience, "Filled to Flow" provides the balance in understanding and activation that we, the Church, desperately need."

-Jon Sato
Superintendent, Free Methodist Church of Southern California

"Filled to Flow is a powerful invitation to respond to the most intimate call of God—a call to enter and participate in His perfect communion. John Hansen sincerely guides readers beyond the endless pursuit of 'trying to do better,' shifting the focus to the transformative work of the Holy Spirit in and through us. This book is a profound resource for anyone longing to live a Spirit-filled life of purpose and impact."

-Yoel Bartolome
Founder/CEO Monarch 246

"John Hansen is one of the most powerful men of prayer I have ever known, and he has been so for as long as I've known him—over 25 years now. We attended seminary together in the late 90s, and I could tell stories from those days of how John's prayers changed circumstances and released miracles. When John writes about the power, presence, and gifts of the Holy Spirit, he is not presenting mere theory or academic assertions; he is sharing what he lives.

Reading Filled to Flow was both a joy and a challenge to me. I was deeply impressed that, after all these years, John still overflows with confidence and expectation in the life-transforming power of the Holy Spirit to save, fill, heal, deliver, and empower. Filled to Flow is worth reading because it is a rich compendium of all that John has seen the Lord accomplish through his life and ministry. Even more, it serves as an invitation for us to step into that same flow of the Holy Spirit, so we too can live in the fullness of God's empowering presence."

-Benjamin Robinson
Author, Mentor, Coach + Creative
Senior Pasto, Lineage Church
https://www.lineage.us/

"If you've ever thought to yourself, "There must be more to my Christian walk," this book is for you. Filled To Flow by John Hansen is a powerful invitation to encounter the Holy Spirit in a fresh, personal way. More than concepts or ideas, this book activates faith and invites the reader to step deeper into God's presence. With great clarity and biblical grounding, John shares practical insights drawn from his own journey as a Christ-follower and transformational leader. His vulnerability and passion shine through, offering not just knowledge but a lived experience of God's power. This book inspires and equips believers to live filled and overflowing with the Spirit. I highly recommend "Filled To Flow" to anyone longing for renewal and a closer walk with God."

-Brett Masters
Executive Director & Lead Pastor
Dream Center Lake Elsinore – www.DreamCenterLE.org

"I've gone to a lot of conferences, read countless books and explored diverse church traditions in my pursuit of the Holy Spirit. It can be confusing and even disheartening. In *Filled to Flow*, Pastor John has provided the best resource I know of to help people understand and get activated in the Holy Spirit. He provides solid Biblical grounding, actionable guidance, and most of all, inspires faith through his own vibrant, lived-out experience of the Holy Spirit. If you're feeling spiritually dry and want to experience God in a powerful and dynamic way through the Holy Spirit, I wholeheartedly recommend reading *Filled to Flow*."

-Rev. Dr. Stephen Kim
UTS Randy Clark Scholars Doctorate Alumnus
Ordained Elder in the United Methodist Church

"I've known John Hansen for a little bit over 20 years and have been mentored by his pastoral leadership and his journey in leading his congregation and many others into the rich beauty of Holy Spirit's encounters. I am not surprised but delighted in how FILLED TO FLOW reveals Holy Spirit with ease and clarity. Each chapter feels like an invitation to understand so many questions that often accompany engaging the Holy Spirit. However, what has been needed for so long are the Activation sections, that can help individuals and groups begin to practice what they just read. It is evident that FILLED TO FLOW is written by a true practitioner with a shepherd's heart. I was encouraged when I read in Chapter 3 that "gifts of the spirit are a vital element of life in God's Kingdom – even the 'wild and crazy ones'!" Yes, they are and always have been. FILLED TO FLOW is a reliable guide written by a reliable source to equip the Church for the next Spirit-fueled movement. FILLED TO FLOW is a thorough, balanced exploration to living and ministering in the beauty of Holy Spirit. This is a great book to establish a church's biblical practice, ministry, and discipleship regarding the Holy Spirit doctrine and practice."

-Charles Latchison
Sr. Pastor, Light & Life West Church, Long Beach, CA

"John Hansen is not only a gifted pastor and leader but also a passionate teacher with a deep heart for equipping believers to live Spirit-filled lives. In *Filled to Flow*, he brings clarity, wisdom, and biblical insight to the often-misunderstood topic of the Holy Spirit. This book serves as a powerful and practical introduction to the Spirit-filled life, offering both theological grounding and hands-on activations that will help readers experience the Spirit's power personally. With spiritual activations and chapter-based Bible studies, *Filled to Flow* is more than a book—it's a resource for individuals and small groups eager to step into a deeper relationship with the Holy Spirit. John's approachable style and genuine heart shine through every page, making this a must-read for anyone longing to discover the adventure of living in the Spirit. If you're ready to move from curiosity to activation, this book is for you."

-Brenda Palmer
Author, Preacher, + Host of Life in Perspective Podcast

"I've had the privilege of serving in ministry with John Hansen for over a decade, and his life has been a constant source of encouragement and inspiration to me. It's clear that John has spent years cultivating a deep intimacy with God, with a heart that overflows in prayer and worship. His prophetic insight has been a personal blessing to me time and again. John's ministry creates a unique atmosphere where the presence of the Holy Spirit is honored, and I've had profound encounters with God in his services. In a time when many churches have traded spiritual depth for routine, lifeless rituals, and performance, we desperately need more of the Holy Spirit's presence—something John's message in Filled to Flow powerfully addresses. This book is a timely and essential resource for the body of Christ, guiding us back from dry religion to a vibrant, life-giving relationship with God. When I first heard about the book, I knew it would be a tool to help us rediscover the transforming power of the Holy Spirit in our churches. Filled to Flow is exactly what the church—and I—need right now."

Aeron Brown
Artist in Residence, Saddleback Church
www.aeronbrown.art

This book is certified organic human writing, not the work of AI-generated production. It is a human creation. There is no AI authorship in this book. I wrote it!
- John Voris Hansen

FILLED

TO

FLOW

FILLED

TO

FLOW

HOW TO LIVE OUT THE SPIRIT-FILLED LIFE!

JOHN VORIS HANSEN

Disclaimer:

This publication is designed to provide accurate and authoritative information in regard to the subject matter covered. It is sold with the understanding that neither the author nor the publisher is engaged in rendering legal, psychological or other professional services. While the publisher and author have used their best efforts in preparing this book, they make no representations or warranties with respect to the accuracy or completeness of the contents of this book and expressly disclaim any implied warranties of merchantability or fitness for a particular purpose. The advice and strategies contained herein may not be suitable for your situation. You should consult with a professional when appropriate. Neither the publisher nor the author shall be liable for any loss of profit or any other commercial damages, including but not limited to special, incidental, consequential, personal, or other damages.

Paperback ISBN: 979-8-9923081-0-5

E-BOOK ISBN: 979-8-9923081-1-2

LCCN # 2024927577

Edited by: Sarah Davila

Cover designed by: by Caleb Linden

Printed by GROW FLOW SOW in the USA

First Edition, 2025

For permissions and inquiries, contact:

John@growflowsow.com

GROW FLOW SOW

MURRIETA CA, 92562

www.filledtoflow.com

www.johnhansen.tv

Acknowledgments

A book is a labor of love that requires the love and longsuffering of friends and family of the author.

First, I want to acknowledge my wife, Ann Hansen, for inspiring me with her journey of revival and renewal in the Holy Spirit. I want to recognize her for being a listening ear throughout the writing of FILLED TO FLOW. She gave me space countless nights and weekends to pour myself into this work—even though that meant I couldn't give her my first and best attention. Her love, prayer, support, and powerful ministry inspire me to keep moving in the flow!

I want to acknowledge my mentor and friend, Mike Chong Perkinson, who meets with me monthly and more to pour into my life. His insight, support, and his belief in me - and this book - helped to bring it about.

I want to acknowledge other mentors who have supported me and believed in me as I've endeavored to grow as a leader and author; Matt Thomas, Larry Walkemeyer, Richard Aidoo, and Ben Sigman, among others.

I want to acknowledge Dave and Julie Heras, John Bertalot, Chris Cruz, Patty Marine, Tina Nicholas, Keith and Toni Jones, and many more. These friends have been there along the way, giving me inspiration, challenge, and impartation that have helped shape my life and the expression of this book.

I want to acknowledge the many friends and co-laborers who have stood with me along the way: Mike Wilson, Jeff Osborne, Andrew Hopkins, Kevin Boyce, Steve Kim, Shino John, Lydia Ingegneri, Jon Sato, Glen Prior, Brenda Palmer, Brett Masters, Benjamin Robinson, Aeron Brown, Yoel Bartolome, Brian Warth, Skylar Lewis, Shawn & Angel Anton, the Hansons, Charles Latchison, and many more. Each of you has given me the gift of friendship, belief, and support. Thank you for your love and help in many ways!

I also want to thank other family and friends who have supported, loved, and helped me along the way. Mom, Dad (may he enjoy Heaven!); Kristi & Rob - our original Hansen five - from DC to New York, to Georgia, to New Jersey to California - our story is the foundation of God's blessing in my life, and I cherish you. Madison, Hannah & Ed Byers, 이 시어머니와 시아버지 (엄마 & 아빠), Benny & Janice Yu, along with Micah and Charis - thank you all for the sacrifices, the love, support, connection, help and the memories we've made as the family that we are together.

In addition, want to thank other supporters, family & friends - Bill & Shannon Kneebusch, Thomas Christensen, Rodo & Andrea Peregrina, John Edgar Caterson, Jose Gutierrez, Jack Kelly, Tim & Natalie South, Irene & Aaron Capen, Tiah Lewis, Reggie & Diane Wadlington, Jim & Shelley Harris, Mark & Chris Payne, Karen & Barry Robertson, Blaine & Susie Whitson, Rusty & Stephanie Cochran, Alex & Sarah Davila, & Malinda & Jim Margiotta. Your friendship, support, and fellowship continues to bless me. Thank you for being there for me! My apologies to every other wonderful soul I'm blessed to know and enjoy community with - but also, I thank you too! Life and love are found in our connection with one another!

Lastly, I want to thank the staff and members of Centerpoint Church, past and present. Leading Centerpoint Church is my life's work - and you are invaluable to me as Kingdom co-laborers, friends, and partners in ministry to love & lead people to life-changing connection with Christ!

To my family-
Ann, Tobiah, Noah, & Shiloh
May you always be filled to flow in the Holy Spirit!

"My fear is not that our great movement, known as the Methodists, will eventually cease to exist or even one day die from the earth. My fear is that our people will become content to live without the fire, the power, the excitement, the supernatural element that makes us great!"
-John Wesley

CONTENTS

Acknowledgments

Introduction

ONE

HELLO, HOLY SPIRIT!   31

You're filled to flow in the fullness of the Spirit!

In this chapter, you will learn about the person and work of
the Holy Spirit from a Biblical foundation. You will discover the
various ways we may experience the Holy Spirit. You'll be invited to
embrace the goodness of the Spirit of God in total fullness!

TWO

DO IT LIKE JESUS   65

You're filled to flow in supernatural engagement!

In this chapter, you'll discover that Jesus models
supernatural ministry in the power of the Spirit. The Kingdom of
God is what you're made for. He modeled supernatural engagement
as a way of life. He's the model of what it means to be filled to
flow. We're following Jesus in Supernatural engagement.

THREE

ARE YOU GETTING THE DOWNLOAD? 93

You're filled to flow in the prophetic!

In this chapter, you will learn about the gifts oriented around receiving revelation. You'll discover how to get the downloads from Heaven that God may want to give you. You'll learn about the revelatory gifts of the Spirit- Prophecy, Vision, Word of Knowledge, Message of Wisdom, and Tongues - and how to begin to enjoy these gifts.

FOUR

DON'T GET TONGUE TIED! 127

You're filled to flow in the language of the Spirit!

The experience of the gift of tongues can be a key part of your experience of the flow of the Spirit. This chapter will give you a proper understanding of the full range of all that is 'tongues' - and show you how to move toward engagement in this gift.

FIVE

BREAKTHROUGH, THROUGH YOU! 165

You're filled to flow in Kingdom authority for breakthrough and healing!

In this chapter, you will discover the authority you have because of your identity - and how to walk in it. This chapter will help you to grow in understanding of and empowerment in the demonstrative gifts of healing & miracles in and through the authority of Jesus. You'll learn why they are vital aspects of the Kingdom of God and how to operate in them!

SIX

FIGHT FOR IT   209

You're filled to flow with power for deliverance!

In this chapter, you'll see that when you're full in the Spirit, you're ready to face off the demonic realm - for your own freedom and on behalf of others. This chapter will help you discover how to flow in the Spirit's power to bring deliverance and freedom from evil demonic affliction and oppression.

SEVEN

YOU'VE GOT IT; GO FOR IT!   245

You're filled to flow in the gifts of the Spirit!

The grace of God gets shown off through the gifts of the Spirit, and in this chapter, you'll learn more about each one. You'll be invited to walk with an openness into the move of God and to be part of how the move of God is manifest!

EIGHT

WHO ARE YOU WITH THAT FLOW?   275

You're filled to flow with the fruit of the Spirit!

If you're filled with the Spirit, the flesh gets defeated, and the fruit of the Spirit grows! This chapter will deepen your conviction about the importance of character and integrity. You'll learn to cultivate a holy life where the fruit of the Spirit grows and becomes more evident in and through the choices you make!

Epilogue 300

Introduction

Hi! I'm John Hansen, and I'm the author of this book. As the Lead Pastor of Centerpoint Church, I carry a mantle of responsibility for the ministry, leading me to deep prayer times for the church's future. In 2010, I was in Big Bear, California, with a small group of leaders from our church to pray over the coming years and what God would be calling us to do. I sensed in my spirit that this church of approximately 500 people would soon grow five times that size. This time of fasting and prayer was crucial. During that retreat, while walking in the woods and writing in my journal, I sensed the Lord giving me a phrase to mark the course: "Build to grow, filled to flow!" God also gave me distinct marching orders for what that phrase should lead to, practically speaking.

In the following years, we did build two more physical buildings, and Jesus built the Body to become a group of roughly 2,500 people meeting each weekend in four services. Building to grow was about the physical place and the active discipleship of people. For a long season, my Spirit-filled life was a secret. I kept the active expression of many spiritual gifts on the sidelines.

In 2013, that began to change. My wife, Ann Hansen (a powerful pastor and spiritual leader herself), returned from a mission trip in Mexico City with a sense that God was calling her to be a conduit for revival in our church and our city. At the same time, I began to feel a burden to make disciples like the kind of disciple I am: Spirit-filled and flowing!

We had *built to grow*; it was time for the second part of the phrase God gave me years earlier. I was excited to lead people to experience being *filled to flow*. I finally realized that my best contribution in ministry would include sharing the wonder and power of the Holy Spirit with whomever I had the opportunity to disciple through the church I lead. It is one of the primary passions of my life. I love to see people come alive in the Holy Spirit!

Ann and I began to follow the leading of the Spirit to cultivate a more full and dynamic Spirit-filled expression in and through our church. We developed and taught classes on prophetic gifts, healing, freedom, and deliverance. We adopted a posture of expectancy for encounter with God in our worship rather than simply prioritizing polished performance. We established rhythms of life for our church where there is ample opportunity beyond Sundays to seek the Lord and flow in his Spirit. The result is that our church is flourishing as a charismatic, Spirit-filled church. We've sustained a healthy and nurturing level of revival for nearly ten years.

I wrote this book with some core assumptions. The first is that you are already a Christian, saved by grace through faith. If you have never heard this before, Jesus's core message from the beginning of the Gospel of Mark is: "The time has come! The Kingdom of God is near! Repent, and believe the good news!" If you've never responded to the gospel of Jesus Christ, I invite you to do so now, before you read this book.

Repent of your sin, and believe the good news! The good news is that your sin can be totally forgiven, and you can be saved for all eternity. You can be born again - a new person from the inside out. You can receive the gift of salvation; a home in heaven forever after you pass from this life. You can receive the gift of entrance into the Kingdom of God as a redeemed, forgiven, made-new son or daughter of the most high God! If you have never turned to Jesus and asked Him to forgive your sins and save your life, if you've never given your life to Him, do so now!

The second assumption I've made in writing this book is that you are part of a healthy, Biblical Christian Church. The proper context for everything I will teach you in this book is the Church, the Body of Christ. You must develop and maintain your commitment to your local church Body to thrive in your application of what you will learn in FILLED TO FLOW. This book is going to teach you about one particular core aspect of your discipleship. Its not a replacement for the natural discipleship that takes place in a healthy Church Body; it is a supplement to it.

This book will give you a foundational understanding of the Holy Spirit's person and work. I will also do my part to create moments of activation in the gifts of the Spirit. You'll find these moments of activation in each chapter. It's up to you to make the most of them! I am praying that the Spirit will impart something to you so that you will be even more equipped to flow in the gifts of the Spirit.

Even now, would you begin to pray that Jesus would open your heart to the power and goodness of the Holy Spirit? What can you learn as you read this book? I truly believe that God wants to do something powerful in your life through this experience. I'm praying that you will be *filled to flow!*

Looking forward to the journey together!

John Hansen

For pastors and church leaders

For many pastors and church leaders in the non-Charismatic and non-pentecostal Christian world, the Holy Spirit has become merely a name or designation for God rather than a reality to experience. I grew up in the Episcopal-Anglican church - but came alive in the Spirit through the Assemblies of God, Missionary Church, Free Methodist Church, and non-denominational fellowships.

I want to encourage you to use this group with a group in your church. Let your men's or women's ministry use this book and the Bible Study included in each chapter to deepen your congregation's understanding and experience of the Holy Spirit. Consider launching a church-wide message series on being filled to flow. It may even be helpful to go through this book with your elders or Board members.

You can call for a special mid-week meeting to implement the activations together. Make room for the messy middle! In the messy middle, people are learning, trying, and experimenting. By definition, they're not quite getting it, and some new, interesting things may happen as the Holy Spirit moves in new ways. That's good! Make room for it.

FILLED TO FLOW is meant to be one component of discipleship depth. It is not the goal in and of itself. I'm praying for you to have the courage to increase the freedom to encounter the Holy Spirit in your church and express the gifts of the Spirit in your fellowship!

Bonus Content: The Filled to Flow Bible Study

At the end of each chapter, there is bonus content. It's a Bible study that you can do personally - or with a small group. If you want to access small group teaching videos to go with the Filled to Flow Bible Study, visit www.filledtoflow.com, and you'll find content to help you facilitate a small group study with this book. If you want to lead a small group with this book, I suggest that each person have their own copy of the book. Use the small group guide at the end of the chapter as it is written.

The small group guide is highly comprehensive. There are 10-20 questions for each session. That's a lot! If you have two hours, go through every question painstakingly. But if you have a more realistic timeframe, just utilize the seven or so questions marked with this symbol: "≈." You'll find that some of the questions, marked with the " ⧠ " symbol, are bible study questions for reflection. These questions are more straightforward, and answers should come quickly.

For the " ⧠ " questions, it's okay if just one or two people answer. It would also be OK to skip those questions in the group setting for the sake of time. Because people have this guide, they are encouraged to take time with those questions independently. Other questions are intended for dynamic group interaction, and it would be helpful if the group could engage in those questions. Those questions are marked with the "≈" symbol. If you are leading the group, feel free to read through the whole chapter and circle or highlight the questions you think would be most helpful for your group to spend time on.

In each session of your group, there are scriptures to read, questions to engage with, and time to pray. If you are leading the group, read the summary paragraph aloud at the beginning, and then guide the group in going around the circle with the 'read' sections. Let the group know, "We'll go around the circle, and each take our turn reading the scripture aloud before we engage and talk about it."

After the scripture is read, guide through the *engage* sections by reading the question out loud and waiting for people in the group to respond. If people are slow to chime in, suggest someone in particular in the group to offer their response. You could simply say something like, "How about you, Joe? What do you think?"

The purpose of the group setting is to experience classical, dialogical learning in a semi-Socratic method meant to get people talking and sharing so they can process out loud with others! This creates an opportunity for greater internalizing of the topic and personal vulnerability. Combined, these help a disciple grow. If you are the group leader, you are making disciples, and your role is not to dominate but to facilitate.

Finally, there has to be a time to pray. The Filled to Flow Bible Study includes some helpful prayer prompts. You can also re-engage some of the activations from the chapter. If you are leading the group, you can facilitate a time of activation as a group. These activation moments may help people come alive in the flow of the Spirit like never before!

To summarize:

◻ This means it's a Bible study reflection question. It's okay if just one or two people answer. It's also OK to move through it quickly or even skip it. However, there may not be time to include the reading of this scripture with the whole group.

≈ This means it's a group interaction reflection question. It would be good to ask several people from the group to respond. It also means that the scripture associated with this question should be read aloud to the group.

Another way to use this guide is to ask all group members to go through it privately, as 'homework' or 'prework' before the group meeting. Each participant should recognize that all of the ◻ items are for personal engagement, reading, and reflection, while all of the ≈ items will be for group reading and engagement.

In each group session, be sure to make time for prayer! In the prayer times, approach it with a popcorn style rather than a programmed style. That is, each person considers both the list of prayer prompts and the awareness of what is going on with others in the group and prays as led, one at a time, for each other. If group prayer is new to you, try this: when other people are praying out loud, and you agree with the sentences they are saying, speak up while they are praying and say things like, "Yes, Lord!" "Amen!" or "Thank you, Lord." Giving voice to agreement in prayer together is a blessing, and it is to be encouraged!

ONE

HELLO, HOLY SPIRIT!

You're filled to flow in the fullness of the Spirit!

In this chapter, you will learn about the person and work of the Holy Spirit from a Biblical foundation. You will discover the various ways we may experience the Holy Spirit. You'll be invited to embrace the goodness of the Spirit of God in total fullness!

Getting to know you, getting to know all about you

When I first met her, Ann Lee was smiling and practically dancing across the green grass of the Fuller Seminary campus. She was waving a sign that said, "We're glad you're here!" - and she said out loud with a cheerful, exuberant voice, "Welcome to Fuller!" Her face was beautiful, her joy was contagious, and her outgoing nature was compelling. She was my wife. I didn't know it yet, nor did she, but she was my wife! Okay - the truth is, she would *one day become my wife*. In that moment, though, and for several months that followed - she was just an acquaintance.

Ann has such an inviting way about her. While welcoming me to this new school, she also told me about the church she was part of and invited me to come check it out. I did - and I loved it. She also asked me to join her small group. At this point, I did wonder whether maybe there could be *a possibility* for 'she and I.' I quickly found out she was dating a soon-to-be doctor, a med school student from UCLA who was also part of the church, and part of the small group. No romance for Ann and I - at least not yet!

After several months, we became true friends. I got to see what she is like, what kind of person she is, and what it is like to be in her company with other people. After about a year, she and the med school student broke up. Haha! It was now time for me to make my move! Ann and I went on a mission trip together, and I could see how powerful she was and the quality of her heart in serving God and people. I just knew beyond the shadow of a doubt that she was to be my wife. We started dating and fell in love.

We went on dates, had adventures, worshiped, and prayed together. Throughout this time, I expressed my love for her in various ways. I left notes at the door of her apartment, showed up with flowers for her at the hospital where she worked, sang her songs, painted her pictures, and wrote her poems.

One time I used a silver metallic marker to write a love note on a dried leaf. I secretly went ahead and placed the leaf in a small garden where I took her on a walk during a date. I made sure that she discovered the leaf and picked it up. That may have been the moment I won her heart! I also spent time listening to her - I discovered chapters of her life story that others may never know. I became familiar with what it is like to just hang out with her and hear her voice. Our love was strong and growing.

I knew Ann so much more than I had known her before. She was no longer a stranger, no longer just an acquaintance. She had become a friend who had become a lover and who would soon become my wife. We have now shared more than two decades of marriage - and have raised three children together. I can tell you beyond the shadow of a doubt I know her *very well* now. I now know her far better than I did in any of the moments I just described. I thank God that I do know her the way I do now - and not just the way I knew her when I first saw her standing on that campus lawn holding a welcome sign as a stranger! I'm so glad she said hello to me - and that I also said hello to her!

It's time to get to know the Holy Spirit!

Right now, consider saying hello to the Holy Spirit in a new way. You may know something about the Holy Spirit because you have read Bible verses about Him or mentioned Him in prayer. However, it's also possible that you don't know the Holy Spirit, and I'm here to tell you it's time to get acquainted. Hello, Holy Spirit!

My relationship with Ann began in a context where we were strangers - and then acquaintances who barely knew each other. But there was a progression in our relationship. I came to know more about her - and then I was able to truly *know her* better as I spent time with her, listened to her, and shared experiences with her. The same thing is possible for you in your relationship with the Holy Spirit. If the Holy Spirit is a stranger to you - it's time to say, "Hello, Holy Spirit!" If the Holy Spirit is a casual acquaintance to you - but you're ready for the relationship to go deeper, it's time to say, "Hello, Holy Spirit!" If you've been walking with Jesus and enjoying the Holy Spirit already - it's time to say again, "Oh, Hello, Holy Spirit!" Ultimately - God's design for you is that you would be filled to flow in the Holy Spirit - but first, you must *know* the Holy Spirit.

Could you imagine the lightness and lifting that could come into your life if you would open your heart to the Holy Spirit in a new way? After all, it is the Holy Spirit's power that raised Jesus from the dead; that's quite a lot of lift! Can you daydream for a moment about how good it could be to have the closeness of the Comforter coming along with you through whatever you might need to make it through? Think about what would be possible in your life as you follow Jesus if you were experiencing a greater degree of intimacy with the Holy Spirit. There could be miracles, mighty power, and supernatural breakthroughs just around the corner - if you'd just open your heart to the fullness and flow of the Holy Spirit!

Activation - Hello Holy Spirit

Take a moment to say hello to the Holy Spirit right where you are! Close your eyes, pause the audiobook, and take a deep breath.

As you exhale, simply say, "Hello, Holy Spirit!"

Take another deep breath and say, "Holy Spirit, I want to get to know you more!"

Relax in the Holy Spirit's presence for a few minutes. Resist the urge to grab your phone. Just breathe—and maybe say, "Holy Spirit, I welcome you!"

Just *enjoy* a simple moment of connection! Is there anything you want to say to the Holy Spirit? Just say it - and simply enjoy the Holy Spirit's presence now!

~ Did anything happen to you during this activation?

~ Did you experience any mood shift or feel like the Holy Spirit was doing anything as you said, "Hello, Holy Spirit"?

~ Write down any sensation or sense you had as you said, 'Hello, Holy Spirit!'

The flow comes from the Trinity

Being *filled to flow* is about experiencing the dynamic indwelling of the Holy Spirit to such an extent that you are *filled*. As a result, you are able to *flow* more and more in the love and power of the Spirit to bless the world around you. Because the experience of the Holy Spirit is at the core of the filled to flow life, you need to have a foundation in the Biblical theology of the Holy Spirit. One of the core beliefs of the Christian faith is that God is revealed in scripture as one Being with three unique persons: Father, Son, and Holy Spirit.

Father, Son and Holy Spirit are not separate gods, and these are not three different personality traits. These are not three different 'forms' or 'modes' of God. These are three distinct persons who exist together perfectly as our one God. The word Trinity is not in the

Bible, but it is the word early leaders in the Body of Christ adopted to express the reality that our God is three in one. God is a tri-unity. There is so much mystery in this revelation, and the mystery makes room for the beauty of all of who God is.

Biblical basis for the Trinity

Consider some of the scriptures that indicate the Oneness of our God who is both Father, Son, and Holy Spirit. Hebrews 1:3 describes Jesus, the Son, as the radiance of God's glory and the exact representation of His being. 2 Corinthians 13:14 indicates that Jesus, the Son, brings grace to you, that the Father carries forth divine love, and that the Holy Spirit establishes and creates a sense of connection and community. 2 Corinthians 3:17 states that the Lord *is* the Spirit - and that a core impact of the Holy Spirit's presence is *freedom*. Colossians 1:15-17 describes Jesus, the Son, as the image of the invisible God. Colossians 2:9 reveals a crucial truth - that the fullness of deity lives in Jesus Christ in bodily form.

John 1:14 shows that the *logos* reality of God became flesh in Jesus Christ. Jesus Himself declares in John 10:30, "I and the Father are one". 1 Peter 1:1-2 demonstrates a trinitarian understanding of God - as Father who chooses you and I, Holy Spirit who sanctifies us, and Jesus who is the Lord whom we follow with obedience. 2 Corinthians 1:21-22 gives insight about the way our Trinity God functions in our lives - Father God anointing us and setting His seal of ownership on our lives, Holy Spirit deposited into our hearts, and Christ, in whom we stand firm. Matthew 28:19 gives us the great commission. The words of Jesus call us to embrace the directive of our one God who is Three Persons, as these words call us to make disciples and baptize in the name of the Father, the Son, and the Holy Spirit. I urge you to look up these scriptures and meditate on the reality of the fullness of who our God is - the Great Three in One!

Metaphors for the Trinity

It should not surprise us to think that there are aspects to the nature of God that are mysterious; He's God! And when there is mystery - we have a desire to know and understand. In our quest to comprehend, we often use metaphors. Sometimes a symbolic representation helps us grasp something that is otherwise ethereal. Over time, many believers have employed metaphors to give definition to the revelation of God as Trinity. I'll share some of them - but you should know that most metaphors fail us. They are not *the* definition of The Trinity; they are simply verbal scaffolding that can help us grasp the outline so that we can know our God more deeply.

Some convey the idea of the Trinity with the metaphor of the egg. The egg is shell, whites, and yolk. The yolk is egg, the whites are egg, and the shell is egg. Three in one. Another Three-in-one metaphor is that of water. Water can be liquid, and it can be frozen solid as ice, and it can become steam. Whether liquid, steam, or ice - all three are H2O water. Another metaphor could be a man with three roles: he's a father to his four children, he's also a husband, and he's also an employer who manages 40 workers. He is one man with three distinct personas through which he is known.

All metaphors fail to convey the complete sense of revelation about God as trinity - but there is one which is somewhat more helpful - and it is the metaphor of light. Light is both a particle, and a wave, and a frequency all at once. The aspect of light as a wave is what illuminates so we can see. Light as a particle is what is used by doctors in radiation therapy. Light as a frequency is pure energy that can carry information, such as with fiber optic cables. Dr. Ralph Rohr, MD wrote about this idea, describing the way in which light exists on a well-defined spectrum as low energy light (microwaves), visible light, and high energy light, such as X-rays and gamma rays, in which light becomes an effective though almost invisible particle.

Maybe God, who is light, is actually quite like this. God the Father is like the gamma rays of creation (or destruction). God the

Son is the 'visible light' we can perceive with the naked eye. God the Holy Spirit is like the warm, communicative light of microwaves and radio waves. This metaphor is helpful - and tied to the biblical truth of who God is as light.

Mistaken representations of the Trinity

Throughout history, people have misrepresented the truth of God as One who is Three—the Trinity. One of these missteps is *modalism*, where God operates through three different modes, forms, or masks. This view devalues the divinity of the unique roles of the Son and the Spirit. Varieties of Arianism also misrepresent the Godhead as three in One.

Another commonly held (but incorrect) perspective is called *Dynamic (Adoptionism) monarchianism* in which the Son is a created being who learned how to serve God really well - so much so that he became worthy enough to be adopted as a kind of God. Groups like the Jehova's Witnesses embrace a conclusion similar to this. Another belief that violates proper understanding of the Trinity is called *patritheism*, where the Old Testament God is the Father - the one who is angry, wrathful, and ready to start a war. Then the Holy Spirit is the softer, gentler balance while Jesus is a peacemaker demigod who arbitrates between the Father and humanity.

Technically, these are examples of *trinitarian heresies* - and the reason I'm bringing them up here is that I want you to really know the Holy Spirit! I want you to be aware of and avoid the common pitfalls of belief that create a diminished view of who the Holy Spirit actually is. The early church dealt with this issue to such a high degree that leaders from the entire known movement of Jesus followers from around the world met in Nicea in 325 AD to create a statement of faith that would clarify the Christian belief in the Trinity. This creed represents that shared belief of the Christian church over many centuries. Read it - and allow the clarity of who the Holy Spirit is to rise.

THE NICENE CREED:

We believe in one God, the Father, the Almighty,
maker of heaven and earth, of all that is, seen and unseen.
We believe in one Lord, Jesus Christ, the only Son of God,
eternally begotten of the Father,
God from God, Light from Light, true God from true God,
begotten, not made, of one Being with the Father.
Through him all things were made.
For us and for our salvation he came down from heaven:
by the power of the Holy Spirit he became incarnate from the Virgin
Mary,
and was made man.
For our sake he was crucified under Pontius Pilate;
he suffered death and was buried.
On the third day he rose again in accordance with the Scriptures;
he ascended into heaven
and is seated at the right hand of the Father.
He will come again in glory to judge the living and the dead,
and his kingdom will have no end.
We believe in the Holy Spirit, the Lord, the giver of life,
who proceeds from the Father and the Son.
With the Father and the Son he is worshiped and glorified.
He has spoken through the Prophets.
We believe in one holy catholic and apostolic Church.
We acknowledge one baptism for the forgiveness of sins.
We look for the resurrection of the dead,
and the life of the world to come. Amen.

What about the pronouns and definite articles?

If you are a linguist or a grammar nerd, you may have noticed that I've been inconsistent in my use of the definite article 'the' when naming and referring to Holy Spirit. This is actually intentional on my part. Language indicates reality - and I want to be intentional that my language about Holy Spirit be clear in establishing his identity as the third *person* of the trinity. We do not believe in our God as a being who consists of "two whos and a what!" The overuse of the word 'the' to indicate Holy Spirit can begin to create a sense of identity of Holy Spirit as a 'what' rather than a who. In my writing and speaking about Holy Spirit, I look for opportunities to remove the word 'the' and just refer in a more personal way to Holy Spirit by name.

You can use the definite article *the*; the Bible itself in the Greek text sometimes does. If I were throwing a party and I opened the door - and I announced, "The Mikester is here," you'd know I was actually elevating my appreciation and value for Mike by my use of the word "the." But if, as the party progressed, I continued to refer to him as "the Mike," it would be really strange! I want to invite you to consider shifting your own language from time to time to honor who Holy Spirit is by removing the word "the" in describing Him. You can expect that I will frequently do that throughout this book!

Holy Spirit is a person to love!

Before you learn any more high-minded words, terminologies, concepts and theological insights about Holy Spirit, you first need to know and embrace that the Holy Spirit is a *person to love*! You know God as your Father in Heaven whom you love. You've come to embrace Jesus as your savior and One you love. Holy Spirit is also a person to love - and before anything else - would you simply take a moment *right now* to express your love directly to Holy Spirit!

Activation - I Love You, Holy Spirit

Take a moment right now to encounter Holy Spirit. Sometimes we express our love best through a song. Even if you aren't a gifted musician, you can make up a song. Sing out the phrase, "Holy Spirit, I love you," making up your own melody as you go. Sing it out several times! Then, just rest in Holy Spirit's presence - and enjoy Him!

~~ What kind of sensation or feeling did you have during this activation?

~~ How did it feel for you to sing out your love for Holy Spirit? How do you think it made the Holy Spirit feel?

~~ Did you sense any degree of closeness to the Holy Spirit in this experience?

~~ Write down any impression you have after this moment.

To know Him is to love Them

The Holy Spirit that you get to be filled by has been there from the start of it all. Elohim is the very first word for God found on the pages of your Bible, and you should know some things about it. The word is plural; Elohim is not singular - but it is a name which indicates one who is plural. This points to the presence of Father, Son and Holy Spirit, even from the beginning. In fact Genesis 1:2 says that as God created the heavens and the earth, the Spirit of God was moving upon the face of the waters. The Hebrew term used there is 'Ruach Elohim;' the literal translation is 'breath or wind of God.' Hebrew scholars have determined that 'Spirit' is the better translation - but the color of the language is clear - Holy Spirit is *like* the very breath of God - in effect and essence. More importantly - Holy Spirit is present in this moment of creation - and active in the process, maybe in ways that go beyond our conception.

In the New Testament, the Greek word *pneuma* is used to speak of the Spirit of God. The word *pneuma* (from which we get such words as 'pneumatic') also conveys the current of air. There is something about Holy Spirit that is imperceptible yet known by the feeling of its effect. Holy Spirit is like the wind - you can't see it - but you feel its effects. *Ruach. Pneuma. Spirit.* Consider the words Jesus spoke in John 3:5-8 (NIV):

Jesus answered, "Very truly I tell you, no one can enter the kingdom of God unless they are born of water and the Spirit. Flesh gives birth to flesh, but the Spirit gives birth to spirit. You should not be surprised at my saying, 'You must be born again.' The wind blows wherever it pleases. You hear its sound, but you cannot tell where it comes from or where it is going. So it is with everyone born of the Spirit."

The goal is the Kingdom

In Jesus' Words about being born again by the Holy Spirit, he clarifies that the goal for a born-again person is to enter the Kingdom of God. On the one hand, the Kingdom of Heaven is *heaven* - the realm we enter when we die because of the Cross of Christ and our faith in Him. But Jesus always spoke about the Kingdom of Heaven as a realm or reality we also experience here and now. Jesus wants His followers to be people who have entered into and are living in the reality of the Kingdom of Heaven!

When you put your faith in Jesus, you received the gift of salvation. Your salvation includes the ultimate great hope of going to heaven when you die - but it also is an empowerment for living in strength, hope, joy, and victory here and now. When you consider the work of the Holy Spirit, you should know that Holy Spirit is the person of God who is present and able to empower you to live the values and goodness of the Kingdom of God here and now! This is a large part of the reason God established the possibility for you to experience the Holy Spirit beyond simply conviction of sin so you could repent and turn to God!

The Holy Spirit was at work when you were born again. The Holy Spirit *regenerated* you and made you into someone brand new. Your old self was encrusted with a sinful nature that governed you - even though you had learned to make good appearances. Your old self was covered in sin and bound for hell. When you were born again, Holy Spirit was at work breaking you free from that old sinful nature. You were regenerated, reborn, with a new nature. Your new self has the capacity to be empowered by the Spirit of God from within to live in personal victory, hope, and power - in such a way that you both live in and establish the kingdom of God!

The goal of the Christian life is to receive salvation - and then live in the merits of salvation in such a way that your here-and-now life increasingly reflects the values of the Kingdom of heaven that you belong to!

Jesus describes the work of the Holy Spirit in terms of the wind - it is active, and you can feel its effects, but you can't control it. As you get to know Holy Spirit, you need to keep this in mind. Holy Spirit is a person you can love and experience - but you don't control Holy Spirit. As a believer, and sometimes for whole churches, it can be tempting to work up or fabricate something with intensity and call it Holy Spirit.

I keep various tools in my garage; I'm a DIY guy through and through. One recent addition is a battery-powered blower. After mowing the lawn, I put the battery in, crank that tool up to full speed, and blast all the grass clippings out of the driveway and off the sidewalks. I love that tool! The air current produced by the turbines in it is practically jet force! That is NOT the way the Holy Spirit works. You and I don't get to *produce* the movement of the Spirit. We get to *partner* with the movement of the Spirit. And to partner with the One who is like the wind - you've got to know what the Spirit is like - and you've got to have your sails open!

Your experience with Holy Spirit starts from a place of peace

After His resurrection, Jesus appeared to the disciples in a breathtaking yet breath-giving way. He wanted to introduce His disciples to the power now made possible by His resurrection - the power of the Holy Spirit. As soon as He appeared to them, this is what happened, according to John 20:21-23 (NIV):

Again Jesus said, "Peace be with you! As the Father has sent me, I am sending you." And with that he breathed on them and said, "Receive the Holy Spirit. If you forgive anyone's sins, their sins are forgiven; if you do not forgive them, they are not forgiven."

These are some of my favorite words from Jesus. I love his greeting - peace be with you. Sure - it was probably just a standard greeting, much like the phrase 'Salam Aleichem' that is used throughout the Middle East even to this day. But I also know that Jesus chooses his words carefully - and this is one of the rare instances where Jesus uses this phrase as a greeting. It reflects His heart and desire for us to live in the *shalom* peace of God. He really does want that for you.

In this moment, when he knows he is about to express the reality of the Holy Spirit, he begins with a word of peace. You should hear this and lay aside any fears or concerns about Holy Spirit. I know that you are reading this book because on the one hand - you are curious and excited about the possibility of experiencing more of Holy Spirit. At the same time, I know a part of you is worried that things with the Holy Spirit could get carried away. Receive His peace - and surrender your fears and worries about the fullness of the Holy Spirit at Jesus' feet! Yes - Jesus wants for you to receive his Spirit - but the context for that is first - *peace.*

Sent like Jesus: full of the Spirit!

Before speaking of the Spirit - Jesus gives his disciples a commission; he says, "I'm sending you like I was sent!" Jesus was sent full of the power of the Holy Spirit - and that is what He desires for you. He wants you to rise up in the Spirit's power in the mission to reach the lost. Jesus was sent to bring revelation about God and the Kingdom of God. He wants you to take your place, in the power of the Spirit, to do the same! Jesus was sent with power in the Holy Spirit to bring miraculous breakthrough - even to a degree that was outlandish - feeding 5,000 people with a couple fish! Well

- Jesus has it in mind that you would be so lifted by the Holy Spirit that you would walk in faith and obedience and also bring breakthrough by the Holy Spirit's power.

Jesus was sent in the Holy Spirit's power to set people free from demonic affliction and bring healing to their bodies. He longs for you to do your part in bringing that freedom and healing, too, but the power of the Holy Spirit must do it! Jesus was sent to proclaim forgiveness and reconciliation - and you have the same calling. It's only possible by the Holy Spirit! Jesus was sent to create authentic community among God's people - and you get to do that too; you are 'sent' by Jesus as He was sent! And you walk in the ways He has sent you by the power of his Spirit!

Jesus had such good breath...!?

There are only a few moments after the resurrection of Jesus from the dead that are recorded in the gospels. The moment in John 20:21-23 is so poignant - because Jesus appears - coming through locked doors - and yet so physically real that he is able to *breathe* on the disciples. He blows his breath across the room - and as he does this - he says 'receive the Holy Spirit!' Could it be that Rabbi Jesus was demonstrating Genesis 1:2 to them in that very room? Could it be that He wanted them to clearly understand that the Holy Spirit literally is part of His very being? Could it be that he was stirring up the flame that would later be lit fully at Pentecost?

When I was a little boy, my dad would make a fire in the fireplace, and he would always do something that seemed almost magical to me. When the fire was barely burning at all, and looked like it was going out, my Dad would stick his face up close to the logs, and with a deep breath, he'd blow right into the fireplace - and suddenly, flames would begin to burst and dance on those logs. It was as if my dad had the fire in his own lungs and he was spewing it out! Could it be that Jesus blew his breath over the disciples in that room because there was a fire for God that needed to be lit in their lives? You've probably heard the expression 'on fire for God,' and so have I. In my experience, to be truly on fire for God, you need the wind of the Spirit blown from Jesus to come across your life! That is how you can truly be on fire for God!

Activation - Breathe and Forgive with the Holy Spirit

Activation moment: Read John 20:20-21 and then sit in the presence of Holy Spirit. Imagine Jesus breathing on you - and the power of the Spirit of God coming into you. Feel it. Hold your breath. Exhale - imagine the power of God coming out from you. Repeat.

Ask this question: "Holy Spirit, who do you want me to forgive?" As a person comes to mind, allow space for your feelings, but then surrender the feelings of anger, bitterness, hurt, etc., to the Lord.

Say aloud, "Lord Jesus, I surrender the feelings of pain and offense, etc., to you."
Then, take a deep breath and say, "I forgive this person now because You've forgiven me."
~ In what ways did you sense the presence of the Holy Spirit in this activation?
~ Were you surprised by the person who the Holy Spirit brought to your mind to forgive?
~ Was it challenging to include forgiveness with an encounter with the Holy Spirit, or was it helpful?
~ Write down any impression you have after this moment.

You were saved to be set apart and holy

Create in me a pure heart, O God, and renew a steadfast spirit within me. Do not cast me from your presence or take your Holy Spirit from me. Restore to me the joy of your salvation and grant me a willing spirit to sustain me.

PSALM 51:10-12

In my bathroom drawer, I have two pairs of nail clippers. They are the same kind of clippers - the generic kind you'd buy at the pharmacy for $3. On one, the word 'fingers!' is written in black Sharpie. On the other, the word 'toes!' is written in blue Sharpie. Yes,

I'm that kind of guy - I use a different pair of clippers for my toes than I do for my fingernails. I like to keep them separate because, in my mind, toes are somewhat 'dirty.' Okay, maybe it's just *my* toes! And since I eat with my fingers and not with my toes, I want to keep the cross-contamination to a minimum! You could say I keep my fingernail clippers 'holy.'

The word holy, in its purest form from Hebrew means 'set apart.' And when we describe God as *holy* we are acknowledging that He is utterly and totally set apart from anything else in the universe - because he created it all. But the word *kadosh* or *holy* doesn't *only* mean set apart. The Hebrew community used the word 'set apart' to describe something that was kept clean, something that was kept pure. And the purpose of being set apart is to be holy. As a follower of Jesus, you are invited to live a holy life - because God values purity. It may mean that you are set apart - apart from the crowd, apart from the traditions of men, and apart from popular opinions. But when you live *set apart* - when you live *holy* - you experience more of the purity that Jesus paid for on the Cross.

In your life as a Christian, Jesus is leading you out of sin and into greater depths of the blessing of salvation. The further you go with Jesus, the freer from sin's tentacles you become. The freer from sin you become - the more you fully reflect the image of God that is in you. The scriptures in 2 Corinthians 3:18 describe a process of growth in holiness that is framed in the language of progress; you go from one degree of glory to a greater degree of glory over the long haul of life. This process of transformation is something that Holy Spirit works on with you by leading you away from sin and the flesh and into the Kingdom of God.

The journey of sanctification is sometimes marked by setbacks; sometimes suffering or temptation seems to cut in on you. Your progress is thwarted - and maybe you have even slid back quite a ways. At any given moment, Holy Spirit is able to wash away sin and shame and empower you to have a fresh start in living the way God desires for you to live. Holy Spirit is able to give you a new start on the pathway of holiness that God has for you. He is the *Holy* Spirit; He wants the purity and cleanness of having your sin washed away. He wants to partner with you in establishing wholesome patterns of living. He wants for you to live the 'set apart' life that someone filled with God's Spirit is called to.

The Holy Spirit is calling you to live a holy life

The Spirit of God is called *Ruach Hakodesh* in Hebrew: the Spirit who is Holy. Because this is who He is, you need to know that *holiness* is something the Spirit values - something the Spirit wants, and something the Spirit is. Holy Spirit is a person - and can be affected by the choices you make. 1 Thessalonians 5:19 and Ephesians 4:30 indicate that it is possible to grieve the Holy Spirit through certain life choices. If I could put this a bit more bluntly - you could really break Holy Spirit's heart if you choose to ignore God's call for holiness in your life.

When you embrace this revelation that God wants you to live in the Holy Spirit's power, and that living a holy life is part of what God wants for you, you realize that you have to be open to repenting for any sin in your life whenever and wherever it crops up. If you're going to live a lifestyle of honoring God with your choices - one of the choices you will need to make often is to bend your knees and ask for His mercy as you repent of your sins. This choice opens the door for the deep cleansing work of the Spirit in your life!

You might find yourself in a season when you are not struggling with any overt, shady sin. But what if you were to embark on a deep dive into Psalm 51:10-12 and you allowed the great searchlight of God to shine into every part of your heart? Could pride or selfishness be lurking there? What about lovelessness or lack of compassion for the poor? These are sins to repent of as well. I am not mentioning this so that you'll feel guilty. Actually, it's precisely the opposite.

I want you to be as free in the Holy Spirit as possible. Repentance is the doorway into proper alignment with Holy Spirit!

Once set apart, you're sent back in

> *"But you will receive power when the Holy Spirit comes upon you. And you will be my witnesses, telling people about me everywhere—in Jerusalem, throughout Judea, in Samaria, and to the ends of the earth."*

ACTS 1:8 NLT

When you choose to walk on a life pathway of holiness, it can initially seem like you might be missing out on all the fun. Nothing could be farther from the truth. Joining with the Holy Spirit for God's great work in this world is a fantastic adventure. When you serve people in the power and love of the Holy Spirit, there is a current from the very river of heaven that flows through you - and it is as refreshing as a glass of ice water on a hot summer day. When your life is limited to 'the kingdom of you,' there is a centrifugal force that makes your world smaller. When you cooperate with the movement of the Holy Spirit, your life takes on the momentum of centripetal force - and there is a flow outward from your life into a horizon that grows more and more broad. Your life becomes marked by an orientation toward the Kingdom of God - an expansive, dynamic realm of impact, blessing, and goodness! Holiness is a key element of how you get there.

You've been saved and set apart - and once set apart, now you're ready to be sent back in! Holy Spirit does mighty work through Christian people who serve God wholeheartedly and embrace Holy Spirit's power! Think of the ways you've been personally affected for the good by Spirit-filled people. There was probably a friend, neighbor or family member who was led by the Spirit to share their faith with you or invite you to church. There was likely a leader, evangelist or pastor who was following the Spirit's lead to share gospel truth with you. There may have been a program, outreach or ministry team flowing in the Spirit's power to reach out to you when you needed it most. At the core, these people were experiencing empowerment of the Spirit to bear witness to the power of the gospel and the love of Jesus.

When the set apart ones know they've been sent back in, filled by the Spirit, and begin to take their place of influence in this world, things get better and the light of Jesus shines brighter! When you take your place - full of the Holy Spirit - you will be compelled by the Holy Spirit to bear witness to the power of the Spirit, the goodness of the gospel and the love of Jesus. Holy Spirit desires to bring conviction of sin and unrighteousness so that people can repent and find God's mercy in Christ. For this reason, Holy Spirit is likely to prompt you, as a believer, to witness or bear testimony of what God has done for you and can do for others.

"But in fact, it is best for you that I go away, because if I don't, the Advocate won't come. If I do go away, then I will send him to you. And when he comes, he will convict the world of its sin, and of God's righteousness, and of the coming judgment."

JOHN 16:7-8 NLT

One of the ways the scripture refers to Holy Spirit is with the Greek term *Parakletos*. This word has a range of meanings; it can be translated 'advocate' - and Holy Spirit is ready to be your advocate. You may not even know to what degree or in what arena you may need an advocate, but He's ready to be just that! *Parakletos* can also mean *Counselor*. Holy Spirit is able to bring counsel to you with wisdom and advisement just when you need it. *Parakletos* can also mean *comforter* - and Holy Spirit is ready to bring comfort to you whenever you are in distress. Technically, *Parakletos* means 'the one who comes alongside' - the way an advocate, counselor or comforter does.

"But in fact, it is best for you that I go away, because if I don't, the Advocate won't come. If I do go away, then I will send him to you. And when he comes, he will convict the world of its sin, and of God's righteousness, and of the coming judgment."

John 16:7-8 NLT

When I first met Ann, the woman who would become my wife, I had no idea who she really was. I saw just enough to know I wanted to know her more, but the relationship took time to develop. It also required intentionality, tenacity, vulnerability, risk, and action. I want you to embrace your relationship with the Holy Spirit in a similar way—and don't be afraid!

Would you stay at the Disneyland Gate?

Jesus spoke repeatedly about the Kingdom of God, the realm where the Spirit of God flows full force. He wants His disciples to be people who experience this realm and know the contours of it. He wants His disciples to be people who know how to navigate in the Kingdom of God realm. Many people who come to faith in Jesus hear about the Kingdom of God but fail to enter in fully. They are content to linger just inside the gate of the Kingdom. I want you to be one of the people who experience the fullness of the Holy Spirit in God's Kingdom!

Imagine for a minute that you are going to Disneyland, and you are part of a group with a guide. You've got your ticket, you go through the turnstiles, and you're in! But right then, the guide says, "Wait, just gather over here." The guide just has your group gather there inside by the flowers at Disneyland's front entrance. There you are, for the whole entire day, just standing there, inside, by the flowers. The guide speaks incessantly about Walt Disney, and the dates that marked the beginning of construction of Disneyland,

and when it first opened, and how many acres it includes, and how many different lands there are.

The guide says, "There is this really cool roller coaster that takes you through space! There is another ride - it's a boat - and people who go on it can see elephants, crocodiles and lions! And there is this runaway mountain train ride that some people go on - and they say it's crazy and fun!" The guide is excited about these things, but she also seems nervous as she describes them. After a while, the group you are with just begins to sit down to listen to her. You also find yourself seated, and listening to the guide, but you're thinking to yourself, "The rides sound amazing. Why can't we go on them?"

Just then, one of those serious Disney fans with pins and buttons all over their clothes comes over to the guide and says, "Hey, just let them in so they can actually go on the rides!" Your guide speaks up with concern, 'No! They could go on that roller coaster, and something could go wrong! Or they could end up eating one of those giant turkey drumsticks and choke on it! Or, or, or… they could walk all the way over to the Big Thunder Mountain ride and be totally disappointed because it could be closed! Or, they could go on the Indiana Jones ride – and see skulls and get scared! Or a Disney cast member could be rude to them! And the LINES! They might have to wait, and you know people don't like waiting!"

She opens several books that she has in her bags. These books have been written by authors who have stories of people who have been harmed by their experiences at places like Disneyland. She turns to one of her highlighted pages, shakes her head sharply, and blurts out, "No! It's just too risky! Anyway, they're here, they're at Disneyland. It's just best for them to stay *here* and enjoy the flowers, where nothing can go wrong." Her voice is punctuated by her own nervous laughter.

Just then, the great mouse himself appears, and she gets excited. "Oh look! There's Mickey!" she says. As she waves her books around, she shouts, "Look, they get to see Mickey! What more could they want?" The Disneyland devotee says, "Well, I think Mickey wants them to go and actually see Magic Kingdom, not just sit inside the gates and hear about it!"

This Disneyland story is just a made-up metaphor. I want you to experience the full range of the Holy Spirit and come fully into the Kingdom of God, even if there are risks and even if the way the Holy Spirit moves is unconventional relative to your experience. Consider some of the ways the Holy Spirit appears in the scriptures. Let that begin to define what you can expect to experience with the Holy Spirit.

Seven ways you can expect to have experience with Holy Spirit

Jack Hayford is one of the fathers of the Spirit-Filled Christian faith in modern times. He was a brilliant thinker and a passionate lover of God. He wrote the songs 'Majesty, Worship His Majesty' and 'I Exalt Thee,' among many others. He was President of the Foursquare denomination and a prolific author. In one of His books, Living The Spirit-Formed Life, He listed many functions of the Holy Spirit in the believer's life. In this section, I'm inspired by Hayford's book to do the same thing.

One: You will be baptized in the Holy Spirit

In Acts 1:5, Jesus says, "John baptized with water, but you will be baptized in the Holy Spirit." For a lot of us, the word 'baptized' is a word that carries a sense of religiosity. It prompts us to think of a ceremony. But for Jesus' followers in his day, it was just a regular word – and it meant 'to immerse.' *Baptized* means wholly submerged in, immersed completely in, or drenched with.

When I hear the word 'baptized,' and I think of it in terms of the word's original meaning, I think of being 14 years old; my Dad had just bought us a little two-man canoe from Sears. We went out to

Lake Mercer, and for some reason we both leaned over the same side of the canoe at the same time, and instantly, that thing was upside down, and we were up to our eyebrows in the water! Drenched! Soaked! Completely submerged! Immersed! You could say we were baptized! There was no staying dry! Throughout the book of Acts, this is the preferred word in scripture to describe what happened to people who started following Jesus. That doesn't sound like a neat, tidy package. It sounds like a splashing, fully-encompassing kind of knowing. You will be baptized in the Holy Spirit.

Two: The Holy Spirit Comes Upon You

In Acts 1:8, Jesus says, "You will receive power when the Holy Spirit comes upon you." We do not use the term 'to come upon' very often in everyday speech. In this context, the essence of its meaning is 'to arrive and overtake.' I think of it like this: Imagine a ship at sea – pirates came, got on board, and kidnapped the crew. The US Navy is going to come to the rescue, and the US Navy is going to ram that ship. Those sailors are going to board that ship, arrive, and overtake it!

The pirates are going to be defeated, and the seamen of that ship are going to be set free because the US Navy has *come upon* that ship! Jesus is describing that the Holy Spirit is not going to be some sort of timid tag-along buddy, but the one arriving in us to overtake the control. Like the Navy guys going aboard a ship of pirates to overtake the vessel, the Holy Spirit comes upon you.

Three: The Holy Spirit will be poured out on you

In Acts 2:17, Peter quotes Joel's prophecy, which says, "And it will come to pass in the last days I will pour my Spirit out on all people." Ah, such refreshment! Imagine a bunch of kids playing at the 'splashtopia' section at an amusement park. A massive bucket fills up with something like 100 gallons of water - and then, without warning, it dumps out over the crowd of kids and parents. Because the bucket is larger than life, EVERYONE gets splashing wet, soaked. Some of the parents keep their distance - and even though they are in their bathing suits too, they don't experience the soaking. But for any of those who are willing to be in the area below the large water bucket, they are drenched - and they are delighting in the refreshment of it all.

The Holy Spirit may be poured out on you in a similar way. There may be a designated area where a prayer team or a minister is offering to pray for the pouring out of the Spirit. There could be an altar call where you are invited forward. In that moment, the Holy Spirit may be poured out, and you'll be refreshed! It may be sloshy and silly - because that can sometimes be the effect of the Spirit poured out - but it's worth it to be renewed and refreshed in this way.

Four: You can be filled with the Holy Spirit

The word for 'filled' in the Bible regarding the Holy Spirit always carries a sense of being filled to overflowing. You can picture a server coming to your table with a carafe of coffee. He says, "Would you like some? It's bold and strong, and you look like you need it!" You nod obligingly and slide your mug towards him. He begins to pour the steaming elixir of life into your mug. You expect him to utter "Say when," but he says nothing. He just keeps pouring - and before you know it, your mug is running over the top and spilling down the side right onto the tablecloth. The server looks at you and smiles, fluttering eyelashes and eyebrows raised in delight. That's what this word means!

Filled to the brim and then some, with more than enough. It is abundance. In Ephesians 5:18 it says, "Be filled with the Spirit." The language suggests this is meant to be an ongoing experience, not a once-and-done thing. And in Acts 2:4, that 'filling' of the Holy Spirit led to the birth of the Church of Jesus Christ! It was filling for a purpose – you can be filled with the Holy Spirit, too, to flow in the Spirit's power so that the Church of Jesus Christ would be built up and the Kingdom of God expanded!

Five: The Holy Spirit falls on you

Acts 10:44 records a moment of encounter with the Holy Spirit. It says, "Even as Peter was saying these things, the Holy Spirit *fell upon all* who were listening to the message." Sometimes the Holy Spirit falls on us. The word used here is one that describes a person collapsing into the embrace of another. Imagine a couple at the airport - they haven't seen each other for months - and he was away in a dangerous situation. He comes through the arrival gate; they spot each other and run to each other and practically collide as they hug.

The word describes a moment of intimate connection and affection. You may experience the Holy Spirit falling upon you in a moment of prayer, or as you read the scriptures. You could experience the Holy Spirit falling upon you in a worship gathering - or even while your pastor is preaching (yes, miracles do happen)! When the Holy Spirit falls upon you - you may find yourself weeping or laughing. This will likely be a moment of love and affection for the Holy Spirit who is allowing you to experience the power and love of His goodness.

Six: You have an anointing from the Holy Spirit

In 1 John 2:20 (NIV), it says, "But you have an anointing from the Holy One, and all of you know the truth." In some churches, believers will anoint another believer with oil as they pray. To do this, they take a small bottle of oil that's been prayed over and open it up. They place their finger on the open top, turn the bottle upside down, then rightside up again. They take their finger off of the bottle - and now it has a nice dripping dollop of oil. They press that oil on your hand or forehead and say, "I anoint you in the name of Jesus!" That oil will stay there on the person's skin for hours. It isn't always there. There is a special moment when it's recognizable - until they go wash their face. The anointing of the Holy Spirit is similar; it is something you have at certain times when you've been in an atmosphere of love and devotion to God. That anointing may cause you to feel light, powerful, and at the same time, almost drunk with the goodness of God. The anointing will empower you to carry out something God wants you to do that could only be done by the anointing of the Holy Spirit!

Seven: You receive the Holy Spirit

Acts 8:17 says, "Then Peter and John laid their hands upon these believers, and they received the Holy Spirit." They *received* the Holy Spirit. The word makes me think of a football player: He goes wide, looks over his shoulder, and raises his hands. He's ready. The quarterback nails it. The ball flies through the air, and when it comes, the receiver jumps, grabs the ball, and takes it as close to his body as he can! It is a deliberate, active experience with a chosen posture and stance. We receive the Holy Spirit.

When you receive the Holy Spirit, you may begin to tremble. You may feel heat or something like electricity coursing through your body because of the power of God. You may fall to the ground because of the closeness of God's Spirit. You may begin to pray in tongues (more on that in chapter 4). But most importantly, as a result of this moment, you will experience the work of the Spirit to convict you, guide you, teach you, comfort you, strengthen you, reveal things to you, and empower you. Your spiritual fulfillment will increase to a greater depth than you've ever known before.

Why would we want less? I don't know why we would want to settle for something less than the biblical experience of knowing the Holy Spirit. But it happens! Actually, the larger context of the verse you just read from Acts 8:17 is that of a group of believers who had believed and been baptized but had not yet experienced the Holy Spirit coming upon them. This group of believers, like the one spoken of in Acts 19, knew Jesus - but had not yet received the Holy Spirit. What about you, have you received the Holy Spirit? Have you been baptized in the Holy Spirit? What are you waiting for?

Activation - More of You, Holy Spirit!

Activation moment: Consider all that you have learned about the varieties of experience with the Holy Spirit. Choose one of the seven listed above, and ask for it.

Pray and repent: "Holy Spirit, I repent of my sins, especially..." and name whatever sin has been part of your life recently.

Pray and ask: "Holy Spirit, I want more of You. I would like ..." and speak of one of the seven types of experience of the Spirit you're longing for. Then wait. As you wait, let your physical body move. Become aware of the weight of glory that is present in this moment.

Say out loud, "More of you, Holy Spirit, more of You. More Lord!" Repeat this as needed - and stay in a place of openness to Holy Spirit.

~~ In what ways did you sense the presence of the Holy Spirit in this activation?

~~ Did you experience any physical sensation with the Holy Spirit in this activation?

~~ Write down any impression you have after this moment.

Keep getting to know Him more!

Be intentional about discovering more of who Holy Spirit is as you read this book and open the scriptures. Consider that just when you think you really know Holy Spirit - there is still more to experience of who the Holy Spirit is. Engage in your pursuit of encounters with Holy Spirit with tenacity. Get ready to take some risks in 'going for it' in the experience of the Holy Spirit. Allow your heart to be open - even vulnerable - in how you make room for the Holy Spirit to move you - or move through you. Take some chances in your relationship with Holy Spirit. There may be an expression or gift of the Spirit God wants to bring about through you. Take action in your walk with Holy Spirit. Instead of being passive and simply waiting for Holy Spirit to 'zap' you. Move ahead with a pro-active stance in the things of the Spirit as you discover more about the Spirit in this book.

God designed you to be filled with the Holy Spirit and able to flow in the Holy Spirit's love and power. You were made to be filled to flow! Keep reading, and stick with me on this journey. I want to help you live in the fullness of the filled-to-flow life!

FILLED TO FLOW
BIBLE STUDY SMALL GROUP GUIDE

Chapter One: Hello, Holy Spirit!

You're filled to flow within the fullness of the Spirit!

God wants you to have a true understanding of the Holy Spirit and how you can experience more of Him. This session will give you an overview and help you move toward a greater experience of His fullness.

Bible study group guide how-to summary:

▱ Means it's a Bible study reflection question. It's okay if just 1-2 people answer. It's okay to move through it quickly or even to skip. It also means there may not be time to include the reading of this scripture or the discussion of the question with the whole group. But consider these sections in your own study time!

≈ Means this is a group interaction reflection question. It would be good to ask several people from the group to respond. It also means that somebody should read the scripture associated with this question out loud.

Engage:

1. ≈ Icebreaker: What superpower would you love to have that reminds you of the Holy Spirit?

2. ≈ Share any highlights from this chapter that made an impression on you.

≈ Read John 16:7-8 NLT

"But in fact, it is best for you that I go away, because if I don't, the Advocate won't come. If I do go away, then I will send him to you. And when he comes, he will convict the world of its sin, and of God's righteousness, and of the coming judgment."

Engage:

3. ≈ What does it mean to you that Holy Spirit is your advocate? How have you experienced this dynamic of Holy Spirit?

≈ Read John 16:13-14 NLT

"When the Spirit of truth comes, he will guide you into all truth. He will not speak on his own but will tell you what he has heard. He will tell you about the future. He will bring me glory by telling you whatever he receives from me."

Engage:

4. ▱ Identify the four aspects of Holy Spirit's activity mentioned here. Keep in mind this is *not* a complete list! How are these four aspects of Holy Spirit's activity helpful or valuable?
5. ≈ Share about how you have experienced - or need to experience - any of these four aspects of what Jesus said Holy Spirit will do.

≈ Read John 3:5-8 NIV

Jesus answered, "Very truly I tell you, no one can enter the kingdom of God unless they are born of water and the Spirit. Flesh gives birth to flesh, but the Spirit gives birth to spirit. You should not be surprised at my saying, 'You must be born again.' The wind blows wherever it pleases. You hear its sound, but you cannot tell where it comes from or where it is going. So it is with everyone born of the Spirit."

Engage:

6.   ☐ Why does the goal of entering the Kingdom of God matter?
7.   ☐ What is the rebirth in the Spirit - and how is it experienced? How did you experience it?

≈ Read John 20:21-23

Again Jesus said, "Peace be with you! As the Father has sent me, I am sending you." And with that he breathed on them and said, "Receive the Holy Spirit. If you forgive anyone's sins, their sins are forgiven; if you do not forgive them, they are not forgiven.

Engage:

8.   ☐ What is the significance of Jesus' greeting?
9.   ☐ What are some elements of the way or purpose for which Jesus was sent?
10. ☐ What is the significance of Jesus' breathing on them?
11. ☐ What is the importance and meaning of 'breath' or 'wind' related to the Holy Spirit and the filled to flow life?

≈ Read Acts 1:8 NLT

"But you will receive power when the Holy Spirit comes upon you. And you will be my witnesses, telling people about me everywhere—in Jerusalem, throughout Judea, in Samaria, and to the ends of the earth."

Engage:

12. ≈ In what ways have you observed the Spirit's power at work through other believers?
13. ⌷ Why does the Spirit's power prompt 'witness' - and what does that mean for us?
14. ≈ How have you personally experienced the power of the Spirit?

≈ Read Luke 3:16 NLT

"I baptize you with water; but someone is coming soon who is greater than I am—so much greater that I'm not even worthy to be his slave and untie the straps of his sandals. He will baptize you with the Holy Spirit and with fire."

Engage:

15. ≈ Share your own experience in being baptized in the Holy Spirit. If you have not been, what's holding you back?

Pray ≈:

~ for more awareness of the Holy Spirit
~ for the baptism of the Holy Spirit if appropriate
~ for more openness to Holy Spirit's action in each person's life
~ for whatever needs there are

Extra Credit:

Read the following verses that describe some of the specific works of and expressions of the Holy Spirit. For each verse, name the specific action and work of the Spirit. From these scriptures, identify three works of the Spirit or encounters with the Spirit that you are particularly grateful for and share why. Micah 3:8, Matthew 3:16, Luke 4:1, John 3:3-5, Acts 1:5-8, Acts 2:17, Acts 2:4, Acts 10:44, Acts 8:15-17, Acts 28:25, John 14:15-17, John 15:26, John 16:13,

Romans 5:5, Romans 8:6, Romans 8:11, Romans 14:17, Romans 15:13-16, Galatians 5:16, 2 Thessalonians 2:13, 1 Corinthian 12:1-3, 1 John 2:20-27.

TWO

DO IT LIKE JESUS

You're filled to flow in supernatural engagement!

In this chapter, you'll discover that Jesus models
supernatural ministry in the power of the Spirit. The Kingdom of
God is what you're made for. He modeled supernatural engagement
as a way of life. He's the model of what it means to be filled to
flow. We're following Jesus in Supernatural engagement.

My brother came for a visit - and we flew away

My brother Rob lives in New York where he works in the banking
industry. We don't get to see each other that often because I live
in California. When he does come, we try to find something fun
and interesting to do together. Years ago, he visited when I lived in
Santa Barbara. We went out to the beach one day, and just above
the bluffs, right over our heads, there were people doing something
that looked like skydiving, except they were never coming down
and landing. It seems like they were actually flying right above the
bluff. I asked some people on the beach, "Hey, what is that? How
come those skydivers are not landing and they keep moving?" The
people on the beach were locals, and they pointed up and said,

"What they are doing is called paragliding. They do it here all the time because of the wind. It's cool, you should check it out!"

I went home and opened the phone book. (Hey, it was still the early 2000's when a phone book was a thing!) I looked up paragliding; low and behold, there it was; paragliding was an actual entry in the Yellow Pages of the phone book! I called Eagle Paragliding, one of the two paragliding companies, to see what I could find out. The guy who answered sounded enthusiastic and had a cool, raspy voice - and I was intrigued. "Yeah, buddy!" he said. "Paragliding is amazing, and I can get you up in the sky tomorrow!" He gave a few more details and told us where to meet him. "It's a hundred and fifty bucks per person - and you will be flying by the afternoon!"

We met our new friend and trainer, Rob Sporrer, at Elings Park where there was a beautiful grassy hill. This was where we would learn to fly! First, our trainer taught us about the sport of paragliding and technical information about how a paraglider functions. Then, he showed us all of the gear that we would be using, explaining each item and how we would use it. After that, he helped us strap into our paraglider harnesses and took us outside.

At this point, he laid out the large, colorful glider on the grass in front of us. He hooked up his paraglider and laid it out in front of him. He shouted through the light wind, describing what he was about to do. Then he pulled on the lines just when a gust of wind came and hoisted this giant kite over his head. Once it was in the air over his head, he had total control over it. He gently pulled on specific lines, and the massive canopy hovered over his body as he stood on the ground. When a small gust of wind came, he jumped, and the current lifted him about 5 feet off the ground for 10 seconds or so - and he shouted about how he was controlling the kite - and then he landed. He collapsed the wing back to the ground and shouted through a wry smile, "Okay boys, your turn!"

When Rob and I took our turns attempting to hoist that wing, it was a sloppy mess. The wind seemed to drag us both all across the hill. Our wings and lines and harnesses became a tangled mess. Our trainer looked at us and laughed, shaking his head and burying his face in his palms. "What am I going to do with you guys?" he cried out. Then he lifted his hands, palms wide open, looked up to the clouds, and yelled, "I'm gonna get you in the air is what I'm gonna do!"

Trainer Rob spent the next two hours coaching my brother Rob and me on every detail of how to inflate and manage our giant kites. Once I began pulling up my wing and was starting to get dragged, Trainer Rob would literally take hold of my hips or my chest to control my body so I'd do the proper movement to control the paraglider. He would run with me while I was getting blown around and pull the lines the right way to allow me to experience the most stability with the wing that was possible. After several hours, I was finally at a point where I could hold the wing steady overhead - at least for a few seconds. My brother Rob was able to do the same. At this point Trainer Rob spoke up with confidence, "You two dudes are ready to soar!"

He told us to wait there and watch him. He quickly inflated his paraglider, turned, faced down the hill, and ran forward. Within seconds, the current of wind had lifted him off the ground - and he was aloft. He flew to the left, then to the right, then to the left, carving a giant S into the skyscape above that hill. He effortlessly landed just in front of a container that was on the ground at the bottom of the hill. He quickly bundled up his gear, tossed it in the old Ford cargo van he had parked down below, and drove back up to us. He got out of the van and came our way with a smile on his face, shouting, "Your turn, brothers! It's time to take to the skies!"

Rob strapped a CB radio to my chest and turned it on. He then began speaking to me through his CB radio - and gave me instructions step by step. At just the right moment, when the wind was cycling up, his voice crackled through the radio, "Inflate, now!" I did - and he gave a few more directives to help me steady the big kite overhead. He then said, "Now turn and run down that hill!" I did as Rob said - and after a few steps, my feet left the ground as the wind lifted me over the grassy hill. Rob's voice came through the static in the airwaves, "You're flying now, baby!" He then gave me play-by-play instructions over the radio, while I was in the air, as to how to pilot this simple fabric aircraft. After several S-turns in the air, my altitude was declining rapidly. Just when I thought I was going to come crashing down to earth, Rob spoke firmly, "Be calm, you got this; aim towards that container, and now flare full brakes, both sides!" My glider seemed to come to a smooth stop and my feet were back on the ground - and I had become a pilot! My brother had as well - and so it was that my brother came to visit - and we flew away.

Rob demonstrated paragliding so I could do it myself

Rob Sporrer demonstrated paragliding to me - and trained me in it. After that introduction to paragliding, I was hooked. I signed up for further training courses. I completed my P-2 level certificate and went on to do my P-3 training. As a certified and licensed P-3 foot-launch aircraft pilot, I am cleared to fly almost any paragliding site in the world. It took hours of reading, coaching, and flight training. It took testing and sign-offs by various instructors. There are more advanced certifications I can pursue - but as it currently stands, I can fly anywhere.

I learned to fly a paraglider by studying, training, and coaching, plus time and experience under a wing with careful input from instructors. As a student pilot, I always had a radio strapped to my chest, with an instructor's voice booming through with direction and correction. I focused on my instructor's voice and guidance. The result of this process of learning is that I love paragliding - and I go do it every chance I get! It's a joy and a thrill for me - and I get to enjoy it freely now because I had great examples to learn from along the way. In particular, I'll always be grateful for Rob Sporrer

- my first example of how to paraglide; he gave me a mental model I remember and rely on every time I take to the skies, even to this day!

Jesus demonstrated the filled to flow life so you can do it!

What does my introduction to paragliding have to do with you - and the Holy Spirit? Well, Jesus is the ultimate example of the filled to flow life. You already know that as part of the Trinity, Jesus is one being eternally existent with the Father and the Spirit. But in His earthly life, Jesus condescended fully into the earthly experience. Philippians 2 says that he emptied himself and made himself 'nothing,' being made in human likeness. What this means is that in his earthly life, Jesus demonstrated what a human life fully yielded to God can look like.

As you consider how to live a filled to flow life, your model is *not* the latest speaker who headlines conferences, the trendy revivalist with dreadlocks, or the noted author with book sales in the hundreds of thousands (who now has no need of the local church). Those voices may have meaningful input - but your model - first and foremost - is Jesus in the gospels. You will *also* take to heart the words Jesus inspired in the rest of the New Testament about experience in the Spirit. But your first focus has to be on Jesus!

Fix your focus now, on this day in the life of Jesus - the day of His baptism:

> *One day, when the crowds were being baptized, Jesus himself was baptized. As he was praying, the heavens opened, and the Holy Spirit, in bodily form, descended on him like a dove. And a voice from heaven said, "You are my dearly loved Son, and you bring me great joy."*
>
> LUKE 3:21-23 NLT

Jesus shows us how it's done - starting with His Baptism

Jesus Christ is King of Kings and Lord of Lords, yet he demon-strated a way of life in his humanity that we can emulate. In the moment of his baptism, we get to see the first recorded moment of interaction between Jesus and the Holy Spirit. This is where it gets weird. "Wait - isn't the Holy Spirit... Him, Jesus?" Yes - and also, no! The word used in Philippians 2 that is translated as 'he made himself nothing' is the Greek word *kenosis* - a term that means 'to empty.' Jesus emptied Himself of the total fullness of divine nature - but not totally. He emptied Himself of the total divine nature enough to show us how to be human and engage divine power to overcome and thrive.

It's a bit like my first experience learning to paraglide. My instruc-tor, Rob, was a master pilot. But to teach me - he had to unharness his wing and stand on the ground with me where I could see him. He had to stand on the ground so he could take hold of me and help me gain the skills I would need to soar. He needed to lay his glider aside so he could run with me and coach me as I was trying to figure it all out. And in a sense, Jesus does something like that with the disciples in his 33 years of earthly life. He is entirely God and fully man - but He emptied Himself of a degree of divine power so we could see him as fully man and learn the ways of the Kingdom of God. He emptied himself so he could show us what it looks like to be *filled to flow*.

In the moment of His baptism, Jesus stood on the ground - waist deep in the water - and showed us *how it's done*. He modeled a posture of total humility and desire for the fullness that was avail-able. He was praying - words were coming from His heart. He was expressing His hunger for the goodness and fullness of God. He was praying. When a person is praying - they are deliberately turn-ing their attention towards the spiritual realm - and directing their focus to God himself. There is communication, connection, with the divine. True prayer goes far beyond the external practice of religion;

it is an expression of intimacy from the depth of the inner being of a person - and the result can ultimately be a spiritual closeness that is unrivaled.

Prayer - and the opening of Heaven

If you want to experience the fullness of the Spirit - it begins with prayer. Shift your attention from the things of this world, and allow your spirit to become aware of the spiritual realm and the goodness of God. Focus your attention on your Father in Heaven, and express your hunger for His presence. Tell him that you are open and ready to engage. Pray - tell God how you love Him and thank Him. Pray - and allow your spirit within you to awaken to the presence of God!

As Jesus prayed - as He pressed in with that yearning for real connection with the Father in Heaven - *the Heavens opened*. What is revealed here is that Heaven is not only a place you go *after* you die, but a realm that is *there* and also *here* - and even *now*. It is accessible. And it is possible that as you pray, this realm opens to you and around you in such a way that the glory and goodness of God can come and encompass you in a new way. It may even be that as the heavens open - you have access to enter. After all, Ephesians 2 says you are *seated with Him in heavenly places*; Philippians 3 says you are a *citizen of heaven*, and Hebrews 4:16 gives an anytime invitation for you to come boldly into the throne room of God in Heaven.

The experience of an open heaven is not just reserved for super charismatic churches somewhere in Northern California. An open heaven is possible anytime you earnestly pray and seek the face of God. It may be true that there is a greater degree of such an opening when there are many believers in agreement about pursuing real encounters with God. But you have as much right as anyone else - through the blood of Christ - to go after that open heaven. You do it through prayer - and Jesus modeled it.

The dove reveals aspects of the nature of Holy Spirit

The heavens opened - and then the Holy Spirit descended in the form of a dove. You might wonder why the Holy Spirit chose to come in the form of a dove. So do I! The Bible doesn't explain the answer to this, but the Bible does speak of a dove bringing the olive branch to Noah when the ravishes of the floodwaters had receded. The dove was emblematic of peace - and in appearing in the form of a dove - it is as though a prophetic message is coming from the heart of God about the peace that is possible in and through the Holy Spirit. Turtle Doves were also one of the most basic sacrifices for purification offerings in the Old Testament temple era. The Spirit descending in the form of a dove is a prophetic message about the anointing that would rest upon the life of Jesus in his earthly mission to provide the perfect sacrifice and bring purification from sin for all who would turn to Him.

It may also be that the nature of a dove expresses something about the nature of the Holy Spirit in terms of the Spirit's way of interacting with people. A dove will come near to one who is calm. A dove will fly away from one who is erratic. In a sense, this may reveal something about the nature of the Holy Spirit; The Spirit is willing to come near, but you may need to still yourself so as to welcome His presence. At the same time, if your lifestyle is at odds with the Word of God, this may grieve the Holy Spirit. Like a dove that simply won't come near to a person who is flailing around, the Holy Spirit is unlikely to rest on you when your life is deliberately out of step with God's revealed will.

The Holy Spirit came in a physical form - and in this moment, the form was that of a dove - maybe for the reasons I've stated. But the obvious should not be missed. Holy Spirit was present in an unexpected physical form. This is an indication of something that is always possible with the Holy Spirit. Some would say, "The Holy Spirit coming in a physical form was a one-time thing, and the bird is the word!" But Holy Spirit later comes as tongues of fire, and in Isaiah's prophetic vision, Holy Spirit was present as a thick cloud.

I have personally witnessed the manifest presence of the Holy Spirit coming in such richness that actual *gold dust* accumulated on the arms and hands of several people who were part of the gathering. I've personally experienced the unexplained appearance of feathers - with a deep sense in my own spirit that it was a sign of the Holy Spirit's presence. The point is, the Holy Spirit can come in physical form - and the form is not necessarily limited to small, docile birds!

Holy Spirit's presence brings a proper understanding of identity

When the Holy Spirit descended upon Jesus, the voice from Heaven came booming forth, "You are my dearly loved son - you bring me great joy!" When the Holy Spirit is moving in truth and power, there is often an accompanying clarification of true identity - and false frames of identity are highlighted or removed. When you experience the Holy Spirit filling you, the unhealthy and unhelpful labels, personas, and identities you've taken on get stripped away as the Heavenly Father's voice is carried by the Spirit into your heart, revealing who you *really* are and reinstating your healthy sense of identity. Before Jesus faced temptation from the Devil, and before Jesus created a ministry impact team, before he called any disciples together, he heard the Heavenly Father's affirmation. That satisfied and strengthened Him. It is best this way.

As you learn to flow in the Holy Spirit's power, it must come from first being filled by the Spirit. Your desire for and engagement in the flow of the Spirit must not be from a place of striving - either striving to prove something to the world, or other believers, or seeking to earn something from God. When you receive the filling of the Spirit, you experience an increasing degree of inner strength and security in your own identity as a child of God. You, too, begin to hear the Father's words over you as He speaks of His joy about who you are - independent of whatever you have (or haven't) done for

Him. Further on in this book, I will talk about the gifts and power of the Holy Spirit, but the Spirit flows best through a son or daughter whose sense of identity is secure in the Heavenly Father's love!

I want that for you. I want you to know how much you are loved by your Father in Heaven. I want you to rest in his grace - yes, it was, is, and always will be undeserved; that was God's idea! I want you to be enveloped in His mercy - assured that your sins are forgiven. I want you to know that He loves you, you are his child - and He's so happy about who you are - and who you are becoming. I want you to let Him hold you up in His hands with delight, the way a Father lifts His newborn up with great joy. This is who you really are - a daughter, a son, totally loved by your Heavenly Father! He loves you so much that He is eager to offer you the experience of more of the fullness and filling of the Holy Spirit!

Activation - Identity

In this activation, you will think about some of the identity labels you have adopted throughout the course of your life. Some are related to your profession or your hobbies. Some are related to lifestyle choices, gender, and sexuality. You'll lay these before God, to surrender them to Him. Then consider the names God gives to you - and accept those as who you are by praying through those new identifiers and declaring them about yourself.

~ Say out loud, in prayer, "God, these are the labels I've taken on along the way," and then name them out loud. For example, "Accountant, Nurse, Maverick, Transperson, Singer, Jerk, Queer, Comedian, Perv, Boss, Pilot, Soldier, Punk Rock Girl, etc."
~ Ask the Lord, "Are any of these okay to keep?"
~ Ask the Lord, "Do I need to let any of these go?"

~ Say aloud, in prayer, "I surrender the false identities of X, Y, Z to you - that's not who I am!"
~ Say out loud, in prayer,

"This is who Your Word says I am: Child of God, Beloved, Daughter or Son, Disciple, Friend of God, Slave of God, New Creation, Saint, Holy Temple, Redeemed, Forgiven, Holy and Blameless, God's Workmanship, Overcomer, Servant of Righteousness, Salt of the earth, Light of the World, Child of the Light, More than a Conqueror, Citizen of Heaven!"

~ Declare over yourself, "This is who I am: I am...," and speak out loud, repeatedly, some of the Biblical words of eternal identity listed above that you are most drawn to.

~ Write down any sensation or spiritual feeling you had as you engaged in this activation.

My journey from brokenness toward wholeness and fullness

When I was a child, my mother was an opera singer and a vocal coach. I heard music and singing in our house or in an opera house practically every day of my life. Naturally, I gravitated toward music. I learned to sing and play a few instruments - and before long, I was singing in choirs and performing in operas and musicals as a child. This experience shaped some aspects of my identity. In my teen years, I attended a High School of the Performing Arts because my identity as a performer was growing. I continued this pathway in college; I spent the first two years of college in a highly competitive Bachelor of Fine Arts program in Theater, training to be an actor. As a young adult, *this is who I was.*

During my second year in that program, I had begun dating a young woman - I'll call her Sarah Parker. She struggled with mental illness, and as I got closer and more intimate with her, her struggles became all-consuming for me. She lapsed into episodes of dissociative identity (this is sometimes referred to as schizophrenia) and suicidal ideation - and I felt responsible. The relationship was very codependent. I was not walking with Jesus at the time - and that was apparent in how the relationship progressed. She became pregnant, and I was hardly able to handle the stress of our situation. My work in the theater school suffered, and I was cut from the program at the end of the second year.

When this happened, I felt like my entire sense of identity was shattered. Who was I now? It was as though this college had said,

"You're no good at acting and theater!" Yet this had been so much of my life all the way from childhood to this point. On the one hand, I was dealing with a sense of my identity being crushed, and on the other hand, I was wrecked with the stress of facing a pregnancy and a relationship with someone who was in a great degree of inner turmoil. I felt as though I needed to rescue her - but I was also falling apart. The baby was lost to a mid-term miscarriage, and in the pain of that, the relationship also ended.

It was in my brokenness that I realized *I needed Jesus*. While I had put my faith in Jesus during Middle School, by this time, I was a candidate for a recommitment to Christ if there ever was one. I found a college fellowship group called InterVarsity Christian Fellowship at Rutgers University, and among a large group of fellow college students who were all seeking Jesus, I recommitted my life to Christ. I came to see myself as a fully forgiven son who was loved by my heavenly Father! I still had so much to learn and grow in, but this much was settled, and it gave me strength. It also created the space in my heart in which the Holy Spirit could fill me and flow through me!

In the years that followed I would continue to face struggles and temptations, but the filling of the Holy Spirit prepared me for resisting the temptations that would come and for enduring the trials that would arise. Being filled with the Holy Spirit gave me a source of inner strength that catalyzed great courage in me to embrace an adventure of serving Jesus in world missions. Being filled with the Holy Spirit created a reservoir of hope, love and power within me that buoys me up through wave after wave of struggle and challenge.

A day in the life of Jesus

Before His great years of impact and ministry, Jesus experienced testing and temptation. But he faced it from a place of fullness of the Spirit. The Spirit came upon Him in His baptism - and He was filled with the Spirit before His 40 days in the desert where He was tempted by the Devil. He demonstrated that the Spirit's fullness is the best preparation for dealing with the schemes of the devil to take us out. God desires for you to be a Christian who is an overcomer. The way you will overcome is by the power of the Holy Spirit filling you and flowing from within you!

Consider this moment in Jesus' life:

> *Then Jesus, full of the Holy Spirit, returned from the*
> *Jordan River. He was led by the Spirit in the wilderness,*
> *where he was tempted by the devil for forty days. Jesus*
> *ate nothing all that time and became very hungry.*

LUKE 4:1-2 NLT

Joy - it is yours, and sometimes you have to fight for it

One of the distinguishing blessings of being filled with the Spirit is an indomitable joy that springs from within you. When you are filled with the Spirit, shadows and shame lose their hold and their sway. Pain and despair have a diminished ability to weigh you down, and hope percolates up from the very ground of your being. The result is a distinct inner ease - and a lightness of being that is best described with the word joy. You may not feel chipper and happy all the time - but you have a foundation of joy about you because of the filling of the Spirit. That sense of joy allows you to operate with a deep conviction that you are safe, secure, and satisfied in God's mercy, love and care. This joy will enable you to declare God's praise despite the difficulties you may have to face.

There may be some seasons in which you have to fight for your joy. That joy is part of what God's Kingdom and the flow of the Spirit is all about - but there are times when you may lose touch with it. When that happens, you need to consider where you lost that joy. Was it when you gave in to a temptation and went down a path of sin? Was it when you began consuming a certain kind of media? Identify that moment where joy was lost - and turn to God first with repentance - and then with gratitude. As you begin to express gratitude to God for the myriad ways He has shown you grace, favor, and blessing, joy seems to be right around the corner - and you bump into it almost without even trying.

Have you been baptized in the Holy Spirit?

You may wonder whether you have received the filling of the Holy Spirit. You may be questioning whether you have genuinely experienced the fullness of the Spirit or not. It is a valid question. There is a moment recorded in Acts 19 where the Apostle Paul comes into Ephesus to check in on a group of believers there. He asks if they have received the Holy Spirit - and their answer is that they didn't even know that there *is* a Holy Spirit! It is possible to be a believer who technically *has the seal* of the Holy Spirit without having the experience of being filled with the Spirit. This didn't make them lesser believers - but it did make their experience as believers lesser than what God truly desires.

In a moment, in an instant, everything changed. The book of Acts simply says that the Apostle Paul laid hands on them and prayed for them, and they received the baptism of the Holy Spirit, and they began speaking to God in tongues. (I will share more with you about the gift of tongues in chapter 4.) For now, I want you to catch a vision for *more*: more of the fullness of the Spirit, more of the presence of God, more of the flow of the Spirit, more of the dynamic expression of the Holy Spirit into and through your life. *More* is possible - and it may be that you need to receive the baptism of the Holy Spirit. And I want you to know that God desires for you to receive the gift of the Spirit's fullness!

> *I baptize you with water; but someone is coming soon who*
> *is greater than I am, so much greater that I'm not even*
> *worthy to be his slave and untie the straps of his sandals.*
> *He will baptize you with the Holy Spirit and with fire.*

LUKE 3:16 NLT

These words of prophetic promise are spoken by John the Baptist, and he was talking about Jesus. John declared that the heart of the ministry of Jesus would be a shift in the human experience of the divine. Until this time, the Spirit of God was considered something that people could only hope to be touched by on occasion. John the Baptist was *prophesying* and *promising* that Jesus would radically shift that equation. "He will baptize you with the Holy Spirit and with fire!" John said.

To baptize means *to completely immerse.* The idea is that Jesus will cause you to be completely drenched by the work of the Holy Spirit. His vision and plan is that your whole life will become saturated with the flow of the Holy Spirit! Baptism is generally something that happens in a meaningful way all at once. It's different from a daily bath. So it is with the Baptism of the Holy Spirit. You may not be able to dictate when it will happen - but it *is* God's best for it *to* happen. Generally, the model in scripture is that the apostolic leader in your life (or one designated by him or her) will lay hands on you and pray for the Baptism of the Holy Spirit.

John's prophecy was that Jesus would baptize you with the Holy Spirit and with *fire!* Fire is about passion, expression, warmth, and power. Yes, fire can also be unpredictable and presents a degree of risk; that is part of the nature of fire. However, the scriptures show us, broadly speaking, that the fire of the Holy Spirit is not an uncontrolled destructive blaze - but rather a force for the good of God's Kingdom burning within the hearts of men and women who are filled with the Spirit.

The Anointing of the Holy Spirit

I want you to experience the Pentecost 'tongues of fire' of Acts 2. I want you to experience the baptism Jesus wants for you - a baptism of the Holy Spirit and fire. I want you to be baptized in the Holy Spirit so that you will be so on fire for God that you'll live for the joy of experiencing Holy Spirit flowing through you! You're made for the filled to flow life - and the baptism of the Holy Spirit is part of how you live it. Jesus spoke of this when he was speaking at a synagogue gathering early in His ministry, as recorded in Luke 4:18-21:

"The Spirit of the Lord is upon me, for he has anointed me to bring Good News to the poor. He has sent me to proclaim that captives will be released, that the blind will see, that the oppressed will be set free, and that the time of the Lord's favor has come." He rolled up the scroll, handed it back to the attendant, and sat down. All eyes in the synagogue looked at him intently. Then he began to speak to them. "The Scripture you've just heard has been fulfilled this very day!"

Can you imagine being at church that day when Jesus, the Word of God, opened the Word of God, read it, and then spoke His own words about it? Now, *that* would be life-changing! Jesus was defining his approach to his earthly ministry. He highlighted that the anointing of the Holy Spirit gave Him the fuel and the fire He needed to engage in powerful Kingdom impact in this world!

The word anointing is taken from the Old Testament, and in its original context, it was agrarian terminology. A Shepherd would carry around a horn of oil so he could smear healing oil on his sheep who were wounded or being pestered by bugs. The oil would be smeared on to bring the healing or the protection the animal needed. The oil was valuable, so it wasn't used indiscriminately. It was only used on a select few sheep as required. The shepherd was literally anointing his animals by smearing the oil on them. The word *anoint* literally means to anoint with oil.

As time progressed, the prophets, such as Samuel, carried their anointing oil, ready to apply it to their flocks as needed - but also to use for another purpose. The prophet's horn of oil came to be recognized as a conduit for the supernatural power and authority of the prophet who smeared it on someone. More broadly understood, the oil came to represent the presence and power of the Spirit of

God. The prophet, as one with spiritual authority from God, could smear the oil on a person to designate them as a leader, a prophet, a priest, or a King.

As this practice was carried out, the word itself began to have a significance far beyond its original meaning of 'to smear [with oil].' When a prophet anointed someone with oil, they were set apart. God had chosen them for a purpose, and God's power would be upon them to carry it out. The anointing conveyed supernatural capacity and energy. It empowered the person in a recognizably holy way.

Jesus quoted the scriptures to say, "The Spirit of the Sovereign Lord is upon me; He has anointed me to preach the good news." He used the word 'anointed' in this sense. He expressed his understanding that the anointing that was upon Him would empower Him to carry out His assignment with supernatural force - and it did. The anointing of the Power and Spirit of God on a person's life creates shockwaves of supernatural resonance that sets captives free and creates miraculous power for breakthrough, deliverance, and healing.

Jesus walked in the anointing of the Spirit of God - and you and I also need the anointing of the Spirit of God to engage fully in the ministry of the Kingdom of God. You will be most satisfied in your filled to flow life when you experience the oil of God's presence being smeared upon you from the top of your head to the soles of your feet! You will rise with a confidence that Jesus demonstrated - because you'll know that it isn't just you.

The anointing is the empowering presence of God by visitation or habitation on your life for supernatural breakthrough. The Holy Spirit lives in you - for your own sake. The Holy Spirit lives in you to comfort you, empower you, encourage you, and bring revelation to you - and more. And then, the anointing of the Holy Spirit falls on you for the sake of others. The anointing is there so that you can boldly move forward in supernatural ministry. To put it most simply, the anointing is the presence of God's Spirit upon your life and ministry. Ask God for His anointing; you need it!

Activation - Ask for the Anointing

For this activation, find a YouTube video or playlist of instrumental worship music. I recommend William Augusto: Soaking in His Presence. Play the soaking music, and then lie down on the floor, face up. Simply ask, "Holy Spirit, I'm asking for Your anointing." Then rest, and wait. Imagine a person with a great need for a breakthrough of any kind in front of you. Ask the Holy Spirit, "What would you want me to do for this person with Your anointing?" Then, imagine the empowerment of the Spirit flowing through you to do it.

~ Did anything happen to you during this activation?

~ Did you experience anything physically as you asked for the anointing of the Spirit?

~ Write down any sensation or sense you had as you said, "I'm asking for the anointing."

Jesus wanted show and tell

Jesus didn't want His message to become *just* a message. He wanted His message to be show and tell, teach and do, hear and experience. And it was a specific kind of experience that Jesus wanted to take place – he wanted to see the supernatural breakthrough that people were longing for, praying for, and believing for, come about. We have done a good job with the 'tell' part of the equation, but the experience of supernatural breakthrough is somewhat lacking in many Christian churches.

Part of the problem is that while Jesus established that supernatural breakthrough is the norm, we've sort of 'de-clawed' the scriptures. We've created a different message that tends to be devoid of supernatural breakthroughs, except for the forgiveness of sin. We sanitize the scriptures and use the Bible selectively to suit our preferences. It looks something like this:

"Oh, he cast out evil spirits? Well, that's too scary." Gone.

"Oh, an angel showed up? Not comfortable with that." Gone.

"Oh, He healed people's physical sicknesses? Too hard to explain!" Gone.

"Oh, it says they prayed in tongues? Um, not gonna go there!" Gone.

"Oh, it says we should eagerly desire the greater gifts, especially the gift of prophecy? Awkward!" Gone.

"Oh, it says that there are all these spiritual gifts? Well, certain ones that don't make me uncomfortable are acceptable, but those other ones are just too weird!" Gone.

Churches and preachers have just eliminated or explained away the things they don't prefer in scripture. They've ended up with an adulterated version of the scriptures and a Christian experience that looks less and less like Jesus. Following Jesus is reduced to feeding the poor and going to heaven when you die. The reality is that Jesus established an expectation that we, His followers, would exercise the right or power to act on His behalf in specific ways and usher in His Kingdom!

Jesus has a vision of something greater for you

"Jesus Christ is the same yesterday, today, and forever," is the declaration of Hebrews 13:8. That means He is still healing the sick and still wants us to! That means He is still cleansing those who have leprosy and still wants us to! That means He is still driving out demons from people and still wants us to! That means He is still raising the dead and still wants us to! He wants us to be moving with Him toward supernatural breakthroughs in our own lives and the lives of others! He wants us to experience and then extend the blessing of God's reigning presence!

He actually made His intentions for you known when he spoke the words of John 14:12, "Very truly I tell you, whoever believes in me will do the works I have been doing, and they will do even greater things than these, because I am going to the Father."

These words from Jesus are exciting and daunting at the same time. Think about the kinds of works Jesus did. He loved people who were seemingly unlovable. He prayed with power, and He comforted people with supernatural grace. He fed hungry people with miracles of multiplication. He touched the forgotten lepers

- and with His touch, they were healed. He taught the truth of the ways of God and the heart of God so powerfully that His words are remembered eternally. He demonstrated the spiritual reality of the Kingdom of God and made the supernatural supernormal. He cast out demons, He healed the sick, and He raised the Dead!

Those were 'the works.' Thinking about the kind of disciples He wanted, Jesus put in his order - and He said, "I'll have them with the works, please." That's what he has ordered up for your life! Love people, okay. Comfort people, teach people, okay - got it. But - heal the sick? Yup. Cast out d, d, ddd, ddddd, demons!?? Yup - and fearlessly, too. Raise the DEAD? Uh-huh. These are 'the works' Jesus did.

And just what Jesus meant by 'even greater things than these,' we don't exactly know! But we do know this: All of these things Jesus did - 'the works' - He did as an example of what a human being filled with the Holy Spirit could do. So that we could see what was possible. 1 John 4:4 says, "Greater is He who is in you than he who is in the world." Jesus perfectly demonstrated this reality for us, so we can see that accomplishing the 'greater things' he spoke about, comes from the reality of the Greater One who is in us. He put the greater IN you so he could get the greater OUT of you!

An Eye on Heaven

Jesus wanted you to see His value for the Kingdom of God and the filled to flow life. He also wanted you to see how He approached His own experience of that flow. He did it by keeping His eyes on Heaven - and the One who from Heaven reigns over everything. In John 5:19-20 (NLT) Jesus said, "I tell you the truth, the Son can do nothing by himself. He does only what he sees the Father doing. Whatever the Father does, the Son also does. For the Father loves the Son and shows him everything he is doing." The motivation and inspiration for the flow is not self-generated. It's based on the perception of the Heavenly Father and an understanding of His compassion.

Jesus modeled this so that you would do likewise. You're at your best when you've got one eye on the circumstance you're confronted with or the person you're ministering to, and another eye on Heaven, asking, "What does it seem like your Heavenly Father is doing?"

This might be something new for you, but it is a spiritual skill you can and must develop. Jesus did this all the time - and as far as we can tell, He did it so subtly that people didn't even pick up on it. That's the goal! For now, you might need to pause, pray, and press in for a view of Heaven - and that's precisely what I'd like you to do right now.

Activation - What is the Father Doing?

What if your imagination was a faculty of your brain that God wants to use as an entry point for making Himself more fully known? In this activation, you will invite Him to do just that.

~ Take a deep breath and slowly let it out, and let your concerns go with it. Let your mind wander a bit. Imagine a place you are familiar with, just to warm up. Then, imagine God the Father appearing there. What is His posture? Is He doing something? Is He saying something?

~ Pray and thank God for allowing you to understand who He is, what He is saying, and what He is doing.

~ As you pray, ask God to help you to grow in doing this more and more often, until it becomes a way of life for you, as it was for Jesus!

Look at the Acts 10:38 snapshot - and live it out.

You can't tell everything from a photograph, but it can tell you a lot. There were no cameras in Jesus' day, so sadly - there's no actual photo of Him that I can show you. If you entered the proper prompts, AI would produce an image or likeness that would get close if you want to see a picture of a Middle Eastern man circa 30 AD. But there is one verse of scripture that gives you a snapshot of the ministry life of Jesus - and it's the words recorded by Luke in Acts 10:38:

And you know that God anointed Jesus of Nazareth with the Holy Spirit and with power. Then Jesus went around doing good and healing all who were oppressed by the devil, for God was with him.

ACTS 10:38 NLT

Five core elements in this snapshot give definition to what the filled to flow life is meant to include. This is one snapshot - that means 'there is more.' It isn't the only picture. But it is a good verbal summary inspired by the Holy Spirit. It can help you think about your own life purpose and how the filling and the flow of the Holy Spirit are related. These are five characteristics for you to pray for as you delve into living a more filled to flow life.

Five factors of the Acts 10:38 Snapshot for your life

First of all, Jesus was anointed with the Holy Spirit. You need the anointing of the Holy Spirit too. It isn't enough to just have confidence in your own spirit. It isn't sufficient to depend on your personality or even your talents. You will be at your best when the Holy Spirit's anointing is on you as it was on Jesus when He walked this earth!

Second, Jesus was anointed with power from God. There is something unique about being anointed with power; it's different from being anointed with peace or anointed with grace. As good as those things are, they have to be energized in order to be effectively expressed. That's where power comes in. Supernatural anointing with power can change your life and change the lives of whomever you'll minister to. When God's power is upon you, you can pick up the pace to God's speed, and you can get things done with dynamic capability. When God's power is anointing you, you are accessing the unstoppable force of your Heavenly Father's energy to accomplish the incredible things that God is moving you to do!

Third, Jesus went around doing good. Jesus did not allow Himself to become self-absorbed. He was others-focused. He overcame the inertia of laziness and comfort - and got out there. He moved, and wherever He went, His eyes were open for whatever kind of good He could do. That's what *you* are called to as well! There are places to go, people to serve, good to be done! If you let it, the allure of comfort and entertainment will become a black hole trapper keeper. It will trap you and keep you from going around and doing good in the flow of the Spirit!

Fourth, as Jesus went around, something He was known to do frequently was to heal all those who were under the power of the devil. This part of the snapshot shows us that for Jesus, being filled to flow meant confronting the power of the devil in at least two specific ways: casting out demons and healing the sick. As you move more deeply into your own experience of being filled to flow, this is something you get to do too! There is a place for attending Bible studies, listening to sermon podcasts, and reading books like this one. But at some point, you've got to allow the flow of the Spirit to move through you to engage and tear down strongholds of the devil so people are set free and healed!

Fifth, the snapshot shows us that God was with Jesus. His human life was marked by an observable reality of God's presence about Him. He was filled to flow, and people recognized that Jesus wasn't just doing good deeds. He was moving in and with God's reigning presence in real time on this earth. My friend, that's what you're made for! Be with God in your own secret place in such a way that people can recognize it.

Now consider this - at the time of the resurrection, the Risen Jesus told the leaders of His followers to stay in Jerusalem until the power from on high came to them (Luke 24:49, Acts 1:4). The disciples who were told to wait for the Holy Spirit's coming probably felt a degree of excitement mixed with apprehension and even concern. How would this promised power from on high change things? What would it be like? What kind of trouble could it get them in?

You are two chapters into this book, and you're making progress. But maybe you're feeling concerned in a similar way. Nevertheless, Jesus is inviting you to wait for His power to come into your life by the Holy Spirit. Empowered ministry is always better than driven ministry. Driven ministry can achieve results - but empowered ministry brings glory to the Father.

Jesus described the Holy Spirit as being like a river of living water. He envisioned a kind of spiritual 'ease' for you. Rivers have a current and energy all their own. Rivers provide an answer to the problem of dryness and the need for refreshing and sustenance. A puddle also has water - but it is murky and stagnant. If you see a pond with dirty, still water and algae covering the surface, do you want to jump in? Probably not. If you see a river, clear and flowing, now do you want to jump in? I thought so!

Now the question is - what kind of person was Jesus, and what kind of person do you want to be? You can be a person who settles for a still but putrid pond of religious rightness. Or you can be someone with the adventurous purity of a river - flowing, clean, and powerful. That's the kind of person Jesus was - and that's what living the filled to flow life is all about!

FILLED TO FLOW
BIBLE STUDY SMALL GROUP GUIDE

CHAPTER TWO: Do it like Jesus!

You're filled to flow in supernatural engagement!

Supernatural ministry in the power of the Spirit is modeled by Jesus - and it's what you're made for. Some might think of Jesus as simply a mild-mannered master teacher - but He's actually the One who modeled supernatural engagement as a way of life. He's the model; we're following Jesus.

Bible study group guide how-to summary:

▱ Means it's a Bible study reflection question. It's okay if just 1-2 people answer. It's okay to move through it quickly or even to skip. It also means there may not be time to include the reading of this scripture or the discussion of the question with the whole group. But consider these sections in your own study!

≈ Means this is a group interaction reflection question. It would be good to ask several people from the group to respond. It also means that the scripture associated with this question should be read aloud to the group.

Engage:

1. ≈ Icebreaker: If you could follow anyone around to learn from them for a day, who would it be and why?

≈ **Read John 7:37-39 from your own Bible.**

Engage:

2. ▱ Discuss any highlights from this chapter or observations related to John 7:37-39. Why do you think Jesus compares the Holy Spirit to "rivers of living water?"

≈ **Read Luke 3:21-23 NLT**

One day when the crowds were being baptized, Jesus himself was baptized. As he was praying, the heavens opened, and the Holy Spirit, in bodily form, descended on him like a dove. And a voice from heaven said, "You are my dearly loved Son, and you bring me great joy."

Engage:

3. ≈ How did Jesus posture himself to experience the Holy Spirit - and how are you doing in posturing yourself to experience the Holy Spirit?

4. ▱ What is the significance of Holy Spirit appearing like a dove?

≈ **Read Luke 4:18-21 NLT**

"The Spirit of the Lord is upon me, for he has anointed me to bring Good News to the poor. He has sent me to proclaim that captives will be released, that the blind will see, that the oppressed will be set free, and that the time of the Lord's favor has come." He rolled up the scroll, handed it back to the attendant, and sat down. All eyes in the synagogue looked at him intently. Then he began to speak to them. "The Scripture you've just heard has been fulfilled this very day!"

5. ≈ If you were one of the people in that synagogue - what would your reaction have been to this moment?

6. ⊐ What were some of the elements of the purpose of the presence of the Spirit in Jesus' life, according to His own words?

7. ⊐ If you are a filled to flow follower of Jesus, what are the implications of the words of Luke 4:18-21 for *you*?

⊐ Read John 5:19-20a NLT

Jesus explained, "I tell you the truth, the Son can do nothing by himself. He does only what he sees the Father doing. Whatever the Father does, the Son also does. For the Father loves the Son and shows him everything he is doing."

8. ⊐ What is your approach to following Jesus' example of doing what you see the Father doing?

≈ Read John 3:34 NLT

For he is sent by God. He speaks God's words, for God gives him the Spirit without limit.

9. ≈ Name one step you can or will take to increase your own experience of receiving the Spirit without limit and why it will be good for you.

≈ Read Acts 10:38 NLT

And you know that God anointed Jesus of Nazareth with the Holy Spirit and with power. Then Jesus went around doing good and healing all who were oppressed by the devil, for God was with him.

10. ≈ Share some examples of what it would look like for us, now, to "go around doing good" under the anointing of the Holy Spirit. Share any possible example you can think of.

11. ≈ Does the model of Jesus - casting out demons by the Spirit's power - give you a sense of excitement or fear? Explain.

≈ Read Luke 24:49 NLT

"And now I will send the Holy Spirit, just as my Father promised. But stay here in the city until the Holy Spirit comes and fills you with power from heaven."

12. ▱ How do you think the disciples were affected by Jesus' promise to send the Holy Spirit?
13. ≈ How does Jesus' promise to send the Holy Spirit affect you?
14. ▱ Why did Jesus want the disciples to wait until they had received the Holy Spirit?
15. ≈ How would your life, work, and ministry be different if you experienced more of the filling of the Spirit?

Pray≈:

~ for spiritual thirst in one another's lives
~ for increased experience of the refreshing river flow of the Holy Spirit
~ for greater intimacy with the Father that leads to seeing what He's doing and hearing His voice
~ for whatever other needs there may be

THREE

ARE YOU GETTING THE DOWNLOAD?

You're filled to flow in the prophetic!

In this chapter, you will learn about the gifts oriented around receiving revelation. You'll discover how to get the downloads from Heaven that God may want to give you. You'll learn about the revelatory gifts of the Spirit- Prophecy, Vision, Word of Knowledge, Message of Wisdom, and Tongues - and how to begin to enjoy these gifts.

My first awareness of the supernatural prophetic presence of God

My family moved to Princeton Junction, New Jersey when I was eight years old. We were nominally Christian; my Mom was a professional musician, and she valued finding a church with great classical music. In a relatively short time, my mom found Trinity Church, Princeton - an old-school Episcopal church with a boy's choir - and she signed me up. Pretty soon, I was learning to sight-read music, and I spent my Sunday mornings singing in the church choir in the boy's soprano section. Our choir director was an

Englishman, John Bertalot. He was a graduate of King's College in Cambridge and was a Doctor of choral music. He was a masterful musician and an inspiring choral conductor. He took this group of rambunctious boys and transformed us into a world-class choir that was requested for choral performances around the world.

John Bertalot was also a firm believer with a heart for God's presence, even in a high-church context not necessarily known for that. While he wanted us boys to excel musically, he also earnestly desired to see us discover an authentic faith in Jesus. He would share devotions from scripture at every rehearsal, challenge us to take turns praying out loud, and pray for us individually with warmth and passion.

In my second year, Dr. Bertalot was asked to mentor a group of us boys to prepare us for *confirmation*. In the Anglican and Episcopal traditions, that is a process of learning the fundamentals of Christianity so that you can be confirmed as a Christian. In these confirmation mentoring sessions, he introduced us to the Bible, shared about communion, and taught us about prayer. But what left the most significant impression on me was what he shared about a moment of personal encounter with Jesus.

He told us about a time when he was meeting with a small group of fellow believers back in England. He described how they were sitting in the house's family room with the doors closed. They read some scripture and then prayed together. While deep in prayer, eyes closed and voices raised, they felt a stirring in the air that made them all open their eyes.

At that moment, they saw *Jesus* sitting on the hearth of the fireplace. It was Jesus - with a Middle Eastern complexion, wearing a loosely fitting robe of rough knit white fabric. His nail-pierced hands and feet were visible. He looked each of these college students in the eyes, smiled at them, and said to them, "I'm so pleased with you!" They spent a few silent moments simply looking at Him

- totally amazed. Suddenly there was another stirring in the air - and He was gone.

Dr. Bertalot shared about this experience with this small group of boys - and we were all transfixed. His passion while sharing about this moment was magnetic. He looked at us and said,"'You never know when Jesus is going to show up *right in your family room!*"This made a lasting impression on all of us. That was the first time in my life that it became clear to me that God was really far more than a dry religious or historical topic to hear - or sing - about.

I completed the confirmation class, and weeks later, I was confirmed as a member of the Episcopal Church. The truth was that I had yet to experience a personal moment of encounter with Jesus - or even a personal commitment of my life to Him. This religious ritual *did* give me some theological foundations and language - but my own true conversion at the heart level would come a few years later in an Assemblies of God youth group.

Hearing Dr. Bertalot's personal encounter with Jesus created a hunger in me for something like that to happen in my life. His testimony of experience with Jesus caused me to have an open mind to what *could* be possible. It helped me begin to imagine how faith could be genuine - and the Christian life could be much more than just trying to be good and going to church. It would take me years to come to a place where such a thing was personal - but it established a framework in me for considering that *there is more. There is so much more!*

John Bertalot's encounter with Jesus took place in a context of fellowship and prayer. This was a small group of Christians who were praying and seeking Jesus together. They were willing to enter into God's presence together in a profound way. There was something about their hearts - united in the Spirit while praying - that was an invitation for Jesus to show up. Whether this encounter with Jesus was flesh-and-blood or a vision that all in the group perceived together is debatable. The fact is, though, that they saw Him, heard

His voice, and felt His presence. They experienced something of an *open heaven* as He suddenly came - and suddenly left. It was as though they received a very special download from heaven that was just for them.

What I want to highlight for you is that all of this - and more - is possible. You may experience a visitation like this. It is likely that you, too, could see a vision given by the Lord - and hear His voice! And it does *not* need to be a one-time occurrence; it can be a way of life. The basis for a flow of revelation like this is your life in the Spirit.

You *can* get the download...

Any person who puts their faith in Jesus is marked with the Holy Spirit, as with a seal, according to Ephesians 1:13. The seal of the Holy Spirit on your spirit *affirms* in a way that is spiritually visible that you truly belong to Jesus. But every believer also has *access* to the *filling* of the Holy Spirit. If you analyze the grammar of the original language of Ephesians 5:18, you discover that this isn't a one-time thing. It says 'be filled with the Holy Spirit' - but the verb tense implies something that is to *continue* to happen. Being filled with the Spirit is intended to be an ongoing reality for the believer. But having access is not the same as entering in.

Where'd my keys go...?

As the lead pastor of Centerpoint Church, in Murrieta, CA - I have the master key to the entire church facilities. This key was given because of my leadership role and the responsibilities I have. In a sense, the key *affirms* what is true about me - that I belong to Centerpoint Church as its Lead Pastor. As such, I have *access* to the facilities since I have responsibilities that call for me to enter and make use of the resources. I use those keys nearly every day of my life - to go into the office and do pastoral meetings or prepare a message. Sometimes I use those keys to go into the chapel early in the morning to sit at the piano and worship. Other times, I use that key to go into the sanctuary to walk around and pray and shout. Sometimes I use those keys to rush in, make some copies for a meeting, and then rush out. The point is - I have access - and I take advantage of that access *very often*.

Here's the thing. All of our other pastors and quite a few other staff members have that same key. They have the same access. But I have never run into them in the chapel in the early morning when I wanted to worship. I've never come into the main sanctuary in the middle of the night, when I've come to walk and pray, and seen them there. On the other hand, it seems that every time I rush in to make some copies - there's *always* somebody there, already at the copy machine! For the most part, though, I find that while all of these team members have the same key, and *could* enter the same way I do, most do not.

Has cessationism confiscated your keys?

There is a similar dynamic for many Christians. They have the seal of the Holy Spirit; they have the key that gives them access to the gifts of the Holy Spirit, but they just don't make use of the access they have. If that's true for you, It may be because you haven't been taught that you can. It could be that you've been part of a church culture where most of the gifts of the Spirit were off-limits: access denied. It might be that you came to embrace the view that most of the gifts are for the spiritual elite only.

Worse yet, you may have been shaped by a certain kind of church where the idea of spiritual gifts is marked with the words "access denied!" There are whole movements that call themselves Christian and embrace cessationism. Cessationism is a non-Biblical view that the revelatory and demonstrative gifts of the Spirit have 'ceased.' You have to do Olympic-level mental gymnastics to try to draw that conclusion from the Bible itself - because it is an intellectually dishonest idea. Yet, it is satisfying to the intellect, which is often inclined to idolize certainty and control.

This view emerged around the same time as modern science became mainstream - and anything overtly supernatural or challenging to explain and control was thought to be unscientific and unacceptable. But at the core of the filled to flow lifestyle is the inherent belief that the gifts of the Spirit are a vital element of life in God's Kingdom - even the 'wild and crazy ones!' In particular, the *revelatory* gifts provide an access point into receiving God's heart for the ministry He wants you to do!

It is possible for you to know you have access, but you've been a bit passive about it - and it's been so long you don't remember where that key is anymore. In Matthew 16:19 Jesus says to you as a believer that He will give you the Keys of the Kingdom of God. It couldn't be any more clear - you have the authority for access! But for that access to be acted upon, you will need to move, to risk, to take a step, to try, and to trust Holy Spirit as you go for it!

Activation - An Open Heaven

You know that the throne room of God is accessible to you - in theory (see Hebrews 4:16). In this activation, get settled in a place for prayer. Open your mouth and praise God for who He is, and thank Him for some things He's done. Now, acknowledge to God that it feels like your keys have been confiscated, or you've lost your keys, or haven't been using them much. As you pray, say out loud, "I reclaim my keys to the throne room!" Imagine a giant key coming into your hand. Imagine using it to open the door to go into Heaven - and into the very throne room of God.

~~ Ask God the Father to show you something. Say, "Lord, would you show me a vision?" and then wait; pay attention. Whatever - *whatever* comes into your mind, take note of it!

~~ Ask, "Lord, what is the meaning of this image?" and take note of whatever the answer seems to be.

These activations are like training wheels; their purpose is to help you begin to open a part of your heart and mind to connect with God.

The Gifts of the Spirit - broadly speaking

Through the presence of Holy Spirit in you, you have access to a range of spiritual gifts. The gifts of the Spirit are mentioned in 1 Corinthians 12, Romans 12, Ephesians 4, 1 Peter 4, and a few other places. I'll share more about this in chapter seven. The Bible itself does not categorize the gifts of the Spirit. Further, the verses mentioning the gifts don't offer strict definitions of the gifts. Nevertheless, people have taken various approaches over many hundreds of years to create various groups of gifts - mainly because it is helpful for referring to and thinking about them. I'm not inclined to agree with any of the categorizations because they impose a closed-set thinking about the movement of the Spirit that the scriptures do not.

Among the gifts of the Spirit, some are particularly *demonstrative* and have an aspect of revelation or manifestation - gifts such as healing, prophecy, words of knowledge, miracles, etc. Others are less mystical and more straightforward: service, administration, leadership, preaching, and giving. These gifts are a bit like the 'copy machine' in my analogy with the master key. Everybody uses the key for these gifts, no matter what! I'm glad for those gifts being used - but I long for the full range of the gifts of the Spirit to be used. *But we may need to stop only calling them gifts of the Spirit.*

Gifts are actually pneumatic & charismatic!

I know you might be wondering what I meant by saying, "We may need to stop only calling them gifts of the Spirit." I would be, too! Let me explain. One of the primary sections of the Bible related to the activity of the Holy Spirit in the life of the believer is 1 Corinthians 12 to 14. 1 Corinthians 12 starts by saying, "Now about the gifts of the Spirit, brothers and sisters; I do not want you to be uninformed."

The thing is, the word translated 'gifts' in most modern translations is *not* the actual Greek word 'gift.' That would be the Greek word *dorea*. The word used here is πνευματικῶν *-pneumatikon-* (noo-ma-tee-kone). And later in the chapter, the term translated 'gift' is χαρισμάτων *-charismaton -* (kah-riz-mah-tone). These words have very specific meanings - and, yet, they are complex terms with no direct English equivalent. Translators opted for the simple English word 'gift,' but that word fails to convey the right sense of what these are, which is ironic since the scriptures say, "I do not want you to be uninformed" about them! Let me share 1 Corinthians 12:1-6, with emphasis on these two words in their original language. The NIV words are in [brackets], and the Greek word is in {braces}.

Now about the [gifts of the Spirit] { πνευματικῶν}, brothers and sisters, I do not want you to be uninformed. You know that when you were pagans, somehow or other, you were influenced and led astray to mute idols. Therefore I want you to know that no one who is speaking by the Spirit of God says, "Jesus be cursed," and no one can say, "Jesus is Lord," except by the Holy Spirit. There are different kinds of [gifts] { χαρισμάτων}, but the same Spirit distributes them. There are different kinds of service, but the same Lord. There are different kinds of working, but in all of them and in everyone it is the same God at work.

1 CORINTHIANS 12:1-6 NIV

Both of these unique words indicate the freely given movement of the Holy Spirit in and through a Christian person. In the sense that they are freely given, yes, they are gifts. But they are not gifts in the traditional sense. When you think of a gift, you imagine one who is the giver, who is active, and the recipient is passive. That is the problem with the word *gift* - it creates a tacit expectation for a believer to be in the passive stance of a recipient. But these words require proactive engagement!

The word *pneumatikon* has a root word that is likely familiar to you. Pneumatic is a word in English that describes the power of pressurized air - usually for the purpose of some kind of work or desired outcome. This word conveys the reality that the breath or wind of the Spirit is at work with the power to bring about a specific desired effect. In English, the word 'charismatic' is familiar to you. In English, it conveys the idea that a person has something special within them that shows up in a compelling, visible way.

The Greek word *charismaton* or *charismata,* if it's singular, has a root word that forms the substance of what it means: *charis* - it's the word 'grace'. You could describe this word as 'grace-expressions.' If you are a believer, by God's grace, there is something very special inside of you - and specific kinds of actions allow it to come out and be seen! It is the Holy Spirit who is that someone very special inside of you! And yes - God's idea is that Holy Spirit within you can and should come through!

1 Corinthians 12:7 NIV, uses the word 'manifestations of the Spirit' - and this expression describes it well; these are specific ways the Holy Spirit can move in and through believers in ways that can be seen and heard! Because of this, there is no room for pride; it is the Holy Spirit at work - and you get to partner with the Holy Spirit. You get to be a vessel through which the Holy Spirit is flowing. You are an active participant in what the Holy Spirit is doing - but the Spirit is bringing forth the supernatural power and impact. The Holy Spirit is at work in *all* of the manifestations. But there is one group of these that the scriptures call us to pursue in particular. Consider 1 Corinthians 14:1 and 1 Corinthians 14:12 and how they frame this pursuit:

Follow the way of love and eagerly desire gifts
of the Spirit, especially prophecy.

1 Corinthians 14:1 NIV

Since you are eager for gifts of the Spirit, try to
excel in those that build up the church.

1 Corinthians 14:12 NIV

The purpose and the parameters of the prophetic flow

From God's vantage point, prophecy is a manifestation of the Spirit that is so beneficial that He wants every believer to desire it eagerly. If God says that you should eagerly desire something, He intends for you to have it. When you prophesy, you are attuning your heart to what God is communicating. You become a conduit for what He wants to speak. The great good that can come from engaging this manifestation of the Spirit is that the Church, that is, the people who are the Body of Christ, can be built up!

In the Old Testament, the prophets spoke words of warning, condemnation, and promise about the nation's future, which continue to come true today. New Testament prophecy is different. First, it does not and cannot ever carry the weight of the Eternal Word of God, the Bible. The canon of scripture is closed, and no further consummate revelation can be given apart from the Bible.

New Testament prophecy *is* a word from God - but it is to be subjected to the words of the Bible and must be in alignment with what has been written in scripture. The primary purpose of New Testament prophecy is *forth-telling*, as revealed in 1 Corinthians 14:3 (NASB): But the one who prophesies speaks to people *for* edification, exhortation, and consolation. Those three factors are the primary aim of New Testament prophecy because they allow the speaker to *tell forth* the heart of God for a person. As you learn more about the prophetic flow, keep this in mind and let it be a filter: Does this prophetic flow edify and strengthen a person? Does it exhort them and encourage them to move in a direction of faith and hope? Does it bring consolation and allow them to receive a measure of the comfort of their Heavenly Father?

While edification, exhortation, and consolation are helpful guidelines for New Testament *forth-telling* prophecy, they are not limitations. New Testament prophecy can also include *foretelling*. For example, the prophet Agabus speaks of the future where Paul would be bound up when he goes to Rome in Acts 21:11. But let me be candid with you. The foretelling aspect of prophecy is something to move into with great care. We are human vessels, we can easily 'get it wrong' with a prophetic word. Further, we can never allow ourselves to be partners in a false spirit of fortune-telling. I would rather see you become seasoned in the *forthtelling* mode of prophecy long before you venture into *foretelling*.

Activation - Give me 'tion

You're starting to see that forthtelling the heart of God most often involves hearing a word of edification, exhortation, or consolation for someone. These three 'tion' words help guide the kind of expression you give. Another way to put these three words is - to strengthen, encourage, and comfort. Get into a place of connection with the Father, right now, and seek Him for a brief prophetic word for a person you know.

~~ Ask God the Father to show you a particular person. Say, "Lord, would you show me a person I can pray for right now?" Then, wait, pay attention, and note who the person is.

~~ Ask, "Lord, would you give me a 'tion' for him/her right now? Edification, exhortation, consolation?" And then listen, watch, pay attention. You should get a phrase, a single word, or even a Bible verse.

~~ Ask, "Lord, is there a meaning to this I can share?"

This is just practice - so it's okay if you're not sure it's something that needs to be shared. But, if you *do* feel it's shareable, consider reaching out to the person to share it! If you share it, simply say, "I was praying for you, and I got the sense that..." - that's it!

The Revelatory Manifestations - and Prophetic Flow

There are various ways that the Holy Spirit brings a message from the heart of God - and they are all part of a prophetic flow. The starting point is prophecy; this flows into the other revelatory gifts - words of knowledge, messages of wisdom, dreams, visions, and the discerning of spirits. If you are going to be a believer who is filled to flow, this is a distinct part of the flow God has in mind. It begins with you *eagerly desiring* the gift of prophecy and an eager desire to be used by God in the flow of the Spirit to *build up the church*. This flow is something that God has ordained to be characteristic of the very time we are living in. According to the prophet Joel, this is God's heart:

> *I will pour out my Spirit on all people. Your sons and daughters*
> *will prophesy, your old men will dream dreams, and your*
> *young men will see visions. Even on my servants, both men*
> *and women, I will pour out my Spirit in those days.*
>
> JOEL 2:28-29 NIV

The Bible itself does not give a definition for each of these revelatory gifts of the Spirit - and there are no step-by-step instructions as to how to approach or engage in these *pneumatikon* or *charismaton*. But we can deduce how these manifestations of the Spirit function from various passages of scripture where they are employed. What I will share with you here reflects my own understanding of these spiritual gifts, both from scriptural insight and from personal experience. We'll discover more about this in chapter seven. For now, I urge you to do precisely what the scripture calls for: eagerly desire the greater gifts, especially prophecy!

VISIONS

A revelatory vision is a moment of supernatural perception where you see a picture or scenario that is laden with meaning coming from the heart of God. One way a vision can happen is in such a way that you are perceiving with your 'mind's eye.' You are perceiving - but it is happening the way a dream does, within your thoughts. Another way this manifestation occurs is through what is called an 'open vision.' When you see an open vision, the picture or scenario seems to be literally taking place in front of your eyes, in the space out in front of you - almost like a holographic TV screen in the air before you, visible to you alone.

One classic example of a vision is described in Acts 10:9-13:

The Apostle Peter went up on the roof to pray. He became hungry and wanted something to eat, and while the meal was being prepared, he fell into a trance. He saw heaven opened and something like a large sheet being let down to earth by its four corners.
It contained all kinds of four-footed animals, as well as reptiles and birds. Then a voice told him, "Get up, Peter. Kill and eat."

Peter had an open vision; it should be noted that Peter fell into a trance - a profoundly meditative state of prayer, something that nearly goes beyond words - but reflects a profound intimacy with and yieldedness to Holy Spirit. The vision Peter saw needed interpretation. If Peter had simply repeated the vision, it would not have made sense. When he shared about this vision, he gave its interpretation as well. He understood that God was calling Him to welcome non-Jewish people into this faith in the Jewish Messiah, Jesus.

Consider passages such as Galatians 2:2, Acts 18:9-10, Acts 23:11, Acts 9:2-19, Acts 27:23-24, and Acts 22:17. These passages, and many others, indicate the usefulness of visions as a means for God to provide direction and guidance. For example, in Acts 16, Paul and the ministry team were headed south, but Holy Spirit gave a vision of a 'man of Macedonia.' Paul interpreted that vision to mean 'change directions!' They did - they headed north instead - and as a result, they went to Philippi. As a lover of the book of Philippians, I am sure glad they heeded that vision and had the openness of spirit to have the vision to begin with!

A vision can come at any time - even in the middle of the day, such as with Peter. A vision can occur when you are in that liminal state that happens when you've just woken up, or when you are deep in prayer. A vision can come while praying. You cannot *force* yourself to have a vision. You can place yourself in a spiritual posture of *looking*, but it is up to the Holy Spirit as to whether you will see any vision.

When you see a vision, you need to determine what it is indicating. If it is just for you, then this can be a quiet personal journey of discovery. If you are ministering to another person or to a group, it is crucial that you know that just because you see it doesn't mean you need to say it. God may show you something, but your next task as a prophetic person is to discern the meaning of what you're seeing, so you can share it. Unless of course the Lord speaks to you and says, 'Share exactly what you saw'.

For example, you might see a cloud of depression over a person. As you perceive this, you need to have an inner prayer life, an inner conversation, where you seek the Lord for what to say about it. In that case, you might say, "I believe the Lord is showing me that He wants to lift you up and restore hope to you." This is just one example - but I want you to remember this idea: Just because you see it, doesn't mean you say it.

DREAMS

Revelatory dreams are visual, narrative thought-scapes in which God has a message for you to discern. Dreams are a universal human phenomenon. Around the planet, throughout history, people have been having dreams. For many people, and much of the time, dreams are simply a processing mechanism, built into the human brain by God. The soul of a person is the seat of their mind, will, and emotions. The soul accumulates worries, concerns, and an overload of ideas. Dreams are often a way in which those things are metabolized. Such dreams can simply be called 'soul dreams.'

God allows these dreams as a way of highlighting something you may need to pay attention to and process.

On the other hand - you may have had an instance where you woke up *very aware* of a dream you've had. It was so vivid and laden with a sense of meaning that you remembered it even after waking up. You may have even wondered to yourself, "What did that mean?" You cannot force yourself to have a dream - but you cannot stop it either. As I said, many of your dreams are simply 'soul processing dreams.' But occasionally - you may have a dream where God is speaking to you: this is a Spirit-given dream. You should learn to discern between the two kinds of dreams, and if it is a Spirit-given dream, learn to interpret its meaning!

The Bible is full of moments where people experienced Spirit-given dreams. Consider Ezekiel 1:1, Matthew 2:3, Daniel 2:47, Matthew 2:12-13, Genesis 20:3-8, Daniel 4:14-37, and others. Through dreams, Holy Spirit provides personal warnings and sometimes indications of future events for a community or even a country. Spirit-given dreams are sometimes used by God to convey a special calling of the Kingdom of God for your life.

Whole books have been written on the subject of dream interpretation. A word of caution: the reference points in dreams are subjective. There is no way to systematize or catalog a comprehensive and always-accurate list of dream symbolism. The symbolic reference points for you may be different from the symbolic reference points of another person, depending on their culture, upbringing, education, and even personality. The best way to interpret Spirit-given dreams is by asking Holy Spirit! A mature Spirit-filled believer with prophetic flow can also assist by giving their prophetic perspective on the meaning of your dream.

In my experience - part of the purpose of a Spirit-given dream is to awaken my spirit. It is as if the Holy Spirit is saying, through a dream, "Pay attention! Seek me! Pray! Seek revelation about this in community with my people, and pray more!" Whatever the content of the dream may be, if it serves to cause you to do those things, it is good and right!

WORD OF KNOWLEDGE

The Word of Knowledge is precise information given by God directly to your thoughts about a circumstance or a person that helps them feel loved, and creates clarity about what to pray for. We usually relate the word 'knowledge' to 'learning and studying.' But the Word of Knowledge as a manifestation of the Spirit is a part of the prophetic flow, not the result of natural learning. This gift functions in such a way that you will suddenly gain an awareness of or glimpse into a situation and have insight about it. You will be given a partial but precise bit of information, coming from the mind of Christ, about the circumstance or the person. This limited revelation may be obscure, but also beneficial. The Word of Knowledge may come to your thoughts as facts, details, information, or a symbolic image in a way that transcends the normal course of observation; you would not have naturally known it.

I often experience a word of knowledge coming to my mind as something visual, a picture or image that I know in my heart is tied to a prophetic flow. Sometimes, I experience a word of knowledge as an emotional sensation. For example, as I am praying for a person, I suddenly feel the emotion of hopelessness. I think, "Well, that's not my hopelessness because I'm feeling pretty good, personally!" I then know it's a word of knowledge for the person I am praying for. I might say, "Are you struggling with unbearable hopelessness right now?" They'll confirm that - probably with tears; and I'll know that Word of Knowledge was accurate.

There have been times when I've received a word of knowledge as a smell, the sudden smell of cigarettes - indicating to me the presence of a demonic spirit. Other times, I've received a Word of Knowledge as a sensation of pain in my own body, which is entirely different from my own pains. For example, I suddenly sense a terrible pain in my wrist while ministering to a group of people. I know this is a Word of Knowledge given so that I can minister healing for those with painful medical conditions in their wrist.

There is a moment in Mark 2:8 where Jesus has healed a man - and the teachers of religious law are thinking, "Jesus is a heretic!" He doesn't hear this from them - but he flows in a Word of Knowledge and in Mark 2:8 it says, "He knew in his spirit what they were thinking" - and then He confronted them. Sometimes the Word of Knowledge can be extremely precise. If you haven't had much experience with this manifestation of the Spirit, it may take a while for you to increase your accuracy in receiving the Word. If used carelessly and without integration with the message of the Kingdom of God, use of the Word of Knowledge could come across as though you are trying to be a psychic.

Consider these scriptures which contain moments where a Word of Knowledge is given. John 4:18-29, Acts 5:1-11, Acts 10:19, Matthew 9:4, 2 Kings 5:20-27; 2 Kings 6:8-12, 1 Samuel 9-10, 1 Kings 14:2-3, John 1:47. When the Word of Knowledge is given, its effect is often an increase of faith. When a person hears that by the Holy Spirit, you knew something they didn't even tell you, they have an amplified sense of anticipation that something beyond mere human power is at work. Faith is created or augmented by the Word of Knowledge. More importantly - the Word of Knowledge helps a person to know how loved they are. Out of love, personal insight is given that helps make sense of a circumstance. Out of love, information about a particular struggle or pain is revealed - and a person feels truly seen, and truly cared for.

MESSAGE OF WISDOM

The Message of Wisdom is insight from the heart of God with directives or guidance for how to handle a situation or opportunity. Where the Word of Knowledge gives information, the Message of Wisdom provides direction. The Message of Wisdom can sound like simple advice - but the one speaking it generally has the sense that their advice, and the wisdom contained in it, seem to be way above whatever they'd naturally be able to offer.

There is a moment in Acts 27 where the Apostle Paul is on a ship bound for Rome, and they encounter a great storm. He experiences a prophetic flow - and gives a Message of Wisdom. He says, "Unless these men stay with the ship, you cannot be saved." When taken together with the details of the account, the advice doesn't initially seem to make sense. But the captain had come to trust Paul when he spoke in this way - and he followed the advice. The result was that all of the men were saved. How did Paul know that this was what needed to happen? Paul didn't - but the Holy Spirit within him did - and made it known by igniting an awareness within him that Paul then spoke. It was a Message of Wisdom.

Read John 4:16-17, 1 Kings 3:16-28, and Genesis 41. These contain moments where a Message of Wisdom was given which helped individuals to know what to do next or how to proceed with an opportunity that was before them. A Message of Wisdom gives people the insight needed to solve a problem or make a choice. The people in these passages still had to take action and do hard things - but some of the who, what, when, where, why and how was answered in advance.

When you engage in the flow of the Spirit for a Message of Wisdom, it is essential to pay attention to what you are saying. The gift of gab and longwindedness is *not* an indication of the Message of Wisdom. In some ways, brevity is more likely to be used by Holy Spirit in bringing the Message of Wisdom because it is less likely to produce confusion. Brevity lends to clarity - especially when revelatory gifts of the Spirit are used. This is particularly true of the Message of Wisdom.

DISCERNMENT OF SPIRITS

The revelatory gift of discernment is a supernatural capacity to perceive and judge well in regard to the spiritual realm - both what is holy, trustworthy, and good, as well as what is demonic, evil, and deceptive. When a person is flowing in discernment, they may readily sense when there is angelic activity, an open realm of God's glory, or momentum in the atmosphere for the miraculous. They may also easily sense when there is demonic activity, a scheme of the devil, an ungodly atmosphere, or false teaching.

In Acts 13:9-10, Paul is interacting with a man who has been involved with witchcraft. He discerns this - and calls it out. The result is that demonic activity is thwarted, and the Kingdom of God is advanced. This manifestation of the Spirit seems innocent enough - but it can be abused. If this gift is misused, the person operating in it can fall prey to a spirit of accusation and criticism. The gift intended to thwart demonic activity can actually usher in the diabolical activity of accusation, creating enmity, strife, and a stifling of faith. This gift must be used with an attitude of submission and humility!

If you consider passages such as Acts 8:1-8, Luke 4:34, John 3:8, 1 Timothy 4:1, Acts 13:9-10, and Matthew 17:18, you will see moments where the gift of discernment is used. The gift helps people discern and avoid demonic entanglements - and ensures that the Kingdom of God may advance in victory! This manifestation of the spirit must be employed carefully; a person who flows in discernment must guard against thinking of everything they disagree with as 'demonic.' It is possible to confuse natural cynicism and personal preferences with discernment.

PROPHECY

The revelatory gift of prophecy is the Spirit-born ability to spontaneously speak forth or write insight that God is revealing in order to build up, encourage, or comfort someone. An additional element of this gift of prophecy is the ability to speak with spiritual authority and power to such a degree that what God is revealing may be brought into reality. Since we are learning about prophecy, let's be sure we say the words correctly. The *verb* is prophesy (prah-fess-ai) and the noun is prophecy (prah-fess-ee). If you have the gift of prophecy, you must prophesy!

The Old Testament has numerous examples of prophets - with whole books attributed to them; Isaiah, Jeremiah, Amos, Malachi, etc. The Old Testament gift of prophecy was characterized by messages about the future for the whole entire nation. The messages of the Old Testament prophets seemed to oscillate between calls for repentance with ominous warnings of doom - and short visions of hope and promise. The New Testament gift of prophecy is different in its extent and intent. There are two cornerstone scriptures that give a foundation for what the New Testament gift of prophecy is all about: 1 Corinthians 14:3-5 and Romans 12:6.

"In his grace, God has given us different gifts for doing certain things well.

So if God has given you the ability to prophesy, speak
out with as much faith as God has given you."

ROMANS 12:6 NLT

"But one who prophesies strengthens others, encourages
them, and comforts them. A person who speaks in tongues is
strengthened personally, but one who speaks a word of prophecy
strengthens the entire church. I wish you could all speak in
tongues, but even more I wish you could all prophesy."

- 1 CORINTHIANS 14:3-5 NLT

Consider the 1 Corinthians 12:1 call to eagerly desire the gift of prophecy, along with passages such as Ezekiel 37, 1 Corinthians 14:39, Acts 15:32, 1 Corinthians 14:29, and Acts 11:27-28. The scriptures are clear in establishing a baseline for what prophecy is. The Old Testament model of prophecy isn't necessarily *closed down*, but it isn't explicitly called for the way the New Testament type of prophecy is. It is often said that New Testament prophecy can be summed up with three directives: Speak the heart of God to build 'em up, call 'em up, and cheer 'em up. People need hope and comfort - and a prophetic word can give that.

A prophetic word can come through a picture that enters your mind with a sense of meaning attached to it. I have found myself thinking of a lyric of a secular song, and then recognizing that God was using that as an entry point to get my attention and give me a prophetic word. I sometimes picture a movie scene and get a sense that God is speaking through my remembrance of it. Many times, God brings a verse of scripture to mind - with prophetic insight accompanying it. Other times, you may receive a direct word about a person or situation with such clarity that you could write it down word for word.

The primary difference between the Old Testament prophets and you is that their words were verifiably 100% inspired by God, while yours are not. You may be receiving and sharing a prophetic word, but your prophetic words are not on par with the Holy Scriptures. Your prophetic words must align with the revealed word of God in the Bible, or they are false.

The scriptures call every believer who receives a prophetic word to take action with it - and this is the action: Do not treat prophecies with contempt but test them all; hold on to what is good (1 Timothy 5:20-21, NIV). The implication is that your prophetic word could be spot on, or it could miss the mark completely. Often, a prophetic word is mixed. It takes great humility to acknowledge that your prophetic flow might not be 100% pure - but you must acknowledge this. Humility in prophecy is what safeguards you from crossing the line into spiritual pride or spiritual abuse.

Activation - God, what do you think of me?

The prophetic flow is primarily there to reveal the Father's heart. In this activation, get in a time of prayer. Get a journal and pen ready. Praise and thank God, and then ask, "God, what do you think of me?"

~ Write down what you feel God is saying to you about how He feels about you. Also write something you think God may be speaking about what is happening in your life. Write in the 'first person,' the voice of God; for example, "My daughter/son, [name], I think you are strong and courageous, and I think you are going to do something important in this next year!"

~ As with any prophetic word, this should be tested. Just because you wrote it in the first person voice of God doesn't mean it was a totally pure and accurate word of God.

~ When you are done writing, pray and thank God for speaking with you!

Power in the prophetic gift and the prophetic office

Ephesians 4:11-12 describes what are often referred to as the 'ascension gifts of Christ.' These gifts are not the same as 'gifts of the Spirit,' instead, they are leadership offices within the Body of Christ that function to provide motivation and organization for the work of the Church in the Mission of Jesus Christ. The verses state, *"Now these are the gifts Christ gave to the church: the apostles, the prophets, the evangelists, and the pastors and teachers. Their responsibility is to equip God's people to do his work and build up the church, the body of Christ."* These verses reflect the five-fold leadership plan for the church envisioned by the Father. In God's vision for order and organization in the church, there is a specific office of prophet. This is reflected further in 1 Corinthians 12:28, and it shows that there is a distinction between the office of prophet and engaging the manifestation of the spirit for prophesying. Recall that every believer is called to eagerly desire the gift of prophecy - but that wouldn't make the person a prophet. All prophets prophesy, but not all prophecy comes from prophets!

The person who has been called to the office of prophet is some-one whose dominant spiritual gift is prophecy. They have been appointed with authority in a leadership role within a church Body, in which their primary gift in prophecy can be used for the com-munity's good and for training others. Some churches may not use the title 'prophet,' but they recognize and affirm this gift's flow and authorize it. It has been said that a prophet in a church is one who has oversight, insight, and foresight; they have oversight of a min-istry area, most likely in the prophetic. They have insight by way of their gift of prophecy into what God's heart is for the commu-nity. They have foresight, or an ability to see and hear beyond the present moment with a revelation about what's next. Ezekiel 37 highlights the moment when the prophet spoke to a valley of dry bones, and they came to life. This Biblical depiction of prophetic action underscores the possibility of a flow of effectual power that may come through the ministry of a prophet. "So I prophesied as he commanded me, and breath entered them; they came to life and stood up on their feet—a vast army." (Ezekiel 37:10)

1 Peter 4:10, NIV says, "Each of you should use whatever gift you have received to serve others, as faithful stewards of God's grace in its various forms." You may find yourself wondering which of these 'gifts' could be yours. But remember - you have the master key! There will be at least one of the 21 or so 'gifts of the Spirit' that is your particular forte - which you *must* use simply to be obedient in your faith. At the same time - you have an all-access pass to the full range of the manifestations of the Spirit! What this means is that you can move beyond 'the copy machine' and into the realm of the Spiritual life where you get to flow in the prophetic! This means that the revelatory manifestations of the Spirit are accessible to you.

If this is all very new for you, you will probably need to approach it a bit like a child who is learning to ride a bike. At first, you may begin with a tricycle, then a bike with training wheels. You may see your pastor or a ministry leader you respect operating in a prophetic flow - and he or she is like the spiritual equivalent of a Tour-de-France cyclist relative to where you are currently. That's okay! They may have been riding for a long time. But what is accessible to them is also accessible to you!

But where do I start?

If you are earnest in your desire to begin to flow in the Spirit through the revelatory manifestations, the best place to start is in worship. Yes - singing and expressing your affection for and faith in God through worship is connected to your experience of the prophetic flow! The flow comes from a place of fullness. You experience being filled with the Spirit - and the result is the flow of the Spirit through your life. And to experience that filling, start with worship.

Ephesians 5:18-20 describes the intricate connection between the filling of the Spirit and worship. "Don't be drunk with wine, because that will ruin your life. Instead, be filled with the Holy Spirit, singing psalms and hymns and spiritual songs among yourselves, and making music to the Lord in your hearts. And give thanks for everything to God the Father in the name of our Lord Jesus Christ." When you enter into the experience of worship from an earnest, humble, open disposition, you experience a sense of peace and comfort. You sense the joy and delight of God's presence and possibly even the chills that come from a holy visitation. The scriptures call for you to be filled with the Spirit, and they connect this filling to entering into worship because worship is the way you magnify the Lord. When you magnify the Lord - you are minimizing your own flesh - and that creates the space for Him to fill you.

There are so many moments when the greats of the Bible are recorded as experiencing a sense of being transfixed in God's presence through worship. Saul asks again and again for a harpist to be brought in, to lead a time of worship so he can settle his spirit. King David wrote song after song of praise in the Psalms, each one expressing a hunger for God and evidence of the satisfying hope that the filling of the Spirit brings. In 2 Chronicles 20, King Jehoshaphat commissioned the soldiers to sing praise and worship to God - and as they did - a flow of the Spirit came that set an ambush against their enemies.

There are many moments in scripture when singing and expressing worship was part of the prophetic flow. In Isaiah 6, the expression of praise created an atmosphere of such filling of the Spirit that a vision of the Lord with His robe filling the temple was evident. Paul and Silas were imprisoned, as recorded in the book of Acts chapter 16. Their midnight worship from the prison cell invited the power of the Holy Spirit to fill them and flow through them with explosive energy that brought them to freedom. In Revelation, the scenes from Heaven show the mighty angelic beings utterly enveloped in the Holy Spirit's presence to such an extent of fullness that they could do nothing but flow with worship of God for the splendor of who He is.

To access the revelatory gifts, spend some time in worship and adoration of King Jesus. And then, rather than stopping at the end of the song, simply rest in the presence of God. Ask, "Holy Spirit, is there anything you want to do right now? Is there anything you want to show me?" You may be surprised at how easily you experience a flood of prophetic flow as you take this simple step! From here, move into a bit of experimentation with Prophecy, Message of Wisdom, Word of Knowledge and Visions. It's okay if it feels like you're on a tricycle, as long as you're learning to peddle!

FILLED TO FLOW
BIBLE STUDY SMALL GROUP GUIDE

Chapter Three:
Did You Get The Download?

You're filled to flow in the prophetic!

In this chapter, you will learn about the prophetic flow and the gifts oriented around receiving revelation. You'll discover how to get the downloads from Heaven that God may want to give you. You'll learn about the revelatory gifts of the Spirit- Prophecy, Vision, Word of Knowledge, Message of Wisdom, and Tongues - and how to begin to enjoy these gifts. All spiritual gifts are vital. And, yet, the prophetic gifts are called 'greater,' and we're told to desire them. This session will give you greater insight about the prophetic flow - and the other spiritual gifts that rely on the prophetic flow. Prophecy, visions, words of knowledge, dreams, message of wisdom, and discernment; these gifts are vital and are part of a victorious, filled to flow Christian life!

Bible study group guide how-to summary:

▭ Means it's a Bible study reflection question. It's okay if just 1-2 people answer. It's okay to move through it quickly or even to skip. It also means there may not be time to include the reading of this scripture or the discussion of the question with the whole group. But consider these sections in your own study!

≈ Means this is a group interaction reflection question. It would be good to ask several people from the group to respond. It also means that the scripture associated with this question should be read aloud to the group.

Engage:

1. ≈ Icebreaker: What's the most memorable advice or wisdom someone has ever shared with you?
2. ▱ Discuss any highlights from this chapter.

▱ Read 1 Corinthians 12:1 NIV

Now, about the gifts of the Spirit, brothers and sisters, I do not want you to be uninformed.

Read 1 Corinthians 12:7-11 NIV

Now to each one the manifestation of the Spirit is given for the common good. To one there is given through the Spirit a message of wisdom, to another a message of knowledge by means of the same Spirit, to another faith by the same Spirit, to another gifts of healing by that one Spirit, to another miraculous powers, to another prophecy, to another distinguishing between spirits, to another speaking in different kinds of tongues, and to still another the interpretation of tongues. All these are the work of one and the same Spirit, and he distributes them to each one, just as he determines.

▱ Read 1 Corinthians 14:12 NIV

Since you are eager for gifts of the Spirit, try to excel in those that build up the church.

3. ▱ In the big picture, what are the primary purposes of the spiritual gifts, and who should use them?
4. ≈ Share about a way you have been blessed by a filled to flow Christian flowing in the use of a spiritual gift.

≈ Read 1 Corinthians 14:1

Follow the way of love and eagerly desire gifts of the Spirit, *especially prophecy*.

▱ Read Romans 12:6 NLT

In his grace, God has given us different gifts for doing certain things well. So if God has given you the ability to *prophesy*, speak out with as much faith as God has given you.

≈ Read 1 Corinthians 14:3-5 NLT

But *one who prophesies* strengthens others, encourages them, and comforts them. A person who speaks in tongues is strengthened personally, but one who *speaks a word of prophecy* strengthens the entire church. I wish you could all speak in tongues, but even more, *I wish you could all prophesy*. For prophecy is greater than speaking in tongues, unless someone interprets what you are saying so that the whole church will be strengthened.

Engage:

5. ▱ From the scriptures you've read, what kinds of things does the Holy Spirit accomplish through the gift of prophecy?
6. ▱ Why does prophecy, properly understood, hold so much value?
7. ≈ Share how you have been personally blessed or helped by receiving a prophetic word from someone.

≈ Read Joel 2:28-29 NIV

I will pour out my Spirit on all people. Your sons and daughters will prophesy, your old men will dream dreams, your young men will see visions. Even on my servants, both men and women, I will pour out my Spirit in those days.

Engage:

8. ▱ Why do you think God considers prophecy, dreams, and visions valuable, vital aspects of spiritual life?

▱ Acts 10:9-13 NIV

Peter went up on the roof to pray. He became hungry and wanted something to eat, and while the meal was being prepared, he fell into a trance. He saw heaven opened and something like a large sheet being let down to earth by its four corners. It contained all kinds of four-footed animals, as well as reptiles and birds. Then a voice told him, "Get up, Peter. Kill and eat."

Engage:

9. ▱ What is the purpose or value of a vision in the prophetic flow? Have you personally found any action or posture helpful in seeking to receive a vision?

≈ Read Daniel 2:19 NASB

Then the secret was revealed to Daniel in a night vision. Then Daniel blessed the God of heaven.

Engage:

10. ≈ Have you ever had a dream that carried real significance? Share about that, with your understanding of how God spoke to you through it.

☐ Read Mark 2:8 NIV

Immediately Jesus knew in his spirit that this was what they were thinking in their hearts, and he said to them, "Why are you thinking these things?

☐ Read John 1:47 NIV

When Jesus saw Nathanael approaching, he said of him, "Here truly is an Israelite in whom there is no deceit."

Engage:

11. ☐ The above scriptures are just two examples of Jesus flowing in the Word of Knowledge. What purposes does the Word of Knowledge gift fulfill? Has anyone ever spoken a Word of Knowledge to you?

☐ Read Acts 27:30-32 NIV

In an attempt to escape from the ship, the sailors let the lifeboat down into the sea, pretending they were going to lower some anchors from the bow. Then Paul said to the centurion and the soldiers, "Unless these men stay with the ship, you cannot be saved." So the soldiers cut the ropes that held the lifeboat and let it drift away.

Engage:

12. ☐ Acts 27:30-32 is an example of a Message of Wisdom. Share why a Spirit-given Message of Wisdom could be valuable. Have you ever received one - or given one?

⊡ Read Acts 13:9-10 NIV

Then Saul, who was also called Paul, filled with the Holy Spirit, looked straight at Elymas and said, "You are a child of the devil and an enemy of everything that is right! You are full of all kinds of deceit and trickery. Will you never stop perverting the right ways of the Lord?"

Engage:

13. ⊡ What is the value and purpose of the gift of discernment? What are some of the challenges or difficulties with discernment as a revelatory gift?

≈ Read 1 Corinthians 14:29-33

Let two or three people prophesy, and let the others evaluate what is said. But if someone is prophesying and another person receives a revelation from the Lord, the one who is speaking must stop. In this way, all who prophesy will have a turn to speak, one after the other, so that everyone will learn and be encouraged. Remember that people who prophesy are in control of their spirit and can take turns. For God is not a God of disorder but of peace, as in all the meetings of God's holy people.

Engage:

14. ⊡ Describe some of the ways the gift of prophecy functions and some of the basic parameters from all that you've learned in the scriptures above.

≈ Read 1 Timothy 4:14-15 NIV

Do not neglect your gift, which was given you through prophecy when the body of elders laid their hands on you. Be diligent in these matters; give yourself wholly to them, so that everyone may see your progress.

Engage:

15. ▱ Has anyone ever laid hands on you so that you could receive an impartation of a spiritual gift? Share about that.
16. ≈ Share about how you have observed someone exercising one of the revelatory gifts in a beneficial, effective way.

Pray≈:

~ for boldness in sharing prophetic words
~ for visions and dreams
~ for humility in willingness to 'test all things'
~ for impartation and activation in the prophetic flow
~ for whatever needs there might be

Extra:

1. Read passages such as *Galatians 2:2, Acts 18:9-10, 2 Corinthians 12:1-4, Acts 23:11, Acts 9:3-19, Acts 27:23-24, Acts 22:17, Acts 16:9-10,* and *Daniel 2.* Consider what kinds of things Holy Spirit often uses visions to provide?

2. Read passages such as Ezekiel 1:1, Matthew 2:3, Daniel 2:47, Matthew 2:12-13, Genesis 20:3-8, and Daniel 4:14-37 and consider what kinds of things the Holy Spirit accomplishes through dreams.

3. Read passages such as *John 4:18-29, Acts 5:1-11, Acts 10:19, Matthew 9:4, 2 Kings 5:20-27, 2 Kings 6:8-12, 1 Samuel 9-10,*

1 Kings 14:2-3 and consider: How does the gift of the Word of Knowledge lead to furtherance of the Will of God?

4. Read passages such as *John 4:16-17, 1 Kings 3:16-28, and Genesis 41* and consider what kinds of purposes does Holy Spirit often use the Message of Wisdom for.

5. Read passages such as *Acts 8:1-8, Luke 4:34, John 3:8, 1 Timothy 4:1, Acts 13:9-10, Matthew 17:18 a*nd consider what kinds of things Holy Spirit accomplishes through the gift of discernment?

FOUR

DON'T GET TONGUE TIED!

You're filled to flow in the language of the Spirit!

The experience of the gift of tongues can be a key part of your experience of the flow of the Spirit. This chapter will give you a proper understanding of the full range of all that is 'tongues' - and show you how to move toward engagement in this gift.

It's weird!

A friend of mine was a pastor of a thriving and growing church. Each year in the fall, his church sent postcards to the neighborhoods to invite people to church. They were colorful flyers describing the church, what they would teach, and their available ministry programs. The card had a graphic that looked like a seal - the kind of graphic that usually has the word 'guaranteed!' or 'warranty' inside a star-burst circle. Instead, this graphic boldly declared, "No weirdness'" On the one hand, this kind of message is the natural promise of a church culture steeped in seeker-sensitive ministry. But on the other hand - is that a pledge a church can even make?

If you read the scriptures and take them to heart - you'll quickly realize that 'no weirdness' is probably *not* a guarantee a church can keep if what you are doing together is at ALL like what is in the Bible! The Rotary Club or Toastmasters- they might be able to arrive at 'no weirdness' - but the Church, it's weird from the start. We believe that angels are real and sometimes appear to people, and one angel spoke to a teenage girl to tell her she would give birth to the Messiah. We believe that God became a man and died and rose again. We believe that people can close their eyes and talk out loud to the Creator of the Universe - and that as they do so, God is listening. We believe there is a real Heaven, and that after you die, you may go there if you've placed your faith in Jesus, the Messiah. We believe these things because we have a book with words and sentences that we believe were inspired by God. It's weird. All of it is weird!

We are called in scripture to sing psalms, hymns, and spiritual songs to the Lord - and it *is* a little weird to see a group of people closing their eyes and singing songs to an invisible being. The Bible calls people to lift their hands in praise, shout 'glory!' to God, and bow down in His presence. The scriptures record moments of prayer and praise so powerful, such as in Acts 4:31, that the place where they were meeting was literally shaken. That *is* weird. Jesus repeatedly told his disciples (and, by extension, the Church) to preach the gospel, cast out demons, heal the sick, and raise the dead. Ummm, if you think about it, that stuff is all kind of weird!

When that church stamped 'no weirdness' on their postcard, they truly intended to convey that the kinds of things people associated with fanatic Christians wouldn't happen there. Wild shouting, hands waving in the air, strange words like 'glory' and 'hallelujah' wouldn't be used, people would be calm, and there wouldn't be such odd things as prophesying or praying in tongues.

I love my friend - but I wondered whether he was reading the Thomas Jefferson version of the Bible. It is noted that about 10 years after his presidency of the United States, Thomas Jefferson created a unique version of the Bible - or the gospels at least. He took the text of the scriptures in the New Testament, cut out all of the passages that exhibited a supernatural element, and compiled a book he then entitled "The Life and Morals of Jesus of Nazareth." It has been called The Jefferson Bible - only published after his lifetime. In some ways, churches such as the 'no weirdness' one follow a similar trend. To create an environment that is palatable to all, there is an intentional effort to tone down or even refrain from practices of the early Church as recorded in the scriptures if they cross the line into 'weirdness.'

Tongues are weird, and useful

One of the elements of 'weirdness' that receives the most negative attention is the manifestation of the Spirit called *tongues*. There *is* genuinely something weird about a person opening their mouth and uttering syllables and sounds that do not seem to have a readily understood meaning. It *is* weird if a person speaks out in a human language they never knew before, and what they are saying conveys a spiritual word of truth that glorifies God. It *is* definitely weird if one person opens their mouth and pronounces sounds and syllables that are unintelligible - but then another person translates that into the language of the people. Yes - all of that *is actually pretty weird!* But that is the kind of thing that is in the Bible as it relates to the spiritual gift called tongues.

As a believer in Jesus, you are part of the Kingdom of God. The Kingdom of God is not a place like a castle on a hill. It is a realm that is *possible* and *accessible* anywhere, anytime. It is the realm of God's reigning, ruling presence. It is a realm marked by the supernatural flow of the power of the Holy Spirit, which makes miraculous goodness possible. It is a realm you can experience being part of while simultaneously living in the kingdoms of this world. As you participate in the Kingdom of God, you become a conduit for the power of His presence in the world. You establish the Kingdom of God by standing as one He can freely convey His power and love through.

At the core, tongues is evidence of the explosive nature of your Kingdom power. Because you are a believer wholly yielded to the Spirit of God, you advance his Kingdom wherever you go. It is advantageous for you to use the complete range of communication systems available in the Kingdom: prophecy, prayer, intercession, song, and praying in the spirit through tongues. The Kingdom *is* meant to be, at times, fiery and powerful. Consider the day of Pentecost as recorded in Acts 2:1-4:

> *When the day of Pentecost came, they were all together in one place. Suddenly a sound like the blowing of a violent wind came from heaven and filled the whole house where they were sitting. They saw what seemed to be tongues of fire that separated and came to rest on each of them. All of them were filled with the Holy Spirit and began to speak in other tongues as the Spirit enabled them.*
>
> ACTS 2:1-4 NIV

Learning a new ...language?

Tongues is one of the more obviously unconventional manifestations of the Spirit. This gift is amazing, and it provides an excellent access point to so much of the flow of the Spirit for any believer. There is an excellent blessing available in the gift of tongues; it is meant to empower and enhance the filled to flow life.

There is a good deal of misunderstanding about this gift, about how it functions, about its purpose, and its use in the body of Christ. Many believers want to avoid controversy by avoiding this gift altogether. Nevertheless, it is a gift, a manifestation of the Holy Spirit whom we love. It comes from the heart of God, from the Father of the heavenly lights, who gives good and perfect gifts, as James 1:17 says. It is intended to be a blessing. Engagement in the gifts of the Spirit is not an issue of salvation but of sanctification.

You do not *have* to engage in all of the gifts of the Spirit - and you are free to avoid, neglect, or ignore some of them. You can choose to avoid, neglect, or ignore tongues, in particular. But is this the wisest choice?

As a Christian, you are on a journey called *sanctification*. On one hand, this is about learning to do what is right, good, noble, holy, and pure. It is about crucifying sinful impulses. Sanctification *is* about experiencing an increasing degree of the removal of willful and habitual sin from your life. But it is *also* about growing in your identity as a powerful agent of the Kingdom of God! The full range of the Spirit's gifts are tools that allow you to engage in that aspect of sanctification in more significant measure and with greater effect.

Activation - a sigh of thanks

You'll discover that tongues is sometimes fully formed language - and sometimes simply sounds coming from a deeper place, much like a sigh. For this activation, think of something that you are grateful for. Anything. Your home, your car, your job, your marriage, etc. Think of it - and think of being thankful to God for that. With that thought in mind, take a deep breath, put your hand on your heart, and let out a good, long, vocalized sigh. Make a vocal sound as you sigh - and in your mind, think, "Thank you, God!"

～ Repeat this activation several times with various things you're grateful for.
～ How does allowing a sound to come forth from a deep place beyond words feel?
～ Were you able to connect with Jesus as you did this?

Tongues - part of your sanctification process

All of the Spirit's gifts can help you increase your impact for the Kingdom of God. Tongues is not an exception. Some Christian movements *do* teach that tongues is required evidence of salvation. I disagree with that position; Tongues *often* accompanies receiving salvation in many instances in the book of Acts. That indicates it is a vital blessing to expect, learn to use to minister to others, and learn how to employ personally. But the thorough reading of scripture doesn't lead me to conclude that it is required for or proof of salvation. I'd put it another way; your salvation gives you access to the full range of the manifestations of the Spirit. The Baptism of the Spirit is available and normative - and praying in tongues can be evidence of the Baptism of the Spirit. God desires every believer to experience and live in the power of the Baptism of the Spirit. The *filled to flow* life does require that.

If you have been baptized in the Spirit and have begun experiencing the gift of tongues - keep going with it, do not neglect it! Engaging in this manifestation of the Spirit requires your willful, proactive choice. The Spirit will generally not force a manifestation of the gifts upon you. Instead, your active choice to begin speaking forth in tongues is met with the flow of the Spirit from within you. The result will be you praying - or speaking - in tongues in a way that will strengthen you in the Lord.

If you love Jesus, and love the Holy Spirit, but have a hang-up about tongues, be open to learning more about tongues. You may need to work through some misunderstandings or concerns about this gift. You may need to come to a full comprehension of it. But more importantly, you will need to exercise courage to use and then keep using this gift initially. Once you do, you will always have a delightful place of entry into the flow of the Holy Spirit's power!

Getting that lawn mower started with starter spray

A few years ago, I had a lawn mower that was difficult to start. It was a bright orange Husqvarna self-propelled mower - and I had paid a lot of money for it. It had sat in my garage for 5 months during winter, and the cheap gas I used had gummed up the carburetor. As a result, this mower would barely start, no matter how vigorously I pulled the rope. I would be out in the driveway, pulling on that rope for five minutes, throwing my hands up in exasperation. I made some notable utterances that definitely did *not* involve praying in tongues. Finally, about 10 minutes into the ordeal, the engine would give in and get going. I'm telling you - that mower got me in my flesh like nothing else!

I watched a few videos about how other people have dealt with this problem. Of course, some people recommended total engine overhauls, new carburetors, and total engine flushes. But come on, it's a lawn mower. Do I really have to go through all of that? Finally, I found one guy who posted a video of the mower that was the same as mine. He mentioned he was having trouble starting it. He said, "I'm going to show you the easy way to fix this problem," and he did! He popped off the air filter holder, knelt, sprayed this mysterious fluid into the air intake area, got up, pulled the rope, and the mower started instantly!

That mystery spray is called starter fluid, and I rushed out that moment and bought a can. I did exactly as he did in the video, and just like that, my mower was running perfectly! Yes, it is weird that I had to pull the air filter off and spray something into the engine to get it going, but I'll take some weirdness instead of exasperation and frustration any day!

Tongues - like spiritual starter spray

The mower probably also needed a proper tune-up, which may have required a carburetor flush. But I needed the engine to get going then and there. The mower itself was solid and worked well, but it needed something to help it get going. The starter fluid was just that. In some ways, the manifestation of the Spirit called Tongues is like that starter fluid. It may be that your spiritual life is solid; you have faith in Jesus, read the scriptures, and pray, but somehow, that sense of God's presence and strength is lacking. You might feel inclined to get your super spiritual friend to pray for you, or you may find some new devotional book to read. Those could help, but maybe give the starter fluid a try instead!

In my own experience, the expression of Tongues gets my spiritual engine running so well. I know it's a little weird - but I'm okay with that! I would exchange religious tedium and malaise for spiritual activation and the flow of the Spirit any day! The gift of tongues may be the very thing that is most needed for you to come into a more full experience of the flow of the Spirit. I want to give you insight into this manifestation of the Spirit so that you'll have clarity and confidence to move into the experience of this gift with joy!

> *Therefore, my brothers and sisters, be eager to prophesy,*
> *and do not forbid speaking in tongues. But everything*
> *should be done in a fitting and orderly way.*
>
> 1 CORINTHIAN 14:39-40 NIV

When I hear the sound of someone praying in tongues - I get excited. Something deep and powerful could be happening between that person and God. But others might hear that same sound and feel concerned about this thing called 'tongues.' The sound of it makes them feel nervous. They have a sense that something bizarre is happening. *You* might be the kind of person who hears the word 'tongues,' and all you can think about is French kissing or the Rolling Stones logo! Among Christians, there's a lack of clarity about tongues.

There are three different variations of tongues

I want to clarify something for you. There are three different variations of the manifestation of this spiritual gift called tongues. There are the tongues of *ministry at Pentecost*, the tongues of a *message to translate to the church*, and the tongues of *mystery to convey to the Father*. There are three primary scriptural reference points regarding tongues: Acts 2:1-13, 1 Corinthians 14:26-28, and 1 Corinthians 14:2-4. Each passage uses the same word - γλῶσσα or 'glossa' (tongues) - but each passage presents a very different and unique activity. It's not strange for a word to have several disparate uses. Here's an example:

Think of the man in the kitchen with a bag of flour opened and a bowl before him, saying, "I have to make some dough." Now think of the woman in a business suit and designer shades getting into her car with her briefcase on her way to her next sales appointment. She says, "I have to make some dough," and drives away. They both used the same word and phrase but with very different meanings. Something like this takes place in the scriptures as pertains to tongues. I have taken to calling these three variations *Tongues One*, *Tongues Two*, and *Tongues Three*. I know it's not that original - but it will help bring clarity. Let's take some time together to examine the scriptures that give rise to these three very different expressions of tongues. Let's start with tongues one, in Acts 2:1-13 with a focus on verses 4-8.

TONGUES 1 - MINISTRY AT PENTECOST

All of them were filled with the Holy Spirit and began to speak in other tongues as the Spirit enabled them. Now there were staying in Jerusalem God-fearing Jews from every nation under heaven. When they heard this sound, a crowd came together in bewilderment, because each one heard their own language being spoken. Utterly amazed, they asked: "Aren't all these who are speaking Galileans? Then how is it that each of us hears them in our native language?"

ACTS 2:4-8 NIV

The church, as we know it, started with what we just read. Can you imagine this day? It was just supposed to be a regular Jewish holiday - Shavuot. This Hebrew festival was celebrated in honor of the giving of the Torah - the Words of God - to Moses and all of the people. It was also a celebration of the harvest. The Greek word Pentecost was used as a stand-in name for that Hebrew festival. Until this moment, Pentecost was a word used to describe this Jewish holiday.

Pentecost means 'fiftieth' - and it refers to the timing of its occurrence seven weeks after Passover. But on this day, the words of God were given in a miraculous new way to the entire human community in languages that represented all of the cardinal directions in the known world at the time. On this day, the Words of God were given in this supernatural expression that would lead to the long-awaited harvest of righteousness, salvation, and the coming of the Kingdom of God!

This is the first episode recorded in the New Testament where speaking in tongues occurs. You should note the way the verses expressly represent what happened here. The people were *talking* in *known earthly languages* that they hadn't known before. They were not praying. They were speaking to people. This is *tongues 1* - speaking in an actual earthly language you never knew before, speaking *to people*. Those listening are hearing directly, in their own language, about the wonders of God. It's very public, it serves an evangelistic purpose, and it was so powerful that we, as Christians, regard what happened in that moment as the birthday of the Church!

Let's recap: In Acts 2, we discover Tongues One. In this variation of tongues, those engaging the gift are speaking to people, in a known earthly language they didn't previously know. The content they are conveying is a message about the glory of God. Tongues One is evangelistic in nature, generally takes place in public and does not require an interpretation. Those listening understand the language plainly if it is a language they know. Believe it or not, I've experienced this gift. I'll tell you about it just after this activation!

Activation - Duolingo for Jesus!

You may have studied another language, maybe even more than one. If you haven't, this may hit a little deeper. God is fluent in all of the seven thousand languages on planet Earth, and He loves to hear those 'tongues,' whether or not they are your mother tongue. Take a moment right now and utter praise to God in some different languages. Speak out loud - or at least make an attempt!

English: I love you Jesus!
Spanish: ¡Te amo, Jesús!
French: Je t'aime, Jésus!
German: Ich liebe dich, Jesus!
Italian: Ti amo, Gesù!
Portuguese: Eu te amo, Jesus!
Russian: Ya Lyublyu Tebya Isus   Я люблю тебя, Иисус!
Chinese: Wuh ai ni, Yesu!   我愛你，耶穌！
Arabic: Uhibuk, ya Yesu!   عوسي اي ،كبحأ!
Japanese: Yesu, Aishiteru!   イエス様、愛しています！

~   Were you able to connect with Jesus as you did this?

It became more awkward, challenging, or uncomfortable with each language you attempted. But - knowing that you were giving glory and honor to Jesus made it worth it, didn't it? This wasn't 'tongues' - I'm just trying to get you to be more free with the range of how you can express praise for God in ways that are beyond your comfort zone!

I experienced tongues one in Ethiopia

A number of years ago, I led a missions trip from our church to Ethiopia. Our team included two doctors and three nurses, and a key part of our trip was medical outreach in the countryside. In each village we went to, we would set a tent for medical screening and triage and another for treatment. We also set up a location for prayer. If the doctors couldn't treat a particular illness, they would send the patients in for prayer. If they couldn't receive medical care from our team, they could at least receive spiritual care.

We went to one village in the Sidama region of the Ethiopian highlands. It was a cloudy day, and cool, light rain fell as we set up for the outreach in the early morning. I did what I could to help with the setup, and then I took advantage of the time by preaching the gospel to the 200 locals who were in line awaiting our mobile medical clinic. Several people prayed to receive Jesus while in line - and I was excited about seeing the response to the gospel! The moment concluded, and I started trying to help with the medical clinic volunteers. I realized pretty quickly that my unskilled hands weren't that helpful. One of the doctors graciously said, "Hey John, maybe you could go man the prayer tent!". That probably made sense - since I was the preacher on the trip.

I went into the prayer tent - and a group of Ethiopians were already on their knees praying. They were crying out in Sidamo - the local language of their region. I didn't even know how to say 'hello' in this language. I wanted to pray for these people - so I began praying for them, laying hands on them one by one, and asking God to bless them, touch them, heal their bodies, and help them recover from whatever the illness was they were struggling with. When I prayed, they got very quiet. I knew they couldn't understand me - and I felt very feeble in my attempts to be a blessing.

After about 20 minutes of this, I decided to begin praying for them in tongues. I figured that since they weren't going to understand me anyway, I might as well at least bring the powerful connection I know always comes when I pray in tongues. I also figured they probably wouldn't even know I was praying in tongues.

As I began praying in tongues for the people, I felt the anointing of the Holy Spirit on my heart and mind. I could hear the people in the tent engaging in the prayer with far more responsiveness than before. I could make out tones of agreement - and even the shared word 'amen!'. I kept praying this way for a couple of hours - as more and more people entered the prayer tent. Finally, it was time for a break, and I came out. Our local translator and ministry partner,

Getachew, approached me just behind the tent, looked at me with surprise, and said, 'Where did you learn Sidamo?' I said, 'Excuse me? I don't even know how to say hello in Sidamo!'.

He gestured to a group of locals and said, "These people told me your prayers blessed them so much. They asked you to keep praying because they understood you so well. They don't know any English. They said you were praying for them and declaring how God was going to touch their bodies and heal them and how they were going to recover from their illnesses through the power of Jesus Christ!"

At first, I was just silent - because I was shocked. If I was understanding him correctly, something like the miracle manifestation of Acts 2:1-10 had happened in that tent. I was dumbfounded - I almost couldn't believe it. I wish I could tell you that from that moment on, I've been fluent in Sidamo. That is not the case. In fact - since that time sixteen years ago, I have not experienced *that* manifestation of tongues again, even though praying in tongues, generally, has been a part of my life on an ongoing basis. Nevertheless - that day I experienced the miracle of *tongues 1*, and the effect was precisely that which is recorded in Acts 2:11: "—we hear them declaring the wonders of God in our own tongues!"

TONGUES TWO: A MESSAGE TO TRANSLATE

This year for Thanksgiving, we had six extra people at the house. That meant we had just enough people to play some fun games! One of the games was 'fishbowl'. We put phrases on paper and threw them in a fishbowl, and the person whose turn it was had to get up and convey that phrase - but without using the words on that paper. Of course, it was comical to see them struggle. But - somehow - they got the point across, and teammates guessed most of the phrases.

In the second round, the player had to take the paper from the fishbowl and communicate it so the teammates could guess it. But this time, they could not use *any* words; they had to act it out.

Nothing like a good old-fashioned game of charades to get people laughing! Even though it was whacky, it was wonderful, refreshing, and fun. The players had to overcome being self-conscious and just go for it. Some of the time, they did a great job, and players guessed the phrase quickly. Other times, they were so bad that they finally had to say 'pass!' and move on to another phrase.

When a person begins to speak in Tongues Two - it is a bit like that. They have a sense of something that needs to be conveyed - but they aren't exactly sure how to say it. They just go for it - and do what they can, and trust that their teammates will do their part to interpret it.

Tongues two is similar to my experience in getting to know deaf culture

Our church has recently begun cultivating a community of deaf people who are part of our church. Because of the excellent leadership of the volunteer leaders, this community is a vibrant, growing group within our church, with roughly 30 participants. During our Sunday service, this community sits together in the first several rows in one section of our venue. We have a part-time staff member who is a certified translator. She expresses the words I'm preaching to the deaf community through careful and thoughtful ASL. We also have a worship leader on the platform who leads worship through ASL. She *sings* through her *signing* by using her hands and whole body to express the lyrics - and it is beautiful to watch.

After the service, I sometimes cross the sanctuary to meet with the deaf community. I want to greet them and say hello. When I first began to do this, I was caught off guard. A person would request to talk to me. The translator would come, and the person from the deaf community and the translator would look at each other, not at me, even though the person was talking to me. The immature, ignorant part of me wanted to wave my hands and say, 'Hello, I'm right here, you can look at me!'. Thankfully, I also have the Holy Spirit speaking to me from within, saying, 'John, that would be foolishness!'

After a few interactions like this, I realized that this kind of communication differed significantly from what I'm accustomed to. To communicate through ASL, the eyes must be trained on the physical gestures that are being made by both people. The Translator can speak audibly so I can hear, but she must continue looking at the member of the deaf community to convey the next thought. The deaf member must keep his eyes focused on the translator's gestures to listen attentively to what *I* am saying through the translator. In fact, to listen and communicate well, neither person can look at me very much. Some in the deaf community who are further along in their journey of communicating comfortably with the hearing community can make more eye contact - but even for them - the focus is generally on the translator.

This experience of communication has taken me some time to get used to. In the hearing culture, eye contact is vital. It has been a journey to get accustomed to the translated interactions with my brothers and sisters in the deaf community, where the visual focus is on the translator - rather than on each other. It is new for me. At first - it was a bit uncomfortable. But over time, I've come to appreciate the fact that these friends are going out of their way to make a way to interact and share their heart with me - even though I'm almost exclusively an auditory and oral communicator.

Tongues Two is a bit like my experience in communication with the deaf community. It is a variety of tongues that takes place very differently from prayer or prophecy as you would typically conceive. It is a kind of spiritual interaction between God and man in which a translator is needed. The focus seems to shift between one person and another - and God. One person speaks forth in tongues - but not tongues that are in an earthly language. Another person then speaks forth a translation in your language so you can understand. The translation is a word of prophetic flow, a message from the heart of God. Consider the description of what I call *Tongues Two* in 1 Corinthians 14:26-27

> *What then shall we say, brothers and sisters? When you come together, each of you has a hymn, or a word of instruction, a revelation, a tongue or an interpretation. Everything must be done so that the church may be built up. If anyone speaks in a tongue, two—or at the most three—should speak, one at a time, and someone must interpret. If there is no interpreter, the speaker should keep quiet in the church and speak to himself and to God.*

1 CORINTHIANS 14:26-28 NIV

The scriptures describe a phenomenon here that is quite different from the Acts 2 experience of tongues. Here, the tongues that are uttered are spoken indirectly to the people. The language is not something of this world that anyone can understand based on their linguistic prowess. It has to be translated by some other person. Tongues Two generally requires two people or two different utterances: the tongues portion and the interpretation portion. The content is a message or revelation from the heart of God for the congregation or those present; it is a word from God *to the people*. It takes place in public, and the message is for the public - those gathered together.

These verses use the word 'if' to describe Tongues Two. 'If' ('*eite*' in Greek) is a coordinating conjunction that creates a conditional clause. You know what *if* means; it indicates that something does not *have to happen*. It suggests that it *can* happen, in the sense that it is allowable, with certain conditions being met. Again, tongues two - like many spiritual gifts - does not *have to* happen - but it is permissible from a Biblical view. Many churches avoid the use of this manifestation of the Spirit because it can be so easily misused or misunderstood. But there are many churches and groups of believers that *do* engage with this gift as part of their experience of the flow of the Spirit.

The time I first experienced tongues two in New Hampshire

I experienced tongues two for the first time when I was 18 years old. I was just about to graduate high school, and I took a road trip with a friend to go skiing. I wasn't walking closely with Jesus then, but I was still inclined toward Jesus - if that makes any sense. Even though I was in a period of wandering and sin - I was still drawn to scripture - and even to attending church.

On this road trip, my friend Bill and I traveled to the white mountains of New Hampshire. We enjoyed a fantastic trek along the tracks of the Cog Railway on Mount Washington. We were headed back to New Jersey early on a Sunday morning. We found ourselves driving through a town around the time for church - and I suggested to Bill that we go to a service somewhere.

The first church we came upon was the Manchester Assembly of God church. We parked the car and walked up. In New England in the early 90s, people generally wore suits to church - so we stuck out quite a bit, having come from several days of hiking and camping, dressed in our dirty jeans and flannels. Nevertheless, a kind, rosy-cheeked older gentleman in a tweed suit welcomed us and ushered us to our seats. Soon the service began, and after a hymn was sung, the pastor came forward and began a time of prayer. He provided a long pause during his prayer - and then it happened. *Tongues Two.*

From the pews on the left side of the expansive open sanctuary, that rosy-cheeked gentleman who had seated us stood up and said in a loud voice… well, actually, I couldn't tell you what he said in his loud voice because to me it sounded like gibberish. He made those sounds for about one minute and then sat down. Almost immediately, across the aisle from the pews in the front, another man stood up and said, 'The Lord says, behold, this is the day for my Mercy to be made known! I, the Lord, do not hold your sins against you because of the precious blood of the spotless Lamb of God who takes away the sins of the world, including yours!'. He sat down, and the pastor quietly said, 'Amen. That is a true word of the Lord.'

My friend Bill was not yet a believer. When this moment occurred, he and I looked at each other nervously. He looked at me with wide-open eyes as if to say, 'What in the heck was that!??'. The message from his eyes did *not* need an interpretation. I knew exactly what he was saying! After the service, we were enjoying the free coffee in the lobby. The rosy-cheeked man approached us and asked how we liked the service. I think my friend's honest answer would have been, 'Ummm, you're a freak show, man!' and I might have just said, 'To be honest, it was pretty weird', because we did not know what to make of that whole 'tongues' thing. But we restrained ourselves - and then we hit the road.

Bill and I talked about what happened over the five-hour drive home. I had a *bit* of exposure to tongues in the past, but it wasn't tongues like *that*. I had no context or understanding of how to explain what we just witnessed. As I said - I wasn't walking closely with Jesus then. But I did say, 'Bill - I know it was weird, but - what did you think of what was said when the other guy 'translated' or whatever that was? You know, 'I the Lord don't hold your sins against you...'?' We talked about that for a while - and I was able to share more with Bill about the forgiveness that is available in Jesus. Even though I was walking in sin personally at that time - and not close to Jesus - God used that moment of Tongues Two in a church in Manchester New Hampshire, to instigate a conversation from one sinner to another about the mercy of God in Christ. And Bill ended up putting his faith in Jesus!

Part of the difficulty with Tongues 2 is that it is a challenge to discover who might have activation in the manifestation of the spirit to interpret. There must be a high degree of trust in that individual and their genuine yieldedness to the Holy Spirit as they provide an interpretation. However, in a Body of believers with a healthy appreciation for the manifestations of the spirit, there can also be learning environments in classes and groups with room for trial and error. In an environment where experimentation is welcomed, there is a recognition that as we attempt to engage with the Holy Spirit in these ways, we may get it wrong - and that's okay! That's the nature of a learning environment.

TONGUES THREE: A MYSTERY TO CONVEY

Tongues Three is like abstract art - beauty in the eye of the beholder

I would not classify myself as an artist, but I do enjoy painting. Some people enjoy painting *realism*, a specific, realistic representation of a person or place. I do not have the artistic skill to achieve realism in my artwork. But apart from skill, I enjoy abstract impressionism, the raw, evocative art form that generally does not convey reality. I paint in this style, usually with acrylic paints.

I set up my canvas, turned on some inspiring music, put out my acrylic paints, and then created. Generally, I do not begin with a specific goal in mind. I may have a certain color scape I want to achieve; for example, I have a strong penchant for swirls and waves of blue and white. Sometimes, I have in mind a specific kind of technique I want to employ. In fact, I am planning to attempt a method of flowing liquid acrylic paint with a hair dryer later this week! I may choose my colorscape or technique, but the artistic work is decidedly *un*realistic.

I admire the skill of an artist who can create images so realistic that they look like photographs. Realism is wonderful. At the same time, I prefer for my own artistic expression to give me an opportunity to *depart* from what is concrete and direct, into something more fluid and mysterious. When I paint in the impressionist or abstract style, my mind is free to create from a place of flow, where what is applied to the canvas becomes an expression of something deep within me that I've simply been unable to convey with words. This kind of art allows me to communicate something from deep within that needed an opportunity to be expressed in a way that was unimpeded by the constraints of logic or even linguistic parameters.

My works of abstract art are relatively simple - and may not even appear valuable to anyone else; my skill level is still fairly basic. But each canvas was valuable to me for the healing, conveyance, and unburdening it accomplished in me. Someone else may look at my impressionist art and say it's meaningless. However, I can tell you that as it was created, *pure meaning* was flowing from within me directly onto the canvas. Sometimes, I can even look at my impressionist art pieces and *tell you* their meaning. Of course, that is subjective, but as the creator of the piece, I am the one who determines whether there is meaning and value in it.

In a sense, *Tongues Three* is like impressionist or abstract art. Some sounds could seem meaningless to others who hear them. Linguists may not even detect known patterns of speech when analyzing the language. But a conveyance occurs when one prays in tongues with *Tongues Three,* which is a pure flow of meaning and feeling. It truly is mysterious, abstract, and yet Biblical.

When you pray in tongues, you activate a flow between your own Spirit and the Lord Himself through a communication channel made possible by the Holy Spirit within you. This communication channel bypasses the traditional cognitive processing that you are comfortable with - and at first - it may be uncomfortable; that's okay! From time to time, we need to be reminded - even in how we communicate with the Lord - who is Spirit (2 Cor. 3:17) - that His Kingdom is *supernatural.* It is our privilege to enjoy our connection with our King that goes beyond the natural order!

Consider the expression that can flow if you'd just pray in tongues! Tongues three can be as intriguingly captivating as the stars in the sky as envisioned by Van Gogh in Starry Night; It is as splendidly romantic as 'The Skiff,' rendered by Renoir. It is as plainly powerful as the splattered madness of Jackson Pollack. It can be as beautiful as the skies made marvelous by Monet's 'Sunrise.' Ah, but beauty is in the eye of the beholder with art - and it may be that the same is true of *Tongues Three*. Consider the words of 1 Corinthians 14:1-4 which describe this unique expression:

> *Follow the way of love and eagerly desire gifts of the Spirit, especially prophecy. For anyone who speaks in a tongue does not speak to people but to God. Indeed, no one understands them; they utter mysteries by the Spirit. But the one who prophesies speaks to people for their strengthening, encouraging and comfort. Anyone who speaks in a tongue edifies themselves.*
>
> 1 CORINTHIANS 14:1-4 NIV

Tongues Three is prayer in a heavenly language

Tongues Three is indeed a form of prayer. When we think of prayer, we imagine someone communicating with or talking to God. You may recall that Tongues One and Tongues Two reflect communication, which is actually *not* prayer in this sense. The first two kinds of tongues are communications *directed towards other people*. Tongues Three, however, is communication directed to God from the heart of a believer in a language that they do not know, that no other human knows, and that no other human is intended to translate or interpret. It is private between them and God.

The sounds that a person makes with this gift may, in fact, come across as gibberish. Nevertheless, communication is taking place that goes beyond the logical constructs of language. Consider this - when you laugh, you are making syllables and sounds that are not in an earthly language - but are full of meaning - and you freely allow yourself to express it. Or think of a time when you let out a sigh or a groan - a strange sound came from your lips. It wasn't in your native language - yet it conveyed worlds of meaning. A moan is the same way - so is a loud battle cry or the impulsive cheer that erupts when your sports team makes the winning play. I'm just sharing that you *already engage in expressing meaningful 'meaningless' sounds*. Perhaps you could allow yourself to intentionally engage that same faculty in this wonderful Biblical expression called tongues!

Tongues Three is often called 'Heavenly language' because the Bible refers to it in 1 Corinthians 13:1 as 'the tongues of angels.' It is sometimes referred to as a 'personal prayer language.' It does *not* require interpretation or translation. It is an interaction between a human being and God Himself that seems to move beyond the usual logical constraints of linguistics. It is a flow of communication in which two things are taking place.

Activation - LOL!

Sometimes, we just need to know it's okay to express ourselves, even in ways that are a bit mysterious. Tongues three falls in that category! For this activation, think of something that makes you happy, joyful, or even giddy. As you think of it, let that smile come across your face! :)

Now, Tell Jesus all about it - but - don't use words, just laugh - out loud about it! He knows your thoughts from afar (Psalm 139:2) - so the words aren't always necessary. So think of that happy thing, and think of Jesus sitting with you, and just laugh out loud right now!

As you laugh, see if you hear Jesus saying or doing anything in response.

~ What exactly did your laugh mean? Could you sense a release of meaning, even though the laugh is not in any known language?
~ Could you sense a connection with Jesus as you communicated in this way?
~ Did you experience any sense of Jesus responding to you in this laughable moment of connection?

Two things that happen when you engage in tongues three

First, the person is uttering mysteries to God. There are ways in which your spirit within you is processing circumstances and moments on behalf of your soul that you don't even know the fullness of. There are frustrations, pains, and dilemmas that your soul has been vexed by that need to be dealt with. The questions, ruminations, and meditations from your inner being must be conveyed to the One who can handle such unimpeded and imperfectly formed wonderments and make sense of them all. These are the mysteries that have an opportunity to be expressed when you pray with tongues three.

Secondly, according to the scriptures in 1 Corinthians 14:4, when you pray in *tongues three,* you edify yourself in the Lord. It builds you up and strengthens you in the Lord when you pray in tongues. There are ways in which the simple act of praying in the spirit brings relief simply because something from the depths of your soul was able to be released to the Lord. That is therapeutic and healing. But in a way that may transcend our understanding, there is an internal strengthening of the human soul and spirit that comes to you as you pray in tongues!

The scriptures say that when using Tongues Three, a person is uttering mysteries with their spirit to God. The typical Western mindset is not open to this. We prefer things to be academic or philosophical, and this is neither. It is deeply metaphysical, mystical, and spiritual. And it is powerfully important. It engages a different part of us than our everyday boxy, proud, sophisticated modern philosophical mindsets would allow. Science backs this up.

Scientific observation has been carried out on people praying in tongues. The analysis has demonstrated no detectable linguistic patterns in the sounds being made. Some people may hear this and conclude that the idea of tongues is a farce - nothing but gibberish. But as I've noted already, the Bible itself calls this expression of prayer 'the tongues of angels' in 1 Corinthians 13:1. There is no expectation that it will match earthly patterns.

Scientific evidence proves the value and benefit of Tongues Three

Again, the scripture says that a person praying in tongues is uttering mysteries with their *spirit*. The scripture differentiates what the mind can do vs. what the spirit can do. Dr. Andrew Newberg, a researcher at the University of Pennsylvania, did a SPECT brain scan study of people praying in tongues to understand what was happening in the brain. The scans showed that the frontal lobe would light up when people prayed in English. When they prayed in tongues - the frontal lobe activity decreased. The frontal lobe, where standard language is indicated, is not activated. This is because the person is NOT 'praying with their logic' (frontal lobe/ linguistic faculty). They are praying with their spirit.

Dr Christopher Lynn, a researcher at the State University of New York at Albany, also studied people who prayed in tongues to find out what happened at a physiological level. The academic approach described *tongues three* as an auto-induced dissociative state of consciousness activated by religious free vocalization. The study was published in the American Journal of Human Biology and concluded that when people pray in tongues, there is a measurable reduction in circulatory cortisol and an increase in alpha-amylase enzyme activity. This means that praying in tongues causes a measurable, verifiable stress reduction!

Another study was done by Dr. Carl Peterson, a medical doctor and brain specialist. His study found that when people pray in tongues, the hypothalamus is stimulated, and the measurable result is a roughly 35% boost to the immune system. When a person prays in tongues, they edify themselves! No wonder the Devil wants to stir up so much strife over a good gift God wants His kids to have. At a time when mental illness, stress, depression, and anxiety are on the rise, we need to access every healthy form of relief that is available - including *tongues three*!

Are you allowed to use tongues three in public?

I was recently leading a midweek encounter service called '*Seek Night.*' There was a moment where we were praying and singing, and I was on the platform, and I asked people to sing in the spirit privately and pray in the spirit - to pray in tongues. And then I did so myself. And for a few minutes, there was this beautiful shift in the room as a large group of us all connected with God in this very personal way. Some were simply praying in tongues out loud. I was singing in tongues aloud - and urging many to join me in doing so. I could speculate that there is a gift to each person when, as a large group, we allow ourselves to find a sense of resonance with one another. The group may experience a sense of euphoria simply because of the reverberation of a similar frequency, coming from a place of depth from the spirit within.

You might wonder, 'Doesn't the scripture say you should only do that in private?'. Fair question. The scripture does say in 1 Corinthians 14:27, *"If there is no interpreter, the speaker should keep quiet in the church and speak to himself and to God."* The verse explicitly speaks about the kind of tongues that need an interpretation; That's Tongues Two - where a message is being communicated *to the people.* Tongues Three is an entirely different manifestation of the Spirit.

That said, the word "private," as applied to tongues generally, is helpful, especially regarding tongues three. The *meaning* of the interaction is private, but its action can also be expressed publicly. For example, a person may be at the airport, but they are on the phone. It is public, but they are having a private conversation.

For many people, tongues are a controversial gift. For others, they are just, well, *weird.* As a pastor with a heart to reach many people, I am careful about encouraging people to use this gift. I elect *not* to call for it during our Sunday services but instead make a place for it in our prayer and encounter gatherings, such as our Seek Night. To be candid, in my ministry, we rarely experience tongues one or two.

I want to be wise in inviting people into the 'greater gifts' as 1 Corinthians 14:1 calls them. This means choosing the right environment where the experience can be shepherded and where the gathering is intended to help those who are already disciples go deeper. I cannot guarantee 'no weirdness!' but I don't want to force any weirdness, either. Further, as a pastor, I *can* and *should* shepherd the weirdness!

Forbid not... And Hide It?

I know a woman who was one of the primary leaders - a Bishop - in a mainline Christian denomination for four years. She shared with me that the revival known as the Jesus People movement began sweeping the nation when she was a young woman. This move of God included passionate worship, prayer, and the use of the gifts of the Spirit - including tongues. She shared that in her exposure to this movement, the Holy Spirit had gotten a hold of her - and she came to a place where she was praying in tongues. Many of the church's young people were being activated in this gift.

Members and leaders of the denomination heard about this and became quite worried. They didn't want their young people getting caught up in anything heretical. To be fair, revival movements *do* tend to push the envelope. In particular, the leaders were concerned about the use of tongues. She told me that the denomination took a stance on the issue of tongues, expressed in shorthand with this phrase: "Forbid not, seek not." She shared with me that because of this stance, she felt she needed to keep this very private - and that she was really only free to flow in the gifts and passion of the spirit at a different church than the denominational church she was in - and loved.

She shared how this gift had been a precious resource for her for decades. She spoke of how she engaged in this gift throughout the years of spiritual warfare as a missionary and rising leader. However, she kept her engagement in this gift of the Spirit a secret until her final year as Bishop. She was aware that it would be controversial for many people in the denomination - so she just didn't speak about it. But she acknowledged that she wished she could - because she felt strongly that this had been a personal blessing to her for many years, allowing her to thrive during the long and challenging decades of ministry leadership she'd been through.

With a proper understanding of Tongues Three - and good shepherding of its expression, it is a gift that should be pursued. It is in category 1 Corinthians 14:1, which calls for 'the greater gifts', which are to be eagerly desired. Of course, tongues should not be forbidden. Beyond that, tongues should be pursued, eagerly desired and taught. There is too much to lose by leaving it fallow!

Tongues how?

You may wonder how this gift of *tongues three* works. First of all, as someone who prays in tongues nearly every day, I will tell you it is my choice to do so. I choose to open my mouth and make sounds. You need to do the same - to determine that you will open your mouth and create the syllabic utterance called tongues! You cannot wait for God to 'zap you into it'. He gives *you* the will and choice of how your body will function - including your mouth. I pray with people to receive - or rather - to activate into the gift of tongues fairly often - and each time, I need to remind the person that they should not wait for God to 'do it' - because He's already 'done it' - and He's waiting for them to 'do it'!

You might feel afraid that as someone is being prayed for to receive the gift of tongues, they could feel pressured. There is some truth to that concern. As I stand with someone who has said they want this gift, I see that they often start by being passive. So as I pray with them, I do, in fact, 'pressure' them. I say, 'Come on, open your mouth; don't wait for God to make you do it. You choose to move your mouth - so go ahead! Copy my sounds if you have to!' In my experience - praying in tongues is so different from our other standard ways of engaging - that some prodding is required at first.

When my kids first learned to ride a bike, I ran along with them, pressuring them to keep going. I taught them how to pedal and strongly urged them to push each foot forward. They needed that motivation and coaching - and I was glad to do it to get them going. When I minister to a person to begin praying in tongues, I actively coach them to take their first steps. Rather than thinking of it as 'pressure,' I think of it as direction, coaching, prodding - and pastoring. In the end, the Holy Spirit inspired these words in 1 Corinthians 14:5 - and it will require teaching, shepherding, and prodding:

I would like every one of you to speak in tongues.

Activation - Ugh!

In English, the action of groaning is represented by the words 'ugh' or 'ergh.' However, those aren't actual words; they reflect something we do almost universally as humans: When we are frustrated or in pain, we groan.

For this activation, think of a problem you are facing; a situation, a condition, a relationship issue - something you feel stress, frustration, anger, sadness, or tension about. Got it in mind? Good. Imagine you were just sitting with Holy Spirit to talk about it. But instead of putting it all into words, just take a deep breath and let out a good old loud groan. Do it again. Do it again!

If you've never received the gift of tongues three, I want to let you in on something. You might have just prayed in Tongues Three; a groan like that is Tongues Three with training wheels!

~ How does it affect you to allow yourself to convey something profound - but do so without cognitive linguistic constructs?

~ Take a moment to thank the Holy Spirit for keeping you safe and allowing you to be vulnerable.

Don't get tongue-tied!

My intention in delving so deeply into this one manifestation of the Spirit is that you would understand it and feel motivated to explore it. You can wait for a pastor or leader to lead you in activating this gift - or you could just *begin*. Don't get tongue-tied! Give yourself the freedom to *go for it* now that you know about it! Take a moment and look through this table - it will remind you of the key differences in the various expressions of tongues:

TONGUES 1	TONGUES 2	TONGUES 3
-Acts 2:1-13	-1 Cor. 14: 26-28	-1 Cor. 14: 2-4
-Direct to people	-Indirect to people	-Direct to God
-Understood	-Interpreted	-Mysterious
-Earthly language	-Heavenly lang.	-Heavenly lang.
-About God	-From God	-To God
-Public	-Public	-Private

I Will Pray, or I Won't...

> *Well then, what shall I do? I will pray in the spirit, and I will also pray in words I understand. I will sing in the spirit, and I will also sing in words I understand.*

1 CORINTHIANS 14:15 NLT

As you reflect on the words from 1 Corinthians 14:15, I hope you notice the word *will*. This passage conveys the sense of volition that is engaged when you pray. This verse beckons you to see that it is a willful decision to engage in communication with God - and that applies to tongues just as well. You *will* - you exercise your own choice to open your mouth and let syllables flow. An initial 'I will' must come into effect when determining whether to pray in tongues. There is an ongoing 'I will' to engage this gift consistently.

For many people, there is no 'I will' with regard to tongues. There is an adamant 'I won't'. There are Bible scholars and teachers that I greatly admire who vehemently oppose this gift and its use. They *won't*. I do not condemn them - they are free to make that decision. I also choose not to pray in tongues in many instances - but my choice is not based on a system that prohibits me - instead, it is based on leading of the Spirit for the sake of love.

Some theologians establish their own studied subjective rationale for cessationism as a framework for understanding the Bible. Often, this is tied to a specific view called *dispensationalism* - an arbitrary construct wherein the activity of God is 'boxed in' to a beautifully constructed chronology. It's very logical - but it is also very man-made. The dispensational view is helpful in some regards in attempting to understand the sequence of events that arise in scripture. I hold the dispensational view loosely - as a tool, one of many, that can help me comprehend the major plotlines of the prophetic words of the Bible. But In the worst case, dispensationalist preachers and scholars inadvertently engage in an idolatry of their own theology, vaunting their view of God over who God Himself has expressed Himself to be.

The plain reading of scripture does not lead to the conclusion of the cessationists. I'll still cherish the insightful teaching these scholars can provide on many other topics - but I cannot share their view on the manifestations of the Spirit. I would urge you to guard against the high-brow, lofty thinking of theologians who seem to feel they must have everything neatly categorized. God Himself has shown through His own word that His ways are not our ways - and when we attempt to ascribe limitations to His activity - we limit ourselves, for He can not ever be constrained to our chronologies! Instead - take the direct challenge of scripture to engage in your connection with King Jesus through prayer in the Spirit!

And pray in the Spirit on all occasions with all kinds of prayers and requests. With this in mind, be alert and always keep on praying for all the Lord's people.

EPHESIANS 6:18 NIV

Tongues is power for world changers

To summarize, Tongues One is *preaching in tongues* - like the ministry of Pentecost. Tongues Two is *prophesying in tongues*, with a message to proclaim to the church, and Tongues Three is *praying in tongues*, with a mystery to convey between you and your Heavenly Father. Each manifestation of the gift of tongues is unique. Each aspect of tongues can be a blessing.

Tongues are a gift that should create a deeper flow of the love of God into and through your life. Tongues edifies you so that you're stronger. When you're stronger, you can love more fully. You become the kind of person who can lend strength to the neighbors you're called to love. Let love be your highest aim. You might come to love this gift of tongues, but If you make your preference for tongues your priority, you could end up idolizing a manifestation of the Spirit. If you become dogmatic about it, you could make supernatural faith look foolish and leave the beautiful mystery looking like bullying and mean-spiritedness.

God's goal is for you to become a person who wants to live as a world changer. The manifestation of tongues can be an excellent component of how you get there. It's about power and strength from God flowing into you. You can do it without it- but It would be like driving your car while leaving one of the battery terminals disconnected. It would be like only ever charging your phone to 65%. I would prefer that you press in and get the full charge so you can live *filled to flow!*

On the other hand, tongues doesn't stop you from sinning; It doesn't cover it up or make up for it if you do sin. Tongues doesn't take away your personality issues. Tongues doesn't make you better than anyone, and tongues doesn't make God love you any more than anyone else. But it *does* give you a delightful access point to another manifestation of His grace. That's something you just might need! So - go for it - and don't get tongue-tied!

Group Activation - initiate the direct connect

Generally, the gift of tongues is activated through the laying on of hands by someone else with this gift of tongues. If you have a group with a person like that - or a friend who prays in tongues, ask them to lay hands on you for you to receive and be activated in the gift of tongues three.

Just as you choose to laugh, you decide to groan, you choose to hum a tune, and you will need to choose to utter syllables. You are not a puppet - and if it feels like 'you are doing it,' that's because *you are*. What matters is the connection with God!

~~ Begin to pay attention as you pray in tongues three. Prayer in tongues three can become a two-way street, and God may allow you to experience downloads of meaning and revelation while you pray in tongues.

~~ Once this gift is activated, continue to choose to use it!

Group Activation - no need for Google Translate here!

This activation is for a group - or at least two people. This is an activation of tongues two. Spend some time in praise and thanksgiving, and then - one person, speak forth a message in tongues. Let it be brief. Then stop. Then, someone else in the group boldly says, 'I believe the Lord says, ...!' and goes out on a limb to provide the interpretation.

This is a learning and activation moment. There is room for trial and error. Consider this your 'time on the tricycle' and 'time with training wheels.'

~~ The person who gives the interpretation should ask the tongues-speaker, 'Did my interpretation sound right to what you felt in your spirit it might be?' The group should also discern whether the message was in alignment with scripture.

~~ This gift requires mutual understanding, submission, and agreement to use. If your group or church generally doesn't practice using this gift. Don't try to force it.

FILLED TO FLOW
BIBLE STUDY SMALL GROUP GUIDE

Chapter Four:
Clandestine Kingdom
Communications: Tongues

You're filled to flow in the language of the Spirit!

The experience of tongues can be a key part of your experience of the flow of the spirit. This message will give you a proper understanding of the full range of all that is 'tongues' - and show you how to move toward engagement in this gift.

Bible study group guide how-to summary:

▱ Means it's a Bible study reflection question. It's okay if just 1-2 people answer. It's okay to move through it quickly or even to skip. It also means there may not be time to include the reading of this scripture or the discussion of the question with the whole group. But consider these sections in your own study!

≈ means this is a group interaction reflection question. It would be good to ask several people from the group to respond. It also means that the scripture associated with this question should be read aloud to the group.

Engage:

1. ≈ Icebreaker: Share a word or phrase you know in another language (keep it kosher, now!) how you learned it, and why you like that phrase.

2. ▱ Discuss any highlights from this chapter. What emotions come to mind when you hear about the gift of tongues? Why do you think you feel that way?

≈ Read 1 Corinthian 14:39-40 NIV

Therefore, my brothers and sisters, be eager to prophesy and do not forbid speaking in tongues. But everything should be done in a fitting and orderly way.

Engage:

3. ≈ What did you think the first time you heard someone praying in tongues? What does 'tongues' sound like to you?

≈ Read Acts 2:1-4 NIV

When the day of Pentecost came, they were all together in one place. Suddenly a sound like the blowing of a violent wind came from heaven and filled the whole house where they were sitting. They saw what seemed to be tongues of fire that separated and came to rest on each of them. All of them were filled with the Holy Spirit and began to speak in other tongues as the Spirit enabled them.

≈ Read Acts 2:11b

"—we hear them declaring the wonders of God in our own tongues!"

Engage:

4. ▱ How do you think the disciples in the upper room might have felt when they had this experience described in vs. 4?

5. ▱ What were the people in Acts 2:1-4 doing, technically?

≈ Read Acts 2:5-13 NIV

Now there were staying in Jerusalem God-fearing Jews from every nation under heaven. When they heard this sound, a crowd came together in bewilderment, because each one heard their own language being spoken. Utterly amazed, they asked: "Aren't all these who are speaking Galileans? Then how is it that each of us hears them in our native language? Parthians, Medes and Elamites; residents of Mesopotamia, Judea and Cappadocia, Pontus and Asia, Phrygia and Pamphylia, Egypt and the parts of Libya near Cyrene; visitors from Rome (both Jews and converts to Judaism); Cretans and Arabs—we hear them declaring the wonders of God in our own tongues!" Amazed and perplexed, they asked one another, "What does this mean?" Some, however, made fun of them and said, "They have had too much wine."

Engage:

6. ▱ What did some people who didn't share the experience think of it (vs. 10-12, & vs 13)?

7. ≈ Why do many believers want to avoid an experience of the power of God and the gift of tongues? How have you wrestled with that tendency?

≈ Read 1 Corinthians 14:26-27 NIV

What then shall we say, brothers and sisters? When you come together, each of you has a hymn, or a word of instruction, a revelation, a tongue or an interpretation. Everything must be done so that the church may be built up. If anyone speaks in a tongue, two—or at the most three—should speak, one at a time, and someone must interpret.

⧄ Read 1 Corinthians 14:28

If there is no interpreter, the speaker should keep quiet in the church and speak to himself and to God.

Engage:

8. ⧄ In this second and different iteration of tongues, who is being spoken to, and what are they receiving?

9. ⧄ What is the purpose of this type of tongues - and if it is used, how should it be used?

10. ⧄ Have you ever been in a gathering of believers where this gift of tongues and interpretation was used? Was it beneficial? How did it affect you?

11. ⧄ Consider the value of the word 'if' in the verses above and share your reflection about what that implies, either way.

≈ Read 1 Corinthians 14:1-4 NIV

Follow the way of love and eagerly desire gifts of the Spirit, especially prophecy. For anyone who speaks in a tongue does not speak to people but to God. Indeed, no one understands them; they utter mysteries by the Spirit. But the one who prophesies speaks to people for their strengthening, encouraging and comfort. Anyone who speaks in a tongue edifies themselves.

≈ Read 1 Corinthians 14:5 NIV

I would like every one of you to speak in tongues.

12. ⬜ What is the value of this third iteration of tongues?

13. ⬜ Sometimes, 'Tongues Three' is called a personal private prayer language. Why is it referred to this way, and what constitutes correctly using this gift? What are its benefits?

⬜ Read 1 Corinthians 14:15 NLT

Well then, what shall I do? I will pray in the spirit, and I will also pray in words I understand. I will sing in the spirit, and I will also sing in words I understand.

≈ Read Ephesians 6:18 NIV

And pray in the Spirit on all occasions with all kinds of prayers and requests. With this in mind, be alert and always keep on praying for all the Lord's people.

Engage:

14. ≈ If you have been activated in this third gift of tongues, share what it means and does for you. If you have not been, share why you'd want this gift of tongues.

15. ⬜ How does the gift of tongues fit into God's great call to love our neighbor?

16. ≈ Which expression of tongues are you most drawn to?

≈ Read Jude 1:20-21 NIV

But you, dear friends, by building yourselves up in your most holy faith and praying in the Holy Spirit, keep yourselves in God's love as you wait for the mercy of our Lord Jesus Christ to bring you to eternal life.

17. ≈ What does it seem that the Holy Spirit is trying to accomplish through each of these three different expressions of tongues?

Pray≈:

~ for openness to the gift of tongues and repentance over cynicism about it
~ for activation of the gift of tongues 3
~ for activation of the gift of tongues 2
~ for activation of the gift of interpretation of tongues 2; give it a try?!?
~ for whatever needs there may be among the group

Extra:

Read Mark 16:17, Acts 10:44-48, Acts 19:1-7, Acts 2:38-39, Romans 8:26, and consider: What do you observe about who the gift of tongues is for? Why do you think we generally see less manifestation of the gift of tongues in our current Christian churches?

FIVE

BREAKTHROUGH, THROUGH YOU!

You're filled to flow in Kingdom authority for breakthrough and healing!

In this chapter, you will discover the authority you have because of your identity - and how to walk in it. This chapter will help you to grow in understanding of and empowerment in the demonstrative gifts of healing & miracles in and through the authority of Jesus. You'll learn why they are vital aspects of the Kingdom of God and how to operate in them!

The breakthrough that brought about Centerpoint Church

I was just 29 years old when I first came to Murrieta, California. I had been serving as the worship and youth pastor of a wonderful church in Santa Barbara, where I also worked as the campus worship pastor for Westmont College. I had never been a lead pastor before, but we moved to this new community to embrace the challenge of relaunching a small, struggling church. I met with the Board President at a diner for the initial interview. He told me about the remarkable history of the church; the founding pastor,

Marty Edwards, was something of a legend in the town - and the church he started carried a sense of passion for Jesus that reflected his earnest desire for God's Kingdom. Jim told me about how the church had come to the place where it was gravely struggling.

There had been a terrible church split that scarred the congregation. What was intended to be a healthy church plant went sideways and siphoned off a large core of the congregation. Then, the beloved founder left and started a new parachurch ministry. The next pastor who came in only lasted a year and a half before he lost heart because the vibrant church had lost so much momentum. Several other treasured team members were let go due to financial constraints, and the Board was running the church, praying for a miracle. He shared that the Board was praying for a breakthrough.

Jim described to me how the finances were in the red. The treasurer was at the point of needing to decide which bills would or wouldn't be paid each month. The rented storefront suite where the church met was becoming especially difficult to afford. Jim shared that he felt the Board wouldn't mind taking a chance on me, even though I'd never been a lead pastor before—because, in his words, they were thinking about closing the doors anyway.

That week, before the leadership had even formally offered me the call to come to be the new pastor, something surprising happened. I went to the 10-acre property the church owned. The Board was considering parceling it off to sell to fund the ministry. The property was vacant land with two old dilapidated houses, a shed or two, and a mobile trailer falling apart. The place was an eyesore; it was clear that vagrants and vandals were using the property as a place to hide out and do drugs. Trash and drug paraphernalia were strewn all around the houses. Windows were crashed out, ceilings were caving in, and the doors were literally swinging in the wind. The state of the property was dismal, and the state of the congregation who owned it was in despair.

I walked to the middle of the property, knelt down, and put my hands on the ground. My fingers sunk into the loamy soil in an area that had formerly been a horse pen. I began to pray, asking God if it was his will for me to be called as the new pastor for this small church that was wondering if it would even survive. Then and there, God spoke to me and gave me an open vision. In the vision that appeared before me, I saw a fluid, moving picture of this mighty congregation - a large crowd of people worshiping Jesus there. It was a community full of joy, full of hope, and full of the Spirit. The gathering was in a beautiful, prominent new place. I heard the Lord say, "Be strong and do the work! Get ready to be strong and do the work; this is what I spoke to you about when I called you away from Santa Barbara! Be strong and do the work! I have a new identity for this congregation, a new place, a new name, new life, New Impact! Be strong and do the work!"

Breakthrough began at that moment.

The cries of faith from those faithful board members were met with the breakthrough power of God - coming into me with an open-heaven vision. The breakthrough continued when I moved into this entirely new region and community - and God gave me favor. I wasn't skilled or accomplished - but God anointed me and continued his breakthrough work for this church - and I was a conduit of it. I was virtually clueless about what to do; I just knew God put it on my heart to be sure to give a simple gospel invitation every time we met. The breakthrough became miraculous when people began coming, one by one, and putting their faith in Jesus, week after week. Soon, 50 people became 100 people, and the breakthrough continued as those 100 people committed more than $1,000,000 towards our first church building.

The breakthrough continued to blossom as that building was constructed- and then 100 people became 1,000 people, and three more buildings were built. Centerpoint Ministries was birthed

- and the congregation became Centerpoint Church. Two other churches have been planted along the way. Twenty years later, the entire ten-acre campus is built out to maximum capacity, and 2,700 people gather every Sunday in three services. The miracle is marked by a ministry that sees salvation, supernatural healings, prophetic words, deliverance, and inner healing by the hundreds every month. Centerpoint Church is living in the miracle that came from that breakthrough that began so many years ago with fingers in the dirt.

It's the *dunamis* that does it

That breakthrough was a manifestation of the power of God. Acts 1:8 describes a promise - that believers will be clothed with power when the Holy Spirit comes upon us. The word for power is *dunamis*; we get our word 'dynamite' from that root word. The power of God brings explosive energy for miracles and breakthroughs, and it is our privilege to be people who are clothed with it. It's also our responsibility to see where we can flow with it.

One of the words that many Christian preachers, authors, and worship leaders lean on is the word 'breakthrough.' The word evokes a sense of hopeful anticipation about what God will do. In living a *filled to flow* life, embracing all the possibilities of what powerful, supernatural blessings God may bring is essential. However, assuming some responsibility for how those things may happen is also crucial. In fact - God may want to bring the breakthrough through you!

As you read through the scriptures - from the beginning - God chooses a Moses, an Abraham, a Sarah, a Jael, a Joshua, a Zechariah, a Miriam, a Deborah, a Paul, etc., through whom He will bring His breakthrough. In the New Testament, Jesus' first action is to announce God's Kingdom and then invite disciples to make Kingdom blessings happen. Too much of the Christian experience is cast as passive: come to church, listen to a sermon, sing some songs, go home. Repeat. But the plan of God is for something so much more life-giving, so much more adventure-filled and so much more dynamic!

People need many kinds of breakthroughs - but the need for healing and miracles tops the list. In this chapter - you'll discover the keys to bringing healing breakthroughs. I want you to be equipped to understand how to flow in the Spirit's power for miracles. Activate your sense of expectation and wonder about the possibilities of how God may bring breakthrough *through you!* Ask God to give you a *breakthrough anointing* for His Kingdom!

Get in the habit of checking in with Holy Spirit every once in a while to ask this question: "Holy Spirit, what kind of miracle or breakthrough do you want to bring through me?" Jesus was passionate about inviting people to come follow Him. But He never expected those whom He discipled to be passive recipients of His teachings and example. He aimed to authorize them to engage in the fullness of the Spirit with a full-force flow of His Kingdom goodness, with breakthroughs abounding through their yielded lives: "Get out there, preach the gospel, heal the sick, cleanse the lepers, raise the dead!" That was the central theme of His call to action to His disciples - and, by extension, to you! Tag, you're it!

Activation - not all superheros wear capes

This activation is intended as a warm-up for you - not an end in and of itself. Think of a very bad situation, real or imagined. It could be at home or even something global. Now, imagine if you could develop and send in a new superhero; what powers would that superhero have? What would they do first, second, and third - what would the ABCs of their actions be?

Now begin to pray about that problem: 'In the mighty name of Jesus, I declare the power of God coming for XYZ problem and bringing the power for A, B, and C!'

If the situation was made up, you can say, 'Thank you for fiction, Lord; that was fun!' But if it was real, believe God for a breakthrough, just as you declared!

~ The dunamis power of God is not magic. It is His power - and you get to begin to partner with God in His power for His purposes and glory!

~ Thank God for His dunamis power being the basis for the breakthroughs and the miracles you will move towards, including healing!

Miracles flow from a faith-filled mindset

The gift of miracles is one of the manifestations of the Spirit that isn't mentioned very often. It doesn't get much air-time from those who teach God's Word, either. That may be because it's just hard to define. I can tell you this, though. That day, I sunk my hands into that dirt, and God activated the gift of miracles in me. He gave me a breakthrough anointing for His Kingdom. In essence, it was a release of His power into my spirit to be able to carry out a work that seemed impossible. After that moment, I carried this tenacious faith for this church that I couldn't have fabricated. It was supernaturally birthed - yet it's like a fire I've needed to tend over the years through *faith*.

The breakthrough anointing requires a faith-filled mindset, and I want to give you an infusion of that! Any good thing I've accomplished in the Kingdom of God has resulted from a faith-filled mindset. A faith-filled mindset says, "I know that this will be difficult; I know that this doesn't make sense on paper; I know that this seems impossible—*but God!*"

You will need this faith-filled mindset more than anything else beyond the love of God. If you don't believe that God can bring supernatural healing, it is improbable that God will use you to bring it about. If you don't think that reconciliation can come, it is unlikely that God will bring reconciliation about through you. If you do not believe that God is able to intervene in a way that defies the laws of nature to turn around a circumstance, you will probably not be the conduit through whom that breakthrough will come.

However, when you have a faith-filled mindset, it is as though you have a switch you can throw that empowers you to believe that your God is able and to know that He has called you to participate and partner with Him. So, while you may have a lot of lack, the God you're partnering with has *no lack*! Because of that, you can have an abiding, deep sense of knowing that you can do this thing that seems so unlikely - that it can happen.

Flying a small plane - you control the attitude and the altitude

My city has a small civil airport where private pilots fly small airplanes. Hector Schmidt was a friend - and he took me out to the French Valley Airport for a flight. Hector was a commercial pilot, but he wanted to take me flying for fun. Hector knew that I had an appreciation for aviation. He rented a small Cessna 152 - and we loaded in. We wore headphones with an attached microphone to communicate in the small, noisy airplane. We started up the plane, taxied down to the end of the runway, and took off.

Before I knew it, we were soaring over the neighborhood I called home. After flying for about ten minutes, Hector gestured to me with his hands on the yoke and said through the intercom, 'Put your hands on the controls!' I wasn't sure if the intercom system was making it hard to understand - or if I'd heard him say what I thought I heard him say. He took his hands off the controls, looked at me, and said, "Your aircraft!". I said, "What?". He said, "Your aircraft, fly the plane!"

It was kind of crazy. I've never had pilot training for an aircraft like that. I mean, I fly a paraglider - but that's not anything like this - it's basically a large kite! Hector's voice came through the headphones with some static: "Push in on the yoke." I did what he said- and it made the nose of the plane point down. Almost immediately, I could tell that we were flying down. The headphones buzzed with Hector's voice again: "You're heading towards the ground, you know?" "Yeah, I see that! What should I do?" He gestured and said, "Pull up on the yoke!"

I started vigorously pulling up. He slowed the action with his yoke (it was connected to mine). "That's too fast. Are you trying to kill us?" he said with a wry smile. Several times, he asked me to push down on the controls and pull up. In a small plane, every movement feels very pronounced; you can see the nose coming up or pointing down. At one moment, after pulling up on the controls while increasing the throttle, we were heading up into the sky. "John, you're controlling the attitude right now." That's a technical term in aviation - attitude

- and it refers to the direction the nose points. "Attitude determines altitude," Hector repeated through the headphones.

Will you raise your attitude so you can rise?

Your attitude will determine your altitude when it comes to your relationship with God. What you believe about God - and what you believe God may want to do through you- will determine your altitude. It will determine whether you rise with Him to see miraculous things happen - or not. Choose to have the attitude of a person like King David. David says - "God, you light up a lamp for me; my God turns darkness into light!" (Psalm 18:28). Don't ever forget that that's who He is! He's your God who empowers you with power and light to face the impossible! David lived with that mindset. "Saul and his cronies are chasing me down and trying to kill me; whatever! My God turns darkness into light, and with me, with my God, I can scale any wall!" *That's the mindset of miracles!*

> *You light a lamp for me. The Lord, my God, lights*
> *up my darkness. In your strength I can crush an*
> *army; with my God, I can scale any wall.*
>
> PSALM 18:28-29 NLT

This is the attitude of faith - and cultivating it is your responsibility. When Hector looked at me, and took his hands off the yoke, and said, "Your aircraft!" he was indicating to me that the airplane's attitude was up to me. My hands were on that yoke. If I pulled up on that yoke, we'd rise. If I pushed down, the attitude would lower, and so would the altitude meter.

Your attitude about what you think God can or can't do will affect whether you can see miracles, healings, and breakthroughs occur. Figuratively speaking, your hands are on the yoke. In certain instances, you've got to decide: "I'm pulling up right now!" "I'm pulling the attitude up right now - I'm pulling back up to *God, and*

I believe you can. I'm pulling back up to *nothing is impossible for my God.* I'm pulling back up to "*With my God, I can scale any wall.*" Yes - it's a wall in front of you, a wall of resentment or bitterness; it's a wall of sickness or hatred…. There's an army coming against you. It's an army of demonic activity, curses and hexes from the devil, but you're pulling back on the yoke, and your spirit within you is rising to say, like David, "*With my God, I can crush that army!*"

You control that 'attitude.' if you allow your attitude to go sour, you are putting your hands on the yoke and pushing down. It looks like thinking, "It's all going to fall apart. It's all going to go down. It's going to be bad; it's going to be awful." And if you set those thoughts on repeat in your mind, you'll probably be right about that. If you are committed to a train of thought that says, "I don't think God's going to do anything," you'll probably be right. But your hands are on the yoke. You have control of the attitude. You choose the attitude - and the attitude that you choose will determine the altitude. When you choose a faith-filled mindset, you can begin to rise into an experience of the miraculous. Think of the words of Jesus in Matthew 19:26

> *Jesus looked at them intently and said, "Humanly speaking,*
> *it is impossible. But with God, everything is possible."*
>
> MATTHEW 19:26, NLT

Jesus is the model for flowing in a breakthrough anointing

I know this sounds like "Jesus 101" - but sometimes we must repeat the basics. Humanly speaking, it is impossible for this person with cancer to be healed; humanly speaking, it is impossible for this person who's oppressed and afflicted by demons to be set free. Humanly speaking, this problem is intractable and can't go away, but with God, anything is possible. In one instance, Jesus even says 'everything' is possible.

If everything is possible, what determines whether a possibility is realized? Sometimes, it is you choosing to activate and exercise your faith! Do you know when you need to exercise your faith more than ever? When you don't feel it. When you *don't feel it* is an indication that you really need to grab the yoke and pull up! And you can! It's a discipline and a God-honoring choice! Let's talk about what that looks like.

For me, it looks like I am sitting alone in the morning and acknowledging that I don't 'feel it'. Some days, I just have to say, "God, I feel upset, annoyed, and irritated. I don't feel like anything good can happen, but I choose to believe that everything is possible with you! Everything - including this situation being changed, this relationship being restored, this sickness being healed, this diagnosis being reversed, this disease being eradicated!" It's a choice. Don't fail to make that choice - for yourself - and the sake of those God wants to work through you to minister to! A moment like this represents you taking responsibility for your own heart within you - and stirring up a sense of confident trust in God!

Every good thing is going to flow out of that choice. Every Kingdom breakthrough will flow out of that choice where you decide, "I'm grabbing the yoke, and I'm pulling up! I believe that with my God, I can scale any wall!" Take to heart that Jesus is your model! You are a follower of Jesus, so your model for this filled to flow life is Jesus. Consider again the summary of His life and impact in Acts 10:38

> *You know the message God sent to the people of Israel, announcing the good news of peace through Jesus Christ, who is Lord of all.* [37] *You know what has happened throughout the province of Judea, beginning in Galilee after the baptism that John preached—* [38] *how God anointed Jesus of Nazareth with the Holy Spirit and power, and how he went around doing good and healing all who were under the power of the devil because God was with him.*

> ACTS 10:36-38 NIV

That is Jesus! I know you have already read about this in more detail in Chapter 2 but consider it again. He went around doing good! Whatever kind of good that needed to be done! He didn't just kick back and chill; He went around doing good! He was looking for the problems, the pain, the hurt, the injustices, the wrongs, the disappointment, and the hopelessness. He knew that He could bring the breakthrough power that was needed! So, he *healed* those who were under the power of the devil.

Breakthrough comes in the going around

There are a lot of people who are under the power of the devil in this world. We must gather and be together as the church. The scriptures invite us to gather together to learn God's Word and build up the Body. The Bible commands us to come together to sing our praise and give our worship to God. It is right for us to spend time in our services, praying, singing, and worshiping. But we also must 'go around' like Jesus did. We've got to be believers who are part of a body who will 'go around doing good' - looking for the opportunities to reflect the Kingdom power of Jesus Christ into hurting hearts and lives where it is needed!

Jesus brought breakthroughs as he *went around*. He went around - to the villages, to the public wells, to the markets, to the lakeside, to the docks, to the streets. If you want to see breakthrough power flow through your life, you need to go around to where that breakthrough power is required. Go around to the malls, to the schools, to the parks, to the coffee shops, to the alleys… to the place where people are that need that breakthrough!

When you 'go around,' something happens inside of you. You're no longer where you're comfortable, and when you are no longer where you're comfortable, you find yourself confronted with the reality that you really do need God! You begin to get in touch with your faith! And that needs to be strengthened and activated in the spirit of people who are filled to flow! Jesus was seen to have 'went around doing good' - and he sent his disciples out to do the same. Consider the moment he asked his disciples to go out and carry out their Kingdom assignment as recorded in Luke 9:1-2:

> *"One day Jesus called together his twelve disciples and gave them power and authority to cast out all demons and to heal all diseases. ² Then he sent them out to tell everyone about the Kingdom of God and to heal the sick."*

Luke 9:1-2 NLT

The role of power and authority in breakthrough

Jesus had spent time with his disciples, teaching them about the Kingdom of God. He demonstrated God's Kingdom's breakthrough power through supernatural healing and deliverance. His disciples had seen Him do these things - and at this point, Jesus had determined they were ready to be commissioned. He released an impartation at that moment. He gave them the two things that are absolute prerequisites for a legitimate breakthrough of God's Kingdom: *power* and *authority*.

Without the recognition of the power and authority you've been given, you won't be able to do the things that Jesus has called you to do. He has brought you out of darkness - and into God's Kingdom (Colossians 3:13-14). The Kingdom of God is your new residence! As a resident of the Kingdom of God, you are authorized to carry out the directives of the King. As a resident of the Kingdom of God, you are allowed and encouraged to draw upon the King's power to enact the will of the King.

> *For the kingdom of God is not a matter of talk but of power.*

1 Corinthians 4:20 NIV

God's plan for how a breakthrough will come is for *you*. When Jesus went to a wedding in Cana, and they had no wine left for the celebration, he saw an opportunity to bring a breakthrough. Gallon after gallon of water was turned to wine in a miraculous display of the breakthrough power of God. When Moses led the people of God out of Egypt and faced the Red Sea, it was an opportunity for a breakthrough. There was no guarantee - but he made that gutsy move anyway to put his staff into the waves of the sea. A tide of miraculous power came in - and the sea tides gave way to dry ground. Elijah was confronted with hundreds of pagan prophets taunting him at a religious altar. He knew it was a moment when a supernatural display of the power of God was possible - and he called down fire from heaven. The fire came. It was a breakthrough in the form of a miraculous moment of fiery deliverance. God brings breakthroughs through individuals who are willing to see the possibility of what God could do - and are inclined to believe Him for the impossible, for the sake of His Kingdom being established!

Did you know you wear the badge?

Imagine that you were a police officer. There would be certain expectations about the actions you would take because you are part of the police department. As an officer, you would be present in public places - and because you are in uniform, it would be obvious that you have authority and power. The sidearm in your holster is there - ready for use should the need arise. The gun and the ammunition clips on your belt are full of power. The badge you wear is gleaming as the sun's rays come through the window; it has both your name and the emblem of the city you represent. It conveys the reality that you have been authorized on behalf of the city to enforce the laws and protect the peace.

You might be enjoying a nice breakfast at a diner. Suppose that while you're squeezing the ketchup bottle to add some tangy flavor to your hash browns, there's a stirring outside. Through the window, you see a woman being harassed by a man wearing a mask. He's brandishing a knife and screaming at the woman, but because of your training, you are on your feet and rushing out the door without hesitation.

Once you get outside, you move directly toward the man in the mask. You keep an appropriate distance but get close enough to take whatever action is needed while controlling the situation. While moving toward the man with the knife, you're observing the surroundings to see if there are any other threats. You're rapidly assessing whether others in the vicinity are in danger.

Your voice is strong and direct: "Sir, back away from this woman right now!" Your heart is racing; nevertheless, you take one step closer after another. Your hand is close to your sidearm - but you are determined not to pull it out unless it's necessary; you'd prefer to use the cuffs than to use that Glock. "I'm going to need you to drop the knife, sir. Do it now, and put your hands behind your head." Within moments, you have the man in cuffs, hauling him off to processing at the detention center. You carried out your responsibility because you have the power and authority.

Imagine if you'd made a different choice. You're shaking the ketchup bottle; you notice what's happening outside and shrug your shoulders. You mutter, "Too bad there are so many bad people like that out there in the world." You push your hash browns into the dab of ketchup on the plate and take a bite. The tangy, salty flavor is so satisfying. "MMM-mmm, this is good!" You look out the other window into the sunrise and say, "What a nice day!"

If the second scenario occurred, people around you would demand that you get up and help. They recognize that you are the one who is meant to do something about problems like this. If you don't, you're abdicating the responsibility that comes with the power and authority you've been given.

As a filled-to-flow Christian, you know *you* have been given power and authority. You have prayed the Lord's prayer, "May Your Kingdom come and Your will be done!". God is glad to hear your prayers for His Kingdom to come - but He also expects you to be available as an agent through whom His Kingdom *can* come. You are a disciple - and you've been given power and authority for the sake of the Kingdom of God being established!

I'm a proponent of 'going around,' as you just read. God's people are made to be on a mission, living out the great commission! At the same time, God has a vision for His people to be gathered and working together in healthy, called-out, called-together communities called *churches*. The metaphor of the Body is used when describing the church because it helps define how very different parts are joined together for a purpose. Believers who are sent out and go around do so best when they're grounded in relationships of support and accountability in a particular church.

The church community is where manifestations of the Spirit are meant to be taught, activated & cultivated. Even a casual reading of 1 Corinthians 12-14 shows that the Church community is the primary place where the gifts are meant to be expressed. One of the breakthroughs needed most is *healing*. And as the church body grows in engagement with the manifestations of the Spirit, this wonderful expression of the Spirit can bring that breakthrough. Think about how the scriptures express this vision in 1 Corinthians 12:28:

Here are some of the parts God has appointed for the church: first are apostles, second are prophets, third are teachers, then those who do miracles, those who have the gift of healing, those who can help others, those who have the gift of leadership, those who speak in unknown languages.

- 1 Corinthians 12:28 NLT

Activation - dressed for success

You'll get dressed for success in authority and power for this activation! Stand to your feet (just to change things up a little!) Take a couple of minutes to pray and praise God. Then, ask Jesus to give you a picture of yourself in uniform. Take note of what kind of uniform it is.

~~ Say out loud, 'This is a uniform for XYZ' and name what it's for. Think about the natural significance of that uniform for a moment. Think about the importance of what that uniform means. Think of the value and responsibility of the person who wears that uniform. Think about the good that comes from their role, power, and authority.

~~ That uniform represents a realm of work that must be done in this world. Take a moment to receive power and authority from the Lord to pray over that realm. Say aloud, 'I receive power and authority from You, Jesus, to pray over this realm!'.

~~ Now, take some time to pray as an intercessor over that particular realm with prophetic insight into its real value. Take this one step further and ask the Holy Spirit, 'Is there a spiritual equivalent to this uniform? What is it? What does that mean?' and then as you get revelation, pray over that, too!

Blockages to the flow of Kingdom Authority

The flow of Kingdom authority can become blocked. One of the primary blockages is disbelief. If a person does not believe that breakthrough is possible, that disbelief will likely be honored in the spiritual realm, and nothing will happen. An unwillingness to risk will characterize the manifestation of the disbelief. Where there is no willingness to risk, there is rarely a breakthrough. Another barrier to the flow of Kingdom authority for breakthrough is rebellion.

When a person is walking in willful, unconfessed rebellion to God or the standards of his Word - access to the flow of God's power is short-circuited. Further, when a person has rejected the earthly structures for spiritual authority that God has established in His Body, the church, they've cut themselves off from the means through which the fire of God is meant to burn. In His compassion, He is unlikely to allow the fire that brings breakthrough to burn in or through one who has rejected the authority God has intended to be respected.

THE BREAKTHROUGH OF HEALING

All healing comes from God, who is the Healer! We partner with God in His desire and ability to bring healing.

My healing from food allergies

I was 21 years old when it began. I didn't know what was happening to me, but I found myself getting migraine headaches every day. I was in my fourth year of college, and it made for a challenging year of studies. After a few weeks, I was not only experiencing daily severe headaches, but I found myself sleeping 12 to 15 hours a day. In addition, the white parts of my eyeballs had begun to turn bright red. I was extremely miserable, and I felt like I was sick to the point of death.

I went to doctor after doctor, and they prescribed one medication after another. Nothing worked. The sixth doctor I went to was an allergy specialist. When I did the test for the various allergies, the nurse practitioner told me that I was fine and had no allergies.

I requested a second opinion with a different allergy doctor. He reviewed my file and admitted that the science of allergy medicine was relatively young (it was 1996). He suggested that, in light of my symptoms, I may have a food intolerance rather than an allergy, as it was commonly understood. He recommended that I test myself by way of an elimination diet. I was to eliminate almost all everyday foods from my diet and only eat a few things that were least likely to cause intolerance.

With this doctor's orders, I went home and began eating a diet of only plain-boiled or broiled chicken, plain broccoli, and plain white rice. He explained that these things tend to be least likely to provoke an allergic response. Within a few days, all of the symptoms that had plagued me for so many months began to clear up. After 2 weeks, I felt so much better that I went out with friends. We went to a Mexican Cantina and started with chips and salsa. We followed it up with enchiladas and tacos.

Before we even left that restaurant, I could feel the shift in my body. My head began throbbing, and my sinuses became totally congested. I was ready to crash, and it was barely 8:00 p.m. The following day, I could hardly wake up, and when I looked in the mirror, my red eyeballs told me this was not a fluke. Whatever I had eaten at that restaurant had set off the intolerance or allergy process in my body all over again.

In the following weeks, I practiced an elimination diet, introducing one item at a time and carefully gauging its impact on my body. It became clear that I was allergic to garlic, onions, nuts, seeds, wheat, dairy, and corn. Wheat is in *everything*—pasta, bread, crackers, cookies, noodles, pastries, and anything else made with flour. Garlic and onion are the foundational elements of any sauce with any flavor.

My life changed dramatically as I became the person who had to bring his special food everywhere. I became the person who needed to have a 10-minute sidebar conversation with the waitress if I ever tried to go out for dinner somewhere. Plain vegetables, plain meat with nothing but salt and pepper, and rice ... that, along with fruit, was all I could consume for the most part. Well, I should say that God did not leave me comfortless - I could still eat dark chocolate. Glory to Jesus!

For the next 13 years, I lived that way. I was prayed for many times and by many people for healing. I continued to attempt various forms of medical care for the issue, but this was to no avail. I even received prophetic words related to the healing that would come. God fulfilled those prophetic words in his own time in a way that I can only describe as mysterious.

I developed a different health condition that was not connected to the allergies. Because of this condition, I needed to have surgery on my wrist. The doctor was going to remove a tumor from the nerve in my arm. He was gravely concerned about the surgery, and he warned me that there was a 70% chance that the surgery would leave me paralyzed in my left hand.

The doctor's warning had me quite concerned. The Sunday before the surgery, I decided to ask the church to pray for me. I came down to the floor, and people surrounded me and laid hands on me. They prayed that this terrible statistical likelihood would not come about and that the surgery would happen without any complications. They prayed that after the surgery, I would have full use of my hands. I also distinctly remember one guy, Rob Benson, who lifted his voice aloud in prayer and said, "God, if there's anything else wrong with John's body, Lord, would you heal that too!"

Two days later, at 5:00 in the morning, I went in for surgery at the USC Medical Center. I was deeply anxious about the possibility of losing the use of my left hand. I could barely contain my angst, but the procedure needed to begin. I was taken in, the anesthesia was administered, and the doctors performed the surgery. When I woke up from the surgery in the post-operative room, the nurse asked me, "Are you okay?" I might have said a few strange things at that moment, but I also lifted my left arm and gave the "A-okay" symbol, making a circle with my thumb and index finger. I knew at that moment my hand was still working!

A few weeks later, I traveled to Mexico to officiate a marriage ceremony for a young couple in our church who had planned a destination wedding in Mazatlan. I brought some special food I knew I could eat, and carried out the ceremony. Once the wedding was done, I knew I was off the hook and decided to try some of the regular food. If it knocked me out as usual, it would be okay since my duties were done, and I could sleep in the hotel room for two days if I needed to. Over the years, I'd test out my allergy response every few months to see whether my healing had come. In 13 years - it hadn't.

At the dinner after the ceremony, I ate the meal exactly as it was served. I also decided to enjoy the wedding cake. Typically, the things I ate that night would leave me nearly comatose for a day or two with nothing but a throbbing headache and a mountain of regret. But that night, no headache or sinus congestion occurred, and I didn't experience my normal swollen, bloodshot eyeballs. I was shocked. I thought that maybe the response was just being delayed.

The following day, I woke up, and to my surprise and delight, there were still no allergic reactions. I wanted to know whether I was being healed. Since I was in Mexico, I decided to try some legitimate fish tacos. The garlic, onions, and the corn in the tortillas would surely do me in - but they did not! After thirteen years - my healing had finally come. When this dawned on me, my first thought was of that man Rob, lifting his voice to say, "...and God, if there's anything else wrong in John's body, heal that too!"

My wife Ann and I joked with the folks we traveled to Mexico with about the 'Mazatlan magic' that had changed me. But joking aside, we knew only God could have brought this about. Of course, there will always be a part of me that will wonder why God didn't also just heal the tumor. But at the same time, I will not question God's goodness in how he chose to heal me of these allergies. I lifted my voice with the ancient words of Psalm 103:

> *Praise the LORD, O my soul; all my inmost being, praise his holy name. Praise the LORD, O my soul, and forget not all his benefits— who forgives all your sins and heals all your diseases.*

> PSALM 103:1-3 NIV

The promise in Psalm 103:3 is beautiful - and powerful. There was a time in my life, perhaps when I was nineteen years old, that I could respond to the promise in those words with a hearty, loud 'amen!' "Yes! He heals all your diseases!" As a young man with no physical limitations and no sicknesses or diseases - it was relatively easy to embrace that promise. It is another thing altogether to embrace that promise *despite* living with a congenital disease called Neurofibromatosis Type 2 - Schwannomatosis.

My current reality is that I live with this condition, sometimes called NF2 or SWN - and it means that I live with an excruciating degree of pain from nerve tumors. Every twinge of pain I experience is a reminder to me that many people are living with pain such as this - and many people need prayer and breakthroughs. I *have* experienced supernatural healing for one major condition - those allergies. That breakthrough came 13 years after I had first prayed - but it came. The tumors in my body are still there - and that means I am still personally contending for a breakthrough - even while I minister to many other people who *do* receive their breakthrough.

Ironically, the pain and struggle I go through with this condition motivates me to want to move out into the ministry of supernatural healing even more. My struggle creates in me a sense of compassion for others who are battling a health condition of any kind. It stirs an urgency to minister in healing to any degree I can. It rekindles in me a passion for embracing this distinct aspect of Christian discipleship that is a normal part of the Kingdom life modeled by and called for by Jesus. In Matthew 10:8, He gave this basic commission to the disciples: 'Heal the sick.' It wasn't optional - it was integral.

All healing comes through the Cross of Jesus Christ and is an aspect of salvation!

You were saved when you trusted Jesus Christ and asked Him to forgive your sins. The word that we translate as 'saved' is the Greek word σῷζω '*Sozo.*' It has a range of meanings - and it can be understood as save, deliver, protect, heal, make whole or well, deliver from penalties, and preserve one who is in danger. Our conventional Christian theology correctly emphasizes the aspect of 'salvation' as it relates to the forgiveness of sin, atonement, and redemption.

This emphasis is correct because that is what the gospel promises. We live in the gospel reality of Ephesians 2:8, which in the NIV says, "For it is by grace you have been *saved*, through faith and this is not from yourselves, it is the gift of God." The word *saved* does have its range of meanings. But as it pertains to the essentials of the entry point into a gospel-centered life, the context is clearly about justification and redemption from sin's penalty and punishment.

Nevertheless, consider the words of 1 Peter 2:24, which describe how salvation was brought about. It says, "He himself bore our sins" in his body on the cross so that we might die to sins and live for righteousness; "by his wounds you have been healed." These authoritative words establish a correlation between salvation as we conventionally understand it and the prophetic promise of healing described in Isaiah 53:5 and repeated here.

We must distinguish between what the gospel promises and what is possible because of the gospel. The gospel's essence is the sinner's justification, redemption, and promise of eternal life. However, the one who believes the gospel is invited into the experience of the Kingdom of God. In light of the reality of God's Kingdom, the word salvation begins to show its true colors - and one element in its range of meanings is 'to heal' or 'make whole.' Supernatural wholeness and healing are possible for the believer because they have entered the supernatural realm of the Kingdom of God. There is potential for breakthrough healing because they live in the miraculous realm of God's Kingdom.

The gospel of salvation through Jesus Christ does not guarantee a believer's health or wealth. That notion, known as 'the prosperity gospel,' is a tired circus clown looking for an under-the-table payday. It's false. Too many direct verses of scripture in the New Testament virtually guarantee that believers will experience trials, sufferings, and hardships even to begin to entertain that idea. Salvation does not in any way exclude anyone from suffering in this life. The New Testament indicates that believers should expect there to be some suffering.

At the same time, salvation allows the believer to envision a supernatural breakthrough in the midst of suffering. It also brings about the *possibility* that sicknesses, which *will* finally submit to the power of the Cross in eternity, can be miraculously touched and healed by the power of Christ *in the here and now*. Salvation creates the potential for healing and wholeness to materialize in the present realm—on earth as in heaven.

The implication is that the filled-to-flow life is characterized by believing for, praying for, and ministering supernatural healing. This kind of prayer is in the realm of those things about which Jesus told us to pray that the Father's will be done on earth as in heaven. We know from Revelation 21:4 that God will wipe away every tear in Heaven. Isaiah 33:24 speaks of that beautiful heavenly state when he says, "No one living in Zion will say, "I am ill"; and the sins of those who dwell there will be forgiven." Again, forgiveness of sin and healing are regarded with connection to the Savior's work.

The Apostle Paul revealed what happens after earthly death in many of his writings. In 1 Corinthians 15:42, NIV, Paul writes, "So will it be with the resurrection of the dead. The body that is sown is perishable; it is raised imperishable; it is sown in dishonor, it is raised in glory; it is sown in weakness, it is raised in power;". I could quote many more verses; the point is that in Heaven, there is no sickness. And we are told to pray that God's will be done on earth as it is in Heaven.

The Thirty-one healing miracles of Jesus are all different

There are 31 specific individual healing miracles recorded in the gospels. Many verses just say on any given day that Jesus 'healed all their sick.' But there are 31 specific individual healing miracles – and how they all happen is unique. There is no formula. However, the one thing that is true in all these moments is that Jesus doesn't *pray* for their healing. He *commands* it. 'Be clean!', 'Go! Your faith has made you whole!'. 'I rebuke the fever!', 'Be opened now!'

I share this so that you will know that when you pray for healing, you should follow Jesus in His ways. That means rather than just saying 'God heal her,' you may need to shift from 'praying' to speaking a spiritual command with authority as Jesus did. Addressing the condition or problem directly, commanding it to go or be changed, in Jesus' name. We'll call it praying for healing - but now you know that Jesus' approach goes beyond prayer as you commonly think.

You are invited to pray for and believe for healing! In the following pages, I will give you a straightforward pathway you can follow when you are led to engage in healing ministry. John Wimber, the founder of the Vineyard Church movement, initially developed this idea. My representation of that approach is not precisely the same - I've made my own discoveries along the way that I've included. While I'm calling this 'five steps for carrying out healing ministry,' I'd like you to discover that healing ministry does not need to be formulaic or steps-based. But at the same time, these steps loosely follow the examples of Jesus - and this plan will help you as a starting point if healing ministry is new to you. I'll give you the five steps for reference, and then break them down.

Five steps for carrying out healing ministry:

1. Talk to the person

2. Identify the cause

3. Choose how you'll minister

4. Engage in the flow

5. Give some direction

1. Talk to the person

Whether you are in a church service, a ministry event, sitting with a friend asking for prayer, or talking with someone you've just met - but feel led to minister healing to- you start with a conversation. You ask the person to describe where it hurts or the condition. You ask them when it began. You may ask them what they feel about it. You are asking these things to understand why this condition exists. You need to know the cause of the condition; is it natural - biological, supernatural, social, relational, emotional, genealogical, or spiritual, related to sin or affliction? Knowing this will help you understand how to proceed in prayer.

2. Identify the cause

You've listened to the person describe their condition. While you're listening, you are thinking and praying. You can trust the Holy Spirit to highlight possible causes or even to give revelation. For example, you may discern that unforgiven sin towards a family member is a significant contributing cause to the illness. At this point, you say so. You may discern that the person is harboring deep-seated anger, making them sick. Say so tactfully. You may get a sense that unconfessed habitual sin is creating an open door for demonic affliction in their physical body. At this point, you say so - gently and lovingly. In the diagnosis phase, you understand that sometimes 'the problem' isn't actually the problem.

On the other hand, you may see clearly that this is a genetic disorder, injury, or contagious illness - and the problem *is* the problem. In this phase of the ministry, you may need to step aside to pray in the Spirit so that you may receive revelation. Once you get a sense of the cause of the sickness, you're ready to proceed.

3. Choose how you'll minister

You need to know that you have a range of options for ministering to someone who needs healing. You can pray for them and ask God to heal them. Or you can address the sickness, rebuke it, and command it to leave as Jesus did in Luke 4:39. You may choose to do both. You may need to break demonic curses. You could invite them to pray out loud as you provide the words. You could lead them in a moment of repentance. You could speak a prophetic word to them that would create hope. You could lay hands on them, touching the part of their body that hurts (if appropriate). You have these things in mind as you're talking with the person - and you quickly choose an approach to the ministry moment that you feel will be effective.

4. Engage the flow

This ministry moment is not a formula - it's a flow. You come to this moment knowing that you are filled with the Spirit. You know you are filled to flow - so you do! You flow. You pray out loud - and prophetic encouragement may come through even as you pray. You flow as the Spirit leads. You might prophesy over the person and command the sickness to stop and leave. You may choose to anoint them with oil. You may pray quietly or speak passionately in prayer, with volume and a tone of authority. You engage in the flow of the Spirit with expectation and faith. Please pray with your eyes open so you can watch how they respond - that may help you understand how to proceed. Once you've prayed for the person, ask them how it feels. You ask them to check out the condition, if they can, to see if it has been healed. If they say it's 50% better, praise God with the person - and pray some more, then check in again! This flow-led moment is where you and the person you're praying for will witness and experience a miraculous breakthrough.

5. Give some direction

When you find yourself 'running out of steam' when engaging in the flow, it's okay to stop! Wrap up the time with a clear 'amen.' You should give the person some direction at this point. If they've been healed, you might tell them to share the testimony of their healing. You may encourage them to call a particular person to initiate a restorative conversation. As the Spirit gives you insight, you could suggest they begin attending AA, stop eating a certain food, or read the gospels to highlight every verse about healing. If they were not healed, encourage them to continue seeking the Lord and not give up. You may advise a time of fasting or a process of taking communion each day for some time. Advise them to expect improvement over a specific range of time. These are just some examples of the kind of encouragement you could give at the end of this ministry time. This moment of direction helps the person have a handle on what this moment has meant for them.

Eight key options for engaging in the flow

As you consider the 4th step, *engaging in the flow* for healing ministry, you must consider the range of possibilities at your disposal. It is more art than science - but you have a foundation in the scriptures to give you a picture of what the flow could include. John Wimber originally taught the following eight elements of engaging in the flow. I am conveying them here, but not as a direct quote. I'm unsure whether they originally come from a book, a sermon, or a seminar session. But I'm sharing them from my hand-written notes and personal experience. Each of these is like a different color on the palette - and you are the artist, and the ministry of healing is the canvas before you. Take to heart that each of these may help bring healing in the Name of Jesus!

1. Speak to the condition with an authoritative command

Jesus demonstrated that healing ministry is not limited to prayer in the traditional sense. We often consider prayer as 'talking with God' - and it is. Jesus demonstrated that in healing ministry - there is a kind of flow that is needed that is not prayer. The moment that makes this most clear is the time when Peter's mother-in-law was sick - and they asked Jesus to come pray for her. He went in to see Peter's mother-in-law, and Luke 4:39 says: "Standing at her bedside, he rebuked the fever, and it left her. And she got up at once and prepared a meal for them." - Luke 4:39 NLT. In this instance,

Jesus was not praying. He was flowing in the Spirit - in this flow, he spoke in His authority in the fullness of the Spirit. He spoke directly to the condition - and rebuked it.

It could have been that the condition was empowered by something demonic. It could have been that the condition was simply not in alignment with the perfect will of God. It was not 'on earth as in heaven', so Jesus dealt with it accordingly. In this moment, Jesus was showing you and me that there is an authority that is possible in the Kingdom of God to directly address those things that are evidence of chaos and decay. When Jesus rebuked the woman's fever, it left her. The Kingdom authority of Jesus affected substantive change in the very molecules and atoms of this woman's body. A quantum effect is evident in the result of Jesus operating in the flow.

When you engage in the flow of the Spirit for healing ministry, it may be appropriate to do the same. You may need to operate in your Kingdom authority as a daughter or son of God and rebuke the condition. In this flow - you do not need to assume it is demonic - although it might be. You *do* need to assume that you have Kingdom authority to bring a flow of the Spirit to that which is causing pain and disease, with an expectation that it will leave, shift, disintegrate, change, and be done. In this way - you are flowing as a quantum Christian in Kingdom power!

2. Rebuke the spirit of the infirmity

When you minister in healing, you will sometimes discern that a demonic spirit of infirmity is causing a condition or sickness. In such a case, you are there to take a stand against the evil spirit of infirmity. There was a moment recorded in the Book of Luke where a young boy was sick with a condition that resulted in seizures. His father brought him to Jesus - and it says, "As the boy came forward, the demon knocked him to the ground and threw him into a violent convulsion. But Jesus rebuked the evil spirit and healed the boy. Then he gave him back to his father." - Luke 9:42

NLT. In this situation, Jesus did not rebuke a sickness or condition - but dealt directly with a demonic spirit that was causing the illness. This kind of flowing in the Spirit results from discernment and authority coming together.

As you minister in healing, you may discern that an evil spirit is causing or amplifying the disease. This is not always the case - but it can be possible. When you notice this, you may flow in the Spirit to rebuke that demonic presence. Practically speaking, you cast out the demon by simply saying, 'spirit of sickness, spirit of self-harm, spirit of .... - I rebuke you and command you to leave this person right now in the mighty Name of Jesus Christ of Nazareth!' With that, it is done - there is no need to magnify the demonic spirit or give it more attention. You should simply continue ministering in the flow of the Spirit as you are led.

3. Anoint with oil

Throughout the scriptures, oil is used in a prophetic way to reflect the power and presence of the Holy Spirit. In the Old Testament, oil was used by the prophets to anoint Kings and authenticate their authority. The oil was *not* merely symbolic. In effect, the oil was a representative conduit of the kingdom's power conferred on an individual. In the New Testament, a directive is given in James' writing regarding the use of oil for anointing in healing prayer. It says: "Are any of you sick? You should call for the elders of the church to come and pray over you, anointing you with oil in the name of the Lord. Such a prayer offered in faith will heal the sick, and the Lord will make you well. And if you have committed any sins, you will be forgiven." -James 5:14-15 NLT.

What a powerful promise! And what a clear directive. The specific directive is that the sick person call for the elders to come, pray, and anoint with oil. In the context of the New Testament, the elders are those with properly delegated spiritual authority and oversight responsibility. This might be a pastor, deacon, or board member in a modern context. It is wonderful to have those people come and pray. This passage represents an ideal but is not meant to prohibit non-elders from anointing with oil. You might consider asking those in spiritual authority over you if you have their approval to anoint the sick with oil in Jesus' Name. With their approval, you can include anointing with oil as an aspect of flowing in the Spirit for healing ministry.

When you anoint someone with oil, it is best to ask their permission first. Share James 5:14-15 with them, and indicate that you'd like to anoint their head with oil - or their hands. If they are okay with it, then go for it. Place a dab of oil on them and declare as you do: 'I anoint you with oil in the Name of Jesus of Nazareth, and I declare that the power of the Holy Spirit is healing your Body!'. Keep in mind that the oil is *not* just symbolic. Because you are flowing in the Spirit as an agent of God's Kingdom, the oil has prophetically become a conduit of Kingdom authority. Just as the prophet Samuel touched David with oil for anointing and conferred the authority of the Kingdom on him, you convey the authority of God's Kingdom to the person you are anointing with oil. Expect the richness and fullness of God to accompany this faith-filled prophetic act - and watch as God's goodness flows!

4. Laying on of hands

As you flow in the Spirit for healing ministry, you can operate with your verbal interactions in command or prayer. However, there is often a place for physical touch in healing ministry. It isn't always necessary, but sometimes, laying hands on a person is most helpful and effective. This kind of thing is recorded numerous times in the scriptures. For example, the gospel of Mark records that: *"A deaf man with a speech impediment was brought to him, and the people begged Jesus to lay his hands on the man to heal him."* - Mark 7:32 NLT

When you touch another person, a dynamic flow of energy is exchanged. For thousands of years, this has been evident, even in how humans greet one another. Hand clasps, arm grasps, high-fives, knuckle-bumping… in all of these, there is a spark of connection - and it isn't mystical. There is measurable interpersonal neurochemical modulation that takes place, even through a simple physical greeting. How much more could a neurobiological activation be affected through the spiritually intentional act of laying on of hands?

As you flow in the Spirit, you may be led to lay hands on a person as you minister healing. Ask them if you can lay hands on their shoulder, hands, or other body area, as needed and as appropriate. Be wise - laying on of hands should generally be done in public and without any impropriety. Place your hand on the person, and imagine yourself being a 'live wire' conveying the current of Heaven directly to the person. Pray as you lay hands on them - and believe for God to do a mighty healing work.

5. Prophetic declarations and acts

While you minister in the flow, there will often be moments when you are compelled to speak a prophetic word. You should do so! You may sense that a specific phrase needs to be declared by you or the person you minister to. You could even envision a physical action that has significance and that you or the person you are praying for needs to carry out. This may sound strange, but there are examples of this throughout the scriptures.

In one moment recorded in the gospel of Mark, Jesus was ministering healing to a person who was deaf and unable to speak. The wilderness is recorded in Mark 7, where it says: *"After he took him aside, away from the crowd, Jesus put his fingers into the man's ears. Then he spit and touched the man's tongue. He looked up to heaven and, with a deep sigh, said to him, "Ephphatha!" (which means "Be opened!"). At this, the man's ears were opened, his tongue was loosened, and he began to speak plainly."* - Mark 7:33-35. Could you imagine being this man? It would be weird enough that Jesus initiated the original 'wet willy' on you - but it gets stranger. He spits and touches your tongue! That's weird!

Actually, that's prophetic. When Jesus put his fingers in the man's ears, he was engaging in a prophetic act. When something is prophetic, it can convey the power of God. Jesus was, in this sense, conducting the power of God directly to the area physically affected. His declaration was prophetic as well. *'Be opened!'*. It was as much a command to the molecules and atoms with the person's ears and mouth as it was a speaking-forth of the reality that would come. Jesus was modeling Kingdom life - and it is anything but ordinary!

You may be inspired to ask a person to make a physical gesture or to take a particular posture; you may make a declaration - or ask them to make a declaration you provide. These are essential elements of flowing in the Spirit and may be the key to the breakthrough coming. The prophetic act helps to establish a stronger sense of encouragement or helps to increase your faith. Your physical engagement may be effectual in the spiritual realm for reasons we do not know. In any case, follow the subtle leading of the Spirit in giving prophetic declarations and doing prophetic acts!

6. Lead the person to confess sin

When you begin to talk to someone you will minister to for healing, you may conclude that the person could have an area of sin they have not been forthright about. Let them deal with that issue first before you start casting out spirits of affliction or raising your voice and praying with passion. You could simply ask the person, 'Before we begin to pray - do you have any sin you need to confess?' It's an easy question to ask - and it may be the handle for a person's breakthrough in healing.

The book of James presents the connection between confession of sin and healing. It says: *"Therefore confess your sins to each other and pray for each other so that you may be healed."* James 5:16. When the person confesses their sin to you, you might just say, 'There it is. Thank you for sharing the truth with me and confessing that sin. I declare you are forgiven for that sin through the blood of Jesus!'. Minister in the flow of the Spirit to remind them of the forgiveness that flows from Jesus when we confess our sins. You may even check in with them at this point to ask if they still have the pain they were asking for prayer over. Sometimes, God brings an instantaneous supernatural healing, in keeping with His Word, because of the person's obedience!

7. Pray fervently

God created you as a human being with a healthy span of emotional responses that are part of how you express yourself. You sometimes yell or shout in excitement when you see a great play at a sporting event, and you sometimes raise your voice passionately when you feel strongly about a matter. These elements of expressivity are foundational to who you are - and need to find their way into your prayers. The book of James says, "The effectual fervent prayer of a righteous man availeth much." - James 5:16 KJV The New Living Translation puts it even more plainly: "The earnest prayer of a righteous person has great power and produces wonderful results."

I prefer the King James version in its use of the word 'fervent.' The word can be understood as *putting energy into it*. Volume, intensity, pitch, and pace are all elements that reflect *fervency*. When you minister in the flow, put some energy into it while praying for a person. Raise your volume, and change your pitch. Shift the pace. All of these are elements that demonstrate your engagement as you intercede. At the very least, they help the person you are praying for to sense the passion and faith you have as you pray.

8. Pray in the Spirit

The person you are ministering to for healing has probably come with a degree of desperation. They are in pain or discomfort or have received a lousy diagnosis from a doctor. They need whatever measure of healing can come their way - and by whatever means. As you minister to them, you may be at a loss as to how to proceed with the ministry for them. You may have prayed and checked in with them, and they've said there's been no change. What do you do? You pray in the Spirit; by this, I mean - you pray in tongues.

As you've already learned, praying in tongues (Tongues Three) allows the mysteries to be conveyed between you and the Lord. The scriptures say in Ephesians, "And pray in the Spirit on all occasions with all kinds of prayers and requests" - Ephesians 6:18, NIV. Praying in tongues may be the best way to continue your ministry in healing for the person. As you pray in the Spirit, you may get insight into engaging in the flow for a more significant effect.

Activation - a touch from God treasure hunt

This activation is something that you cannot complete at this moment. After all, you're filled to flow - which means going out and flowing in the Spirit for the good of someone who needs his touch! I suggest you open a note file on your phone, call it 'FLOW,' and use it for flow promptings as you may get in this activation. For this activation, get into a prayer time, ask God to speak to you, and show you a person you are meant to find in public today or tomorrow. Write down what God shows you! You might get something vague and straightforward, like 'woman in the red flannel shirt.' Now ask the Lord, 'What does she need healing for?' He may highlight an area of the body or speak a word or phrase to you about the condition needing healing. Write that down as well. Now, pray over that person and ask God to give you faith for the flow. Then, that day, go on a treasure hunt! Go out to the stores, the park, work, or wherever else, and be on the lookout for that person God showed you.

~ When you see someone who is like the one you felt God showed you, approach them and say something like, 'I was praying today, and I had this thought that I'd run into a person in a [red flannel shirt] and that I should say hi to them and offer to pray for them. That's you! Could I pray for you?'

~ You could ask, 'Do you have any pain or trouble with XYZ?' and offer to pray for healing.

What if they don't get healed?

I've shared with you that my journey is marked by a persistent illness called NF2 - SWN. This disease has been the cause of 8 surgeries, proton radiation radiosurgery, and chemotherapy treatment. It is also the cause of a great degree of physical pain every day of my life. The condition is genetic - and chronic. Despite being prayed for personally by healing evangelists of world renown, and despite many times of fasting, the condition is still there. I believe I will be healed - it's just a matter of time.

What I mean by this is that I will receive a glorified body free from pain or disease in Heaven. I have this ultimate hope that I will be healed! It will *certainly* happen in Heaven - and it may happen here in this life. Each surgery I have had has brought some degree of healing. Each time I've gone under the knife, a measure of healing has come as pain-causing tumors have been removed. But as the condition persists, I am experiencing a different kind of breakthrough - the miracle of perseverance. It is a miracle - and I want to attest to it! The powerful grace of God has been at work in me to create the possibility of persevering when I'd have naturally given up years ago. I praise God for the breakthrough miracle of perseverance!

Suppose you minister in the flow to a person, and they don't get healed in that moment. In that case, there can be many reasons, such as personal unbelief, family curses, genealogical curses, unconfessed hidden sin, personal health habits, and misalignment of divine timing. There may be far more to the illness's circumstance than you can see. There may be possible redemptive purposes because of the disease, and God may be at work in this unique way. When a person you minister to does not immediately receive their healing, you should encourage them to continue seeking, trusting, and worshipping the Lord.

As the Spirit leads, you may give them a specific assignment, as in step five. Assure them that you, too, will continue praying for them. Suggests that it is possible that God wants to do another kind of miracle (such as the miracle of perseverance) or that God may want to deal with a deeper issue first or bring about the healing through a progressive experience. Finally, you and I need to understand that each person is only meant to live for a brief moment in this earthly life, and we have an eternity of living with which this life is juxtaposed. You and I will be spending far more time in perfect, illness-free bodies than we will in bodies that experience sickness.

All healing comes from God, but not everyone gets healed here and now

All healing comes from God, whether complete, instantaneous, supernatural, partial, or from medical procedures and treatments. However, God does not necessarily plan to heal every person exactly when you ask for it to happen. Scripture provides examples where sickness is not addressed with supernatural flow in the Spirit but by Holy Spirit-inspired physio-medical recommendations or simply by not treating it at all.

For example, the Apostle Paul writes about a ministry companion who fell ill - *not* to say how he was ministering supernatural healing, but rather, to say: *"I left Trophemus sick in Miletus"* 2 Timothy 4:20, NIV. He also addressed Timothy directly with advice about a health condition. He didn't minister supernatural healing to him - instead - he gave natural remedy advice, saying, *"You ought to drink a little wine for the sake of your stomach because you are sick so often."* 1 Timothy 5:23, NLT. The prophet Isaiah was confronted with King Hezekiah's illness - and rather than engaging solely in a flow of the Spirit (and indeed he could have - he was the great prophet Isaiah!), he gave directions for a medical procedure to be carried out: *"Prepare a poultice of figs."* They did so and applied it to the boil, and he recovered." 2 Kings 20:7, NIV.

In First Corinthians 12, Paul records his battle with the 'thorn in the flesh.' He ministered healing to countless others - but his condition remained. God commended Paul for allowing that 'thorn' to push him to the Throne and find grace - an even greater substance than a supernatural miracle. The message from God was that the 'thorn' was a messenger from satan; that is to say, it was *not* something good. But good could be extracted from it. In Paul's case, the good would be a more significant personal experience with how effective and powerful God's grace would be.

These examples from scripture should free your heart. If you have a medical treatment prescribed to you, it may be the wisest and most God-honoring thing for you to accept it. Give thanks to God for the treatment available. Remember that all healing comes from Him!

Lastly, sometimes people question healing ministry with a cynical view and ask, 'If healing ministry is real, why don't you just empty the hospitals?'. That question evidences a lack of understanding of what healing ministry in the flow of the Spirit is all about. It is about agreeing on who God is, what the Cross accomplishes, and who Jesus is. It is about an elevated focus on personal and corporate trust in Jesus at a moment in time. That is rarely the characteristic of most hospitals. Further, the hospitals may be carrying out exactly the work God intends them to - with modalities of healing that are allowed and empowered by Him.

Group Activation - word of knowledge for healing

This activation is for a group and intended for training, but it may lead to a real and effective ministry flow. Pray as a group with praise and thanksgiving all in one voice. Then, the leader should ask the group members to ask God for a word of knowledge about a condition or health problem someone in the group may have, even though they haven't said anything. The leader should ask the members to write down or remember what they 'got.' A group member or two should then share. They can say, 'I got...,' naming the condition and asking if that pertains to anyone. In some cases, they may also have a person in mind for whom it was for.

~ As a group, minister in the flow of the Spirit for healing, as you've learned in this chapter.

~ If a condition like pain or mobility can be inspected or tested for healing, ask them to do so. If there is total healing, celebrate! If there is partial healing, celebrate, but pray more!

FILLED TO FLOW
BIBLE STUDY SMALL GROUP GUIDE

Chapter Five: Kingdom Authority

*You're filled to flow in Kingdom
authority for breakthrough & healing!*

When you're full in the Spirit, you have authority because of your identity. This session will help you envision how to operate in your authority as a Spirit-filled follower of Jesus.

Bible study group guide how-to summary:

▱ Means it's a Bible study reflection question. It's okay if just 1-2 people answer. It's okay to move through it quickly or even to skip. It also means there may not be time to include the reading of this scripture or the discussion of the question with the whole group. But consider these sections in your own study!

≈ means this is a group interaction reflection question. It would be good to ask several people from the group to respond. It also means that the scripture associated with this question should be read aloud to the group.

Engage:

1. ≈ Icebreaker: share about the most demanding physical problem, sickness, or difficulty you've experienced and how you overcame it.

2. ≈ Discuss any highlights from the chapter. What kind of wall of impossibility would you want to see the Holy Spirit break through, through you - in the world, our community, your work, family, or friends?

≈ Read John 13:3 NLT

Jesus knew that the Father had given him authority over everything and that he had come from God and would return to God.

▱ Read Matthew 11:27 NLT

"My Father has entrusted everything to me. No one truly knows the Son except the Father, and no one truly knows the Father except the Son and those to whom the Son chooses to reveal him."

Engage:

3. ▱ What is the relationship between Jesus' awareness of His authority, his sense of identity, and his actions?

≈ Read Psalm 18:28-29 NLT

You light a lamp for me. The Lord, my God, lights up my darkness. In your strength I can crush an army; with my God, I can scale any wall

▱ Read Colossians 3:13-14 NLT

For he has rescued us from the kingdom of darkness and transferred us into the Kingdom of his dear Son, who purchased our freedom and forgave our sins.

▱ Read 1 Corinthians 4:20 NIV

For the kingdom of God is not a matter of talk but of power.

Engage:

4. ≈ Share about how the authority of Jesus affects and motivates you.

≈ Read Luke 9:1-2 NLT

"One day Jesus called together his twelve disciples and *gave them power and authority* to cast out all demons and to heal all diseases. [2] Then he sent them out to tell everyone about the Kingdom of God and to heal the sick."

Engage:

5. ▱ How do you imagine the disciples might have felt at this moment of commissioning?
6. ≈ Have you ever experienced a decisive moment of commissioning in any arena of life? Share about that and how it affected you. It could be a graduation, a promotion, etc.

▱ Read Matthew 10:1

Jesus called his twelve disciples together and gave them authority to cast out evil spirits and to heal every kind of disease and illness.

Engage:

7. ▱ Jesus mentions two specific realms of supernatural activity; why do these two realms of challenge require authority from Jesus?
8. ▱ What would it look like for you and other believers today to follow Jesus into addressing these realms authoritatively?

≈ Read Matthew 10:5-8

Jesus sent out the twelve apostles with these instructions: "Don't go to the Gentiles or the Samaritans, but only to the people of Israel—God's lost sheep. Go and announce to them that the Kingdom of Heaven is near. Heal the sick, raise the dead, cure those with leprosy, and cast out demons. Give as freely as you have received!

Engage:

9. ≈ Share when you've witnessed someone moving in Kingdom authority to bring a breakthrough.
10. ⊐ What kinds of things hinder the flow of Kingdom authority for a breakthrough?

⊐ Read Matthew 10:7 NLT

Go and announce to them that the Kingdom of Heaven is near. Heal the sick, raise the dead, cure those with leprosy, and cast out demons. Give as freely as you have received!

11. ⊐ Why is it important for people to gain a general understanding and learning of God and about God while also experiencing the dynamic power of God?

≈ Read Matthew 6:9-10 NIV

This then is how you should pray: Our Father in heaven, hallowed be your name, your kingdom come, your will be done, on earth as it is in heaven.

≈ Read 1 Corinthians 12:28 NLT

Here are some of the parts God has appointed for the church: first are apostles, second are prophets, third are teachers, then *those who do miracles*, those who have the gift of healing, those who can help others, those who have the gift of leadership, those who speak in unknown languages.

⊐ Read Acts 2:43 NLT

A deep sense of awe came over them all, and the apostles performed many miraculous signs and wonders.

⊐ Read Acts 9:40-41 NIV

Peter sent them all out of the room; then, he got down on his knees and prayed. Turning toward the dead woman, he said, "Tabitha, get up." She opened her eyes, and seeing Peter, she sat up. He took her by the hand and helped her to her feet. Then he called for the believers, especially the widows, and presented her to them alive.

Engage:

12. ⊐ What are some biblical examples of miracles beyond healing?
13. ⊐ Who does miracles, and how is the gift of miracles activated?

⊐ Read Psalm 103:1-3 NIV

Praise the LORD, O my soul; all my inmost being, praise his holy name. Praise the LORD, O my soul, and forget not all his benefits— who forgives all your sins and heals all your diseases.

≈ Read 1 Peter 2:24 NIV

"He himself bore our sins" in his body on the cross, so that we might die to sins and live for righteousness; "by his wounds, you have been healed."

⟁ Read Ephesians 2:8 NIV

For it is by grace you have been *saved*, through faith and this is not from yourselves; it is the gift of God.

Engage:

14. ⟁ How do being saved and supernatural authority for healing ministry come together? Describe the word 'sozo' and its importance in understanding the healing ministry.
15. ≈ Share about how you have observed or received healing ministry. What excites you about healing ministry?

⟁ Read Luke 4:38-39 NLT

After leaving the synagogue that day, Jesus went to Simon's home, where he found Simon's mother-in-law very sick with a high fever. "Please heal her," everyone begged. Standing at her bedside, he rebuked the fever, and it left her. And she got up at once and prepared a meal for them.

≈ Read Matthew 8:16-17 NLT

That evening many demon-possessed people were brought to Jesus. He cast out the evil spirits with a simple command, and he healed all the sick. This fulfilled the word of the Lord through the prophet Isaiah, who said, "He took our sicknesses and removed our diseases."

≈ Read James 5:14-15 NLT

Are any of you sick? You should call for the elders of the church to come and pray over you, anointing you with oil in the name of the Lord. Such a prayer offered in faith will heal the sick, and the Lord will make you well. And if you have committed any sins, you will be forgiven.

16. ▱ Why are there so many different kinds of prayer or ministry engagement forms for healing? Describe a few of them from these few scriptures.

17. ≈ What would it take for you to engage in healing ministry as a flow of the Spirit? What's holding you back?

Pray≈:

~ for boldness in Kingdom Authority
~ for activation of the gifts of miracle and healing
~ for healing for anyone in the group
~ for other needs among the group

Extra:

Read the following passages and consider all the various ways supernatural healing is and can be a core part of the reality of the Kingdom of God: Matthew 8:1-4, Matthew 8:14-15, Matthew 8:16-17, Matthew 9:1-8, Matthew 12:9-14, Matthew 9:19-22, Matthew 9:27-31, Matthew 11:2-5, Matthew 12:9-13, Matthew 15:29-31, Mathew 20:29-34, Matthew 21:14, Mark 7:31-37, Mark 8:22-26, John 5:1-18, John 9:1-7, Acts 3:1-10, Acts 9:32-35, Acts 9:36-42, Acts 14:8-10, Acts 19:11-12, Acts 20:9-10, Acts 28:3-6

SIX

FIGHT FOR IT

You're filled to flow with power for deliverance!

In this chapter, you'll see that when you're full in the Spirit, you're ready to face off the demonic realm - for your own freedom and on behalf of others. This chapter will help you discover how to flow in the Spirit's power to bring deliverance and freedom from evil demonic affliction and oppression.

Did I see a demon?

At 18 years old, I deferred my college acceptance for a year to spend 16 months traveling around the world. The first part of my trek was several months of hitchhiking around the United States of America. At one point, I got to a national park in the Great Smoky Mountains near the border of Georgia and Tennessee. After getting dropped off near the entrance to the park, I hiked in as far as I could, backpack on my shoulders. It was dark, and I didn't have time to search for the optimum place.

I had a trail map that indicated where there should be some campsites. I headed to that area, and as I waved the beam of my flashlight around, I could see there was indeed a campsite. I saw the rocks set up in a circle like a fire pit and a makeshift table set off to the side. I put my backpack down, got my tent out, and set up camp. I was alone in the woods, and it was chilly - so I decided to start a fire. So I gathered up some kindling and pieces of wood and brought them back to the fire circle. I shined my flashlight into the fire circle, and what I saw made my skin crawl.

Several rocks were set up like a small altar amongst the ashes in the middle of the circle. On the altar were the charred remains of a Bible that had been burned in the fire, with knife stab marks all over the cover and pages that hadn't been completely burned. Something evil had taken place here, sending a chill down my spine.

I was gripped with fear; instinctively, I glanced this way and that. As I peered through the trees, I saw some kind of shimmering figure darting through the trees, and its presence provoked a deep sense of dread and foreboding in me. It was a demonic presence - and I'd never encountered anything like this. I was barely a Christian myself at that time - but I knew this was something evil, invited to that place by whatever wickedness had happened with the desecration of the Bible in that firepit.

I was alone, deep in the woods of the Smoky Mountains. I was deathly afraid. I did all I knew to do: I blurted out, "I rebuke you in the name of Jesus! I rebuke you in the name of Jesus! I cast you out in the name of Jesus!" As I finished yelling those words, I sensed the evil spirit was gone. I can't tell you that my sense of fear was gone! That stuck with me throughout the whole night!

I ended up not making any fire. I went into my tent, opened my Bible, and opened it up. I remembered how my mother would read Psalm 91 often - and I turned there. I read that Psalm again and again. I laid to rest in the tent with the Bible on my chest, eyes still wide open with concern. As I said - I was not that far along in my faith; I just began to say out loud, 'Jesus Christ is my savior and Lord. I resist these evil spirits. Jesus Christ is my savior and Lord!'. I finally fell asleep, muttering those words until I drifted off. That night was my first exposure to the reality of spiritual warfare.

The fight is real

The filled to flow lifestyle offers so much freedom, power, and love. The personal blessings and Kingdom impact that are part of it are incredible! At the same time, there is another reality. There is real spiritual opposition from the demonic realm. You often have to fight for the spiritual breakthrough and the flow of the Spirit—both for your own life and for the lives of people you want to impact in that flow positively.

Spiritual warfare is a topic that sometimes gets overblown - but it is also something that can be downplayed, overlooked - or even dismissed altogether. To live the fullness of the filled to flow life, you've got to be able to live in personal spiritual victory over the demonic assaults of hell that arise against the true believer. You've also got to be ready and able to help others experience freedom from the affliction, oppression, and schemes of the devil.

Good news!

There is no cause for any fear around this topic; the good news is that you fight *from* victory even while you're fighting *for* victory. You must fight for it. However, you have constant access to the Cross of Jesus Christ, where permanent triumph has already been bought and paid for. The battle has been won for all eternity through the blood of Jesus!

The fact that you have eternal victory through the Cross doesn't mean there's no struggle. While on this side of eternity, we must take our stand against the devil's schemes. We must do all we can to personally resist the devil. And we follow Jesus into activating his example of setting people free from demonic darkness. In this chapter, you will be trained in the spiritual art of deliverance and spiritual warfare. You are meant to live and set others free from the devil's strongholds. When you're filled to flow - that's what you do!

Let me introduce you to ...the devil

Popular fiction has created an image of the devil as a mythical creature with a pointy tail and horns on his head, wearing a red suit and a wicked smile, wielding immeasurable immortal power rivaling the strength of Almighty God. This depiction is not accurate in the least. You can find some support for the horns, depending on how you read Revelation 13:11. However, the comic-strip devil is nothing like the cosmic fallen angel the bible describes. You should know that 1 Corinthians 11:14 says that the devil disguises himself as an angel of light. He's sometimes hard to distinguish as the obvious diabolical being we suppose him to be.

The Bible does not explicitly state the devil's origin, but several passages give some indication of who the devil is and where he comes from. He's also called Satan, Lucifer, and sometimes Beelzebub. Jesus calls the devil 'the father of lies'. He's also referred to as 'the god of this world,' which acknowledges that he does operate with real authority. He's referred to in Ephesians 2 as 'the commander of the powers in the unseen world.' The devil is not simply 'dark energy.' He is a being who has real influence.

The devil appears as the serpent who deceived Eve in the Garden of Eden. His first tactic was (and perhaps still is) to provoke humans to question God and whether they should believe or obey what God said. The phrase that lingers from those early pages of the Bible is this demonic thought: '...did God really say...?'. The image of the snake as the emissary of evil begins there; we may never know whether the devil simply appeared as a snake or possessed the snake's body. Snakes themselves are just reptiles and not inherently evil. But the snake that spoke to Even in Eden was most definitely evil. But where did this evil come from?

God established the principle of freedom at the core of *ontological reality in His total goodness and love*. Every sentient being has liberty as part of its core operating system. We get to *choose*. That's freedom - and we have it because *God* is love, and He desires that *we* would love. Love is not love if forced; it must be chosen - and so - freedom is one of the hallmarks of God's creation in humans and angels alike. In our freedom, we can actually love God and love one another. But that does not always happen - because we can also choose *not* to love God or one another.

From a nuanced reading of the allusions of Isaiah 14, Ezekiel 28, 2 Peter 2, Revelation 12, and Jude, among others, we can infer that the devil was an angel, designed originally as part of God's good creation - who fell. There was a time when this being freely served and loved God. But at some point, the devil rebelled against God - and he took a third of the heavenly host of angelic beings with him into rebellion against God.

The devil and his 'angels' (we call them demons) have existed in tormented rebellion against God ever since. The Devil plans to try to thwart or even undo the work and plan of God. According to Jesus in John 10 - the devil seeks to steal, kill, and destroy. He operates out of rebellion, jealousy, and envy of God - and his power is death, hatred, temptation, and deception.

Where your spiritual warfare begins

The warfare terminology conjures up imagery of swords swinging, guns blazing, and bad guys being slain on the other side of the battle lines. But the reality is that you will never personally 'slay' any demon. Just because you're living the filled-to-flow life, you do not have secret access to some supernatural devil-killing bazooka. You engage in spiritual warfare proactively, and there is an offensive strategy to be employed. But your primary field of battle is within you.

In Ephesians 2:2 (NLT), there is an indication of the subtlety of the priority of the devil - which is to deceive you into disobeying God and living in sin. It says, "You used to live in sin, just like the rest of the world, obeying the devil—the commander of the powers in the unseen world.[a] He is the spirit at work in the hearts of those who refuse to obey God." The scriptures here reveal a correlation between living in sin - and spiritual warfare: When you're living in sin, you're ceding the battle before it's even begun. Worse, when you're living in sin, you're obeying the devil. If you began obeying an enemy commander in actual warfare, you'd be a deserter and have lost the war entirely as it pertains to your part!

Your spiritual warfare begins with your choice to repent of your sins and turn to God to obey His word in your life. That is the cornerstone of spiritual warfare. The primary battlefield for your spiritual warfare is within you - because it is from within that you must find fellowship with the Holy Spirit and the strength of Christ to resist temptation, deception, and sin. When you understand that disobedience to God is obedience to the devil - you recognize that spiritual warfare begins with your choice to honor God in your day-to-day obedience to Him.

If you want to engage in spiritual warfare and have real victory, you've got to accept that there is such a thing as sin. You've got to take the standards of the scripture as definitive for what is and is not sin. Accepting and acting on the standards of Scripture may even be very difficult. The words of Scripture may bring conviction of sin, and you may discover that your primary act of spiritual warfare is to surrender the unforgiveness and forgive the one(s) who hurt you. You may see that you need to constrain your sexuality so it lines up with God's standard rather than the world's. You may become aware that you need to stop operating in selfishness with your resources and move into generosity as God's Word commands. All of this and more is primary spiritual warfare.

Your warfare is based on the power of the Cross!

If you're like me, your journey with Jesus will often be three steps forward and two steps back. Perhaps you have your good days when it seems each step is right in line with the leading of the Spirit. Those moments are a gift - a gift empowered by the work and presence of Jesus. Then there are those other days when the old ways of the flesh seem to get the best of you. On those days, your obedience has faltered - and your soul is vulnerable to spiritual opposition. What do you do?

You begin your warfare with personal repentance from sin!

The basis for victory in spiritual warfare is the blood of Christ, shed on the Cross. When you have sinned, you need to confess your sin and ask for your Heavenly Father's cleansing and forgiveness, which comes through the blood of Christ! Jesus thought asking for God's forgiveness was so important that he included it in his daily model prayer; you know the words: "Forgive us our sins as we forgive those who sin against us."

Daily repentance is as vital for your soul as brushing your teeth is for your mouth. You may have moved in disobedience in seemingly small ways - pronounced ways, or even in ways you are unaware of. When you become aware of any sin - confess it and ask for forgiveness through the blood of Jesus! When you confess your sin, you are honoring God for who He is as the only righteous Judge who does get to determine what is or isn't sin.

When you confess sin and ask for forgiveness, you honor the sacrifice Jesus made to overthrow the powers of hell. When you confess your sin, you are re-aligning your life with the holiness of God and the victory of Christ. When you repent and confess your sin, you are making a declaration that you will not continue in your disobedience because Jesus is the Lord of your life. When you repent and ask for forgiveness - you are partnering with Jesus in the exact work He came to do - as is revealed in 1 John 3:8:

But when people continue sinning, it shows that they belong to the devil, who has been sinning since the beginning. But the Son of God came to destroy the works of the devil.

The devil's primary work is to attempt to keep you in disobedience to God. Other aspects of the devil's work include accusing you and taunting you, lying to you about your own identity and about God, perpetuating sickness and disease, and distancing you from God. Further work of the devil involves attempts at killing, stealing from, and destroying God's children, as summarized by Jesus in John 10:9. The devil engages evil forces in the spiritual realm and demons of all kinds in his work.

The devil works through fear to assault people. The devil's most basic work is to taunt you and entice you into a place of carnality; the win of this work of the devil is to see people reacting from and living for *the flesh*. The flesh wants to sin - and the devil relishes in his work of instigating the flesh in people because it will destroy them from within, or at least limit their effectiveness for Kingdom impact. But 1 John 3:8 has the final word: *"...But the Son of God came to destroy the works of the devil"*. That promise indicates that you have access to the capacity to live in increasing victory and the courage to proceed in spiritual warfare with confidence!

The Holy Spirit wants you to know that the things the devil tries to hold against you have been dealt with. Jesus has fully paid for all of the sins that you would ever engage in. There *were* records of the charges against you - but Jesus took them all away through His work on the Cross. As you think about spiritual warfare - let the Spirit-inspired words from Colossians 3:13 fill your mind:

> *You were dead because of your sins and because your sinful nature was not yet cut away. Then God made you alive with Christ, for he forgave all our sins. He canceled the record of the charges against us and took it away by nailing it to the cross. In this way, he disarmed the spiritual rulers and authorities. He shamed them publicly by his victory over them on the cross.*

> COLOSSIANS 3:13-15 NLT

Before I share the tactical methods of spiritual warfare engagement with you, I want to be sure you understand the foundation for why victory is possible - and how you attain it. Revelation chapter twelve describes the ultimate spiritual warfare that takes place in the spiritual realm through the direct conflict between the devil, who is called the Dragon, the Accuser, & the Serpent - and Michael, the archangel. The warfare ends with the Dragon being hurled down. Victory for faithful humanity was announced by a heavenly voice that said:

For the accuser of our brothers and sisters, who accuses them before our God day and night, has been hurled down. They triumphed over him by the blood of the Lamb and by the word of their testimony; they did not love their lives so much as to shrink from death.

REVELATION 12:10-11 NIV

When we engage in spiritual warfare, we do so on the authority of the blood of Jesus - the spotless Lamb of God, and the word of our testimony about Him! When you engage in spiritual warfare, you may get impassioned and raise your voice,xs quote scriptures in an old translation, or even say powerful prayers full of well-considered words. The victory is not in the volume; the might is not in memorizing verses from a specific translation or reciting the right phrases. The victory in spiritual warfare is from the blood of Jesus, the Lamb of God who takes away the sins of the world, and the testimony of your faith in Him!

Uncovering the four core tactics of the Enemy

While victory is available, it is also possible that any person can experience varying degrees of demonic opposition. Understanding some key ways that evil may manifest is essential so you will take your stand against it effectively. There are four terms you should be familiar with: attack, oppression, affliction, and possession. While these words may have some overlap, there are key differences. Here are some descriptions of how you might experience or perceive various aspects of satanic activity.

Attack

Attack is the general term for the devil's scheme of coming against a person intending to wear them down or destroy them.

As believers, we sometimes become aware that Hell has launched an assault against our lives. You might have even told a friend something: "I'm under attack right now!". It may very well be that you *are* under attack. The goal of the devil's attack is to cause you to turn from God to any degree possible. He desires to minimize your faith and the impact of your faith in this world.

A demonic attack can be recognized when it appears that crisis and chaos are erupting in a person's life over and over again. Continual 'bad luck' is sometimes evidence of an attack from hell. Outlandishly complex relationship challenges when there would otherwise be peace may result from a spiritual attack. You might not see any shadowy, shimmering figure darting through the trees - but you have an intuitive spiritual discernment alerting you that the eruption of problems is coming from the realm of evil - not just from happenstance.

Many kinds of demonic entities bring attacks against people from the realm of hell. There are incidents in the Bible where such outbreaks of evil are shown - and there is an association between those moments and the name of the person or the place with a particular demonic affliction or stronghold. Because of the association, we refer to such afflicting spirits by the namesake they're associated with. Some examples include 'The Jezebel spirit,' 'The Leviathan spirit,' 'The Judas spirit,' 'The Zebedean spirit,' 'The Sons of Korah spirit,' etc. The demonic force of affliction may or may not actually have that name - but we use the name as a placeholder to remember specific schemes of the devil that we need to be aware of.

For example, the demonic attack associated with Jezebel is one that brought devastating, crippling fear and exhaustion. It was characterized by a strident, obvious assault coming from a proud, controlling person who had a legitimate role of some importance and authority. The effect on the victim's life (Elijah the prophet) was immobilizing intimidation. The term 'Jezebel spirit' is not so much a name and gender as it is an accurate depiction of a specific set of schemes used by the forces of hell for a particular attack.

The attack associated with Leviathan in the Bible is connected with the twisting serpent of Isaiah 27. The serpent attacked first in the Garden of Eden with false, exaggerated, confusing, and misleading communication. As a result, the 'Leviathan spirit' is often correlated with a demonic attack that confuses communication or the spread of misinformation and slander. Leviathan may or may not be its name, but the set of schemes the scripture associates with that word are identifiable.

There are so many such spiritual attack formations in the scriptures. As you read the Bible, notice how the enemies of God's people are empowered for the attack they launch. Those patterns of assault reflect the devil's schemes, and we are more fully equipped when we make those observations. We do this "in order that Satan might not outwit us. For we are not unaware of his schemes." 2 Corinthians 2:11 states.

I'd like to share a word of caution here. As you observe the devil's schemes in connection with a namesake figure or place in the scriptures, take care when applying that label to people. It is easy to say something like "She has a Jezebel spirit" or "He has an Ahab spirit." Your observation may be on point, but maybe a better way to put it would be to identify that there's a Jezebel scheme of the enemy at work. You might even say it that way: "There is a Jezebel scheme of the enemy at work here." The difference is subtle - but it helps us avoid thinking of a human being as the enemy. It places the allegation on the Enemy and not on a person.

Oppression

Oppression is the satanic scheme used to keep a person trapped in an immobilizing state of negativity and despair so that hope is diminished and faith is reduced.

The word 'oppress' conveys a sense of spiritual heaviness that any person might experience. When someone is under oppression, there is often an indistinct sense of heaviness, leaving a person feeling uncomfortable, anxious, and gloomy. There is often a feeling of hopelessness and anger, of being stuck, bound, or constricted. Technically, the word oppression is related to an unjust use of authority. The evil one does have a degree of authority in this world - and it is not surprising that he would use it unjustly to cause the experience of oppression in a person's life.

Oppression often results in a person becoming irritable, which has a destructive impact on relationships. Oppression can leave a person in a state of lethargy; it tends to paralyze them from taking the practical action they are meant to take. It causes a fogginess of thought, leading to difficulty in concentration. The oppression decreases the momentum and impact the person's life was meant to have. Further, oppression erodes feelings of happiness and peace, leaving a person with an eerie sense of foreboding or impending doom. It rails against the Heavenly reality of the joy of the Lord, which is the true strength of the believer.

Many people do not recognize oppression for what it is. Maybe you haven't even recognized it when you've experienced it. You might have just said, 'I'm just bored and irritable.' Or 'I'm unhappy and unmotivated, that's all.' That's part of why the enemy uses this scheme; it's challenging to detect as something demonic. I'm not telling you that every time you're in a bad mood, 'it's the devil, it's oppression!'. Sometimes, you are just in a bad mood because you overate the day before. On the other hand, when a day becomes days - or even weeks, you may be under demonic oppression.

Oppression can also cause hardship related to personal belongings, finances, or even governmental processes. When a person continually experiences a breakdown of or damage to personal possessions, it may be a form of demonic oppression. When cash flow is constantly in jeopardy due to unforeseen losses, despite earnest efforts in work, career, and budgeting, it may result from demonic oppression. If an entire region becomes mired in injustice and ineffectiveness at a governmental level, it is likely because of spiritual oppression.

Affliction

Affliction is the satanic scheme enacted to create pain, torment, and suffering so that Kingdom impact is impeded.

Oppression tends to be chronic, while affliction tends to be acute. Physical experiences of pain or mental states of anguish often accompany affliction. It is often unexplainable - and it usually seems like something unnatural. Believers who are making a strong impact for God's glory are frequently the subject of demonic affliction.

There can be an experience of providential or preventative affliction that is not demonic in origin. Our sovereign God may work through challenge, trial, or difficulty to redirect a person or prevent them from making a misstep. He may allow a challenge or trial as a natural consequence of sin and foolishness. The word 'affliction' is sometimes used in the traditional sense to describe these seasons, but these moments of affliction *may* not indicate a demonic assault that must be stopped.

When someone is experiencing real satanic affliction, they may suddenly get sick or become beset with a physical condition that brings awful pain. Besetting conditions such as paralysis, seizures, blindness, deafness, migraines, and chronic pain can sometimes be the result of a demonic affliction. The condition may be a legitimate biological expression of malady - but its origins are demonic.

At times, demonic affliction takes the form of an unreasonable degree of criticism and accusation from people - even from people who are believers. Affliction can also be recognized when ministry or Kingdom impact efforts are being thwarted in unseemly ways. Affliction sometimes shows up in such a way that rational thought and decision-making are affected. Sometimes, demonic affliction is so severe that the despair it causes gives way to suicidal ideation.

There are a host of demonic spirits whose efforts are mobilized to instigate your flesh: lust, pride, gluttony, rage, greed, laziness, and selfishness being the primary offenders. These are sometimes called the 'seven deadly sins' - and they can be just that. But behind the sins, there are demonic spirits that afflict a person to cause a person to give in to the flesh and engage in these seven fleshly patterns. But don't be too quick to blame the devil! You are responsible for your behavior; this isn't a license to let someone say, 'The devil made me do it!'. However, it may be important to address personal responsibility while *also* dealing with the spiritual reality of affliction that could be at work!

Possession

Possession is the demonic scheme of taking up residence in the soul of a person to directly influence their thoughts and actions to tear down the Kingdom of God and establish the kingdom of darkness and evil.

When a person has given themselves over to the work of the devil through vows, incantations, black magic, spells, or other occult practices such as partnership and agreement with evil spirits, they open the door for demonic spirits to take hold of their life. When a demon possesses someone, they are no longer entirely in control of their own faculties. Their physical behaviors and speech may become evil. Their general disposition may reflect the evil that has taken hold of them. Interactions with a person who is possessed may result in an affliction for the person who comes into contact with them, especially if they are not a believer and not prepared.

The scriptures are full of examples of people who became possessed by a demonic spirit. The most classic example is the Gerasene Demoniac recorded in Mark 5. In that case, the man was infested with not one - but a thousand demonic spirits. The possession was marked by superhuman strength in which he broke out of the chains intended to hold him back. His behavior was forceful and violent, and people were afraid of him. These factors tend to accompany some incidents of possession - but not all.

Demonic possession is sometimes marked by a shift in personality, with an uncharacteristic disregard for God or morality. In some cases, possession results in supernaturally empowered sexual licentiousness, expression of hatred for God, and defiance of norms of order. A person who is possessed may be empowered by their demonic infector to speak about things of which they had no prior knowledge. A demonized person will likely blaspheme God - and may even be given false spiritual teachings to create false doctrines and entire false religious systems.

Generally speaking, a Christian believer who is actively engaged in their faith cannot be possessed by a demon. However - a believer may 'possess' a demon. Technically, the term 'demonazai', sometimes translated as 'possessed by a demon,' actually means 'to have a demon.' It is possible for a believer to dabble with the darkness without repentance and without renouncing or binding the evil spirit they've partnered with. Some believers do this without knowing it. The result will be that a demonic spirit will torment the person. While different from *possession*, the effects are similar.

A person who is possessed - or a believer who is being demonically tormented - will suffer feelings of confusion and helplessness when they moments when they are cognizant of the darkness that has beset them. They will sense that the devil has a claim on their life - and in many cases, this is because he does. While there is a demonic entity affecting and even directing their thoughts and actions, there is still a human being created in the image of God, designed by God to be free.

The key to spiritual victory is in humility and resistance!

So now you're aware of the four core elements of the enemy's tactics. What do you do about them? The key to spiritual victory over every assault of hell is humility and resistance! The pride of Satan was his downfall - and the opposite stance is to be humble before God. True humility is strength submitted - and it is always right to submit yourself before God. As you do, He will empower you to engage in the resistance necessary for your spiritual victory. Before reading the rest of this chapter, meditate on these two cornerstone passages regarding spiritual warfare.

> *So humble yourselves before God. Resist the*
> *devil, and he will flee from you.*
>
> JAMES 4:7 NLT

> *For we are not fighting against flesh-and-blood enemies, but*
> *against evil rulers and authorities of the unseen world, against*
> *mighty powers in this dark world, and against evil spirits in*
> *the heavenly places. Therefore, put on every piece of God's*
> *armor so you will be able to resist the enemy in the time of*
> *evil. Then, after the battle, you will still be standing firm.*
>
> EPHESIANS 6:12-13 NLT

Seven tactical elements of the resistance:

You can observe in scripture that there are various means for personal victory, and you can count on these completely because they are part of the order that God has established. You should be familiar with these seven vital means for personal victory in spiritual warfare: armor of God, repentance, worship, prayer & fasting, binding & loosing, renouncing, and declaration. As a filled to flow believer, you are part of *the resistance!* The resistance is the remnant of God's people who are flowing in the Spirit for the Kingdom of God to be established. You're part of it - and you need to know that the resistance is also an active engagement in these core actions that advance God's Kingdom victory on a personal level.

Armor of God

The Ephesians 6 armor of God is your ultimate battle gear as a believer. The spiritual armor that has been issued to you includes the *helmet of salvation*, the *breastplate of righteousness*, the *belt of truth*, the *sword of the Spirit*, the *shield of faith*, and the *shoes of peace*. It is your responsibility to know your equipment. You must be competent in operating in this life with this equipment on - because your spiritual victory depends on it.

I have a son in the Navy who is part of a mission-forward tactical unit. After his combat training, he received his gear - his kit. He is passionate about his 'kit'. When he first got it, he described every element of his kit to me and why it was vital. From the ballistic helmet to the ceramic panel inserts to the Glock 19 - he knows each item that has been issued to him. He knows how to use each item, put it on, and operate with that kit on - whether falling through the sky on a halo jump or wet and sandy beach. He wouldn't think of going out onto the field without his kit on. In the same way, you should never head out into a day of battle in this life without *your* kit on - the full armor of God.

The armor of God is both defensive and offensive - as any kit should be. Your **helmet** is *confidence in your Savior, Jesus - and what He has done for you!* Your **breastplate** is both *the righteousness of Jesus applied to you and your own personal righteous living.* Your **belt** is *telling the truth, and living in alignment with and belief in the truth of God's Word.* Your **shield** is *hope in God with expectation for and spiritual perception of God's preferred future.* Your attack weapon is your **sword**; it is *the scriptures and promises of God and the rhema words of God and declarations that come from the prophetic flow of the Spirit.* The kit isn't complete without the shoes - the **shoes** are *your movement in and towards the peace that the Prince of Peace commands.* If you are wondering how to wear this armor, consider using the following declaration. Say it out loud - and visualize each piece of the armor - your kit.

Activation - suit up

For this activation, you'll suit up in the spiritual armor, the full armor of God. Please state these declarations out loud!

~ I am confident in my savior, Jesus, and what He has done for me!
This is my helmet.

~ The righteousness of Jesus covers me. I am righteous in Him! By His grace, I will do what is righteous!
This is my breastplate.

~ I tell the truth; I believe in and live in alignment with God's Word!
This is my belt.

~ I live with deep hope and trust in God, with expectation for and spiritual perception of God's preferred future!
This is my shield.

~ I declare the scriptures, promises, and prophetic words of God with authority in the power of the Holy Spirit!
This is my sword.

~ I *move in* and *towards* the peace that Jesus calls for to speak forth the gospel's good news, to establish the Kingdom of God!
These are my shoes.

This is my armor: helmet of salvation, breastplate of righteousness, Belt of truth, shield of faith, sword of the Spirit, and shoes of the gospel of peace. This is my armor - and it's on! In this armor, I resist the devil and his schemes. In this armor, I take my place in the resistance!

Repentance

When you understand the gospel, you know that Jesus paid a high price for your sin to be forgiven. As a believer, you are likely growing in your sanctification - but you may also have moments where you struggle, miss the mark, and cross the line into sin. When that happens, you can best acknowledge the sin by confessing it to the Lord and a fellow believer. When you confess your sin with a contrite heart, you express to God that you know His way is right and good.

Confession is part of a greater act called repentance. The spiritual meaning of the word repent comes to us from both the Hebrew and the Greek languages - and the scriptures from both the Old and New Testaments. The Old Testament Hebrew for 'repent' derives from a root word meaning 'to turn'; when one 'repents of sin,' they *turn away from it*. The New Testament word is derived from the root words for a 'change of mind.' When someone repents, they have a 'change of mind.'

It has become popular to highlight the New Testament's translated meaning, indicating that repentance is *only* about a change of mind. But a holistic view of the scriptures informs you that to repent truly - you change your mind about whether something is acceptable and what is true - and acknowledge God's standard and truth as the final arbiter. You change your mind about thinking you got to decide for yourself what is or isn't righteous - and acknowledge that what God says goes. You then turn from the lie you had believed, turn from the unrighteous actions you had engaged in, and turn to God's ways and standards! You change your mind - and from that mental shift, you also change your behavior. This is a vital act of resistance! Take a moment now - and engage in this repentance activation in a simple time of prayer:

Activation - turn, and burn

For this activation, you'll need to be in God's presence - and you may even consider kneeling. As you do, pray in this way:

~ Lord my God, I confess that I have sinned against you in thoughts, words, and deeds - in ways I know about and in ways I am unaware of.

~ I repent of my sin. Yes - I do feel sorry about it, but I know that I've got to move beyond feeling sorry about it - and move forward toward Your good and perfect will.

~ So I repent of my sin! I turn from it now, return my thoughts toward you, and give myself to your good, holy, and beautiful standard for my life!

Worship

When you read the book of Revelation, you discover that the center of what we conceive of as *heaven* is the throne of God. Those closest to the throne of God in Heaven cannot help but perpetually fall down in worship to exclaim how utterly holy and worthy God is. Worship is the result of actual recognition of worth and value. When you worship God, your inner being is fixed on His immutable qualities of goodness, holiness, love, power, and righteousness.

There are moments in your life when the challenges and struggles captivate your attention. If you let them, those things can become the focus of your thoughts. The devil may launch the attacks against you that materialize as troubles and challenges. If you focus exclusively on the overwhelming nature of the problems, you are paying a lot of attention to the devil.

When you worship God, you are making a decided shift in where you place your attention and affection. Through your worship, you are declaring the worthiness and holiness of God as even more valuable than the trouble you may be facing from the devil's attack. As you worship, you express affection and devotion to God - and it invites Him to demonstrate His power and love over and against your problems. But more than anything, the expression of affection that worship conveys shifts the atmosphere of your own heart, aligning your spirit within you with love for the Lord rather than with fear or frustration.

Your worship is a vital aspect of your part in the resistance! So, blurt out that old hymn. Sing out that familiar chorus. Turn on that new worship song and hum along. Sing in the spirit with adoration for Jesus. As you worship Jesus, you magnify the Lord your God and minimize the devil's schemes. O, magnify the Lord; your worship is your weapon!

Prayer & Fasting

Technically, these are two different things - but - about spiritual victory over evil, Jesus speaks of them in the same sentence as equally vital. When you pray, you are talking with God, your Heavenly Father, about whatever is on your heart. Your prayer may sometimes go beyond words as you know them; you could sigh, groan, or laugh in God's presence as you communicate with Him, or you might pray in tongues, as discussed in chapter four. In whatever form, the essence of prayer is drawing near to God in relationship and communication.

Scripture promises that He will also draw near to you as you draw near to God. God, who created all that is, seen and unseen, draws near to you as you pray; can you even imagine the protection and strength that might convey into your spirit? It's unimaginably good! And as you pray - you may ask the Lord your God for deliverance from evil, just as Jesus taught. He hears you - and He will intervene!

Fasting *accelerates* and *amplifies* prayer. When you pray, you deprive yourself physically to delight yourself spiritually. True Christian fasting is marked by a deliberate focus on fulfillment in

God during the temporary fasting period. Because you are a spiritual being in a physical body, you sometimes need to engage in pursuits and practices that emphasize your spiritual nature.

When fasting, you deliberately shift your pursuit of satisfaction into the spiritual reality of who you are in your relationship with God. Your prayers are like a fire - burning a bit more with each moment of intentional connection to the Lord. When fasting, you are accelerating and amplifying that connection's duration, frequency, and intensity and its effects. When you pray, your spirit must move through the soulish matters of desire to finally come into a more pure and direct engagement in God's presence. When you fast, you momentarily set aside the most basic soulish desire - hunger. You redirect the sensation of hunger by reframing the reality of your soul's hunger for God!

Activation - now & later

For this activation, you'll pray now and fast later. If you don't have regular fasting practice, try it! Decide on 12 or 24 hours - and determine to fast then. Drink plenty of water - and skip eating. In place of the time spent preparing food and eating - seek the Lord, pray, worship, and experience delight in His presence. This connection with God is something you can do that is proactive - and it is a practical part of spiritual warfare strategy. Fasting is part of the battle plan for the resistance - and so is intercession!

~ Take time right now to intercede and pray, completing the prompts as you feel led,
~ Lord, now, I'm hungry for You! Later, I'll eat.
~ Lord, I pray for my church that...
~ Lord, I pray for my work situation that...
~ Lord, I pray for my friendship with _____, that...
~ Lord, I pray for my child, that...
~ Lord, I pray for my future, that...

Binding & loosing

At the time of Jesus' earthly ministry, the Pharisees were understood to have the authority to both permit and forbid people's behaviors. They were recognized to have divine empowerment to determine what was allowed and what was forbidden in people's lives. There was an understanding among the Jews that the council of the Sanhedrin, with its pharisaical rabbis as emissaries, were representatives for the enforcement of the eternal Law of God. They were thought to have the power to bind - that is, to restrict and forbid - and to loose - that is, to permit and release. Their task was to strictly interpret the Torah, the Law of God - and enforce its practice among God's people. Their authority was understood to be effective in the natural world and carried an other-worldly impact.

In Matthew 16, Jesus speaks to Peter and describes the spiritual reality of the Church. He declares that Peter - and, by extension - all of the Body of Christ - now have the true authority to represent the spiritual authority of God in the spiritual realm. He speaks of the power of the Church (and its members) over the gates of hell - and he describes the means for implementing this authority in the terms 'binding' and 'loosing.' Binding and loosing were no longer the sole domain of the Pharisees. Where there were *implied* undertones of spiritual authority for the Pharisees, Jesus made the spiritual authority of the believer *explicit*: *"Whatever you bind on earth will be bound in heaven, and whatever you loose on earth will be loosed in Heaven."*

Jesus has conferred a measure of delegated authority to you. When you operate in His authority, you can enforce the requirements of the Kingdom of God in the natural realm on earth - and in the spiritual realm. You don't make up the laws, but you do get to see that they are kept. Binding and loosing are two of the ways you do this. Jesus calls believers into His ministry with the mandate to 'preach the gospel, heal the sick, cast out devils, and raise the dead' (Matthew 10:8). You bind evil spirits, curses, hexes, witchcraft, and spells - because the Word Himself, Jesus, who *is* the Law did so and commanded you to.

Activation - binding & loosing

Renouncing

In the early church, from the second century onward, leaders such as Tertullian and Basil insisted that people who were baptized had to *renounce Satan*. When people were baptized, they were asked to declare their renunciation of Satan and all his works formally. Renouncing Satan is still part of the baptism experience in many Christian churches. Whether it happens at the moment of Baptism or in private moments of flowing in spiritual authority, renunciation of Satan is an integral part of spiritual health and freedom!

The word renounce means refusing to obey or follow any further or repudiating and denying rights to one. This is what resisting the devil is meant to include! Sometimes, people can partner with the devil or the demonic, unwittingly - or knowingly. When this happens - it creates a right for the demonic affliction. Once you have repented of sin, the next step is to renounce Satan and all his works! Doing this will cut off rights and establish the baseline expectation of spiritual freedom from demonic affliction.

Activation - resist & renounce

You'll pray, intercede, and then minister in the Spirit for this activation. Note the transition from prayer to ministering in the spirit to renounce evil.

~~ "Lord my God, I minister now in the mighty name and authority of Jesus Christ:"

~~ "I renounce Satan and all his demonic forces that rebel against God.

~~ "I renounce all demonic schemes of deception, temptation, theft, corruption, and destruction."

~~ "I renounce the evil desires of the flesh that would draw me away from God."

Amen!

Declaration

If you take it at face value, the word *declare* means to state something emphatically. If you know a Biblical truth, you *should* state it emphatically! At the same time, you've come to understand that the *filled to flow* life is about walking in your authority as a Christian full of the Holy Spirit. Because of that authority, you are in a unique position - to both stand against the devil's schemes and to establish, in the area under your influence, a more significant impact of the Kingdom of God. This glorifies God and diminishes the effects of evil.

With this in mind, your declarations are not *merely* emphatic statements. They are faith-filled, authoritative expressions of the will and purpose of God, in alignment with the Word of God. They are effectual in the spiritual realm in ways beyond what the eye can see. Your declarations function like a speed limit sign functions. A person may be speeding - but when they see a speed limit sign, it reminds them that there is a law and that while they *can* break the law, there will still be consequences.

Your declarations are similar; they express the law of God's Word. Demonic entities are reminded - by you - that there is a law and that there will be consequences when those laws are broken. Declarations must be based on Biblical truth. There is *direct* biblical truth and inferred *aspirational* (that means 'I hope for it') Biblical truth. Both can be used in declarations. For example, you could quote and state aloud each verse of Psalm 91 as a series of declarations. Or, you could simply state, 'I declare that I live under supernatural protection; therefore, I will not be afraid!'. This declaration is based on God's Word in Psalm 91. In this sense, it is inferred, aspirationally applied Biblical truth.

Activation - well, I - I declare!

For this activation, you'll engage your ministry muscles to begin to preach - except there's no visible congregation. You're going to preach to the spiritual realm and even to your own soul and tell it the truth! Choose any one of the following verses of scripture, and make a personal declaration of it - either as a direct declaration of biblical truth or as an inferred, aspirationally applied declaration of biblical truth.

"Lord my God, I minister now in the mighty name and authority of Jesus Christ:"

~ Psalm 103:20 I declare that _____
~ Mark 11:22-24 I declare that _____
~ Romans 15:13 I declare that_____
~ Galatians 3:1-5 I declare that_____
~ Could you think of another several scriptures you could do such a direct declaration with? Do it! Did you skip this activation because you didn't want to open your Bible? ;) Come on now, just do at least one!

Flowing in deliverance ministry is part of following Jesus

So now you have a comprehensive understanding of the reality of the devil and demonic schemes. As a person learning to flow in the Spirit, there will be times when this information must be put into action for the sake of someone else's freedom. Jesus commanded the disciples to *preach the gospel, heal the sick, cast out demons, and raise the dead* (Luke 9:1, Matthew 10:1-8). This commission is at the core of Christian discipleship, according to Jesus! The implication is that you and I should be ready to do these things. Casting out demons is something that you have the privilege and responsibility of doing, in Jesus' Name.

Hollywood horror movie depictions of what some would call an *exorcism* are pretty far off base. Most of the time, demonic spirits are relatively weak. The power of the finished work of the Cross of Jesus Christ makes casting out demons light work! Do not fear demonic spirits - and do not hesitate to cast them out. If you see that a person is suffering from demonic possession or affliction, come to their aid and kick out the demons! If the person is a Christian, the demons are not *inhabiting* them - but they are hanging around near them - and you will be casting them out of that area and out of the person's life. If the person is not a Christian, you will be casting them out from the person's soul.

What a gift you can offer by casting out demons! This spiritual work is often referred to as *deliverance*. You are partnering with Jesus to *deliver* someone from demonic bondage, possession, or affliction. Jesus quoted the prophet Isaiah to describe his ministry in Luke 4:18, saying, 'I have come to set the captives free.' And in his ministry, he did not open jail cells so prisoners could escape. He *did*, however, set people free from demons time and time again. He demonstrated a value and a standard for deliverance ministry as part of what His Kingdom would bring to people. Now it's your turn to go and do likewise!

Use the following four steps as a pathway for engaging in deliverance ministry. This is not a formula - instead, it is a guide to help you get started. Take to heart everything you've learned in this chapter, and proceed with confidence if God gives you discernment that a person needs deliverance.

Four straightforward steps for deliverance

1. Observe

As you minister God's love and goodness to someone who needs deliverance, observe what kind of spirit seems to be at work. Observe how the Holy Spirit speaks to you about what kind of demonic spirit is at work. Observe how the demonic entity is pestering the person and what kind of harm it is doing to them. Observe what God may show you about His heart for the person. Observe the words and behaviors of the person. Observe what you perceive in the person's atmosphere. Your observations provide the intel you'll need for the spiritual warfare you're about to engage in. Remember - you are more like a special forces operator and less like a frontline infantry soldier. You go in authority with direct intel and take out the demonic entity quickly, deftly, and with as little collateral damage as possible.

2. Identify

First, you need to identify whether the person is a Christian. If they are a Christian, you are dealing with an affliction or oppression. You should also identify whether there is any unconfessed sin the person needs to acknowledge to God. Unconfessed sin provides a legal right for demonic entities to hang around and cause affliction. Lead the believer in a moment of confession and receiving God's forgiveness. If the person is not a Christian, there may also be possession. If you identify the person as not a Christian, you may offer them the opportunity to ask Jesus to forgive and save them - first. If they do so, it may make the deliverance a lot easier! At the same time, if they are not ready to take that step - you can still certainly proceed with the deliverance; after all - Jesus did!

Second, based on the intel you've gathered from your observations, identify the evil spirit - by name or description. It may be a spirit of hatred, perversion, lust, or offense. It may be a spirit with a biblical association, such as Jezebel, Ahab, Ishmael, or Cain. Discern it, define it, identify it. You may give it a temporary name based on your discernment. There may be more than one.

3. Rebuke & Renounce

In this ministry flow moment, begin by simply praying, "Lord my God, I minister now in the mighty name and authority of Jesus Christ." Then, you do as Jesus did and address the unseen but real supernatural entity afflicting the person. Identify the evil spirit by name or description based on the intel you've gathered from your observations. You may simply state something like this: "You evil spirit of _____ (perversion, hatred, lust, etc.) I rebuke you, and the Lord rebuke you for the affliction, oppression, and harm you have caused this person! I rebuke every evil spirit and break every curse, hex, or spell associated with this affliction and oppression."

4. Expel

Imagine Jesus; he is confronted at the synagogue by a man who is overcome by fits of rage. No one knows what to do - but Jesus does. He looks at the man but addresses the demon. First - he rebukes the demon by saying, 'Be quiet!'. Then, he simply says, 'Come out of him!' (Luke 4:35). And then - the evil spirit left the man. That's deliverance! In Mark 9:25, a boy has been afflicted by demonic spirits to the degree that he cannot hear or talk. Jesus identified the evil spirits, saying, 'Listen, you deaf and mute spirits!'. Then - he expelled them with the words, "I command you to come out from him and never come back!". *That's deliverance!* And that's the final step. Expel the demonic entity. Jesus demonstrates calm, confident power to defeat the demons and bring deliverance. You have the privilege and the responsibility to do likewise! In this final stage, simply say, 'In Jesus' Name, I cast you out, you demon of _____!'

Find your problem!

I remember when my son Noah was young, and he was playing recreational league soccer, and I took him to one of his games- and during the game, I heard the coach screaming at my son, who was on the field, 'What's your problem, Noah!???'. As a father, my first thought was, 'Don't talk to my son like that!'. But I kept my cool; I figured I'd mention something later... but I was kind of mad. I kept wondering, 'Why was she talking to my son this way?' and I wanted to give her a piece of my mind! But then, as the game went on, I saw she started saying things like that to the other kids, too. During half-time, she gathered the team and said to all the kids: 'What's your problem?' they said, 'The guys on the other team.' They said. 'That's right!' she said. 'Now find your problem!'. And she sent them back onto the field. "Go find your problem!" She shouted again as they ran to their places. She wanted them to play proactively, not just get trounced by the other team! She wanted them to be aggressive about stopping their action.

In a sense, Jesus would say to us, 'WHAT'S YOUR PROBLEM? FIND YOUR PROBLEM!' Don't live defeated, don't live trounced by evil, don't live victimized by demonic affliction, clobbered by evil spirits. Don't let other people live under the devil's power - do what Jesus did; do what Jesus called you to do! "Go find your problem! Go find your problem!"

The Big Picture

Concerning deliverance ministry, there is much more for you to discover. Deep-level inner healing is a ministry that facilitates and is the foundation for long-term deliverance. Prophetic discernment for supernatural strategy is an art that allows a community of believers to pull down territorial spirits over a whole geographic region. The battlefield of the mind is the place where a believer operates in deliverance the most - pulling down strongholds and taking thoughts captive. These are further elements of spiritual warfare left for you to continue discovering more about. Meanwhile - you've got the basics - and it's time to flow in the Spirit and set some captives free!

FILLED TO FLOW
BIBLE STUDY SMALL GROUP GUIDE

CHAPTER SIX: DELIVER US FROM EVIL

You're filled to flow with power for deliverance!

When you're full in the Spirit, you're ready to face off the demonic realm for your own betterment and on behalf of others. Flowing in the Spirit sometimes requires you to be prepared to face the reality of evil - and to flow in the Spirit's power to bring deliverance and freedom. This message will help you understand how to bring deliverance when needed.

Bible study group guide how-to summary:

▱ Means it's a Bible study reflection question. It's okay if just 1-2 people answer. It's okay to move through it quickly or even to skip. It also means there may not be time to include the reading of this scripture or the discussion of the question with the whole group. But consider these sections in your own study!

≈ means this is a group interaction reflection question. It would be good to ask several people from the group to respond. It also means that the scripture associated with this question should be read aloud to the group.

1. ≈ Icebreaker: Share the name of a fictional villain (from movies, books, or TV shows) that you would "banish" forever—and why.
2. ≈ Discuss any highlights from the chapter. What would be one 'evil' in the world you'd love to see defeated and diminished?

⬭ Read Revelation 12:10-11 NIV.

The great dragon was hurled down—that ancient serpent called the devil, or Satan, who leads the whole world astray. He was hurled to the earth and his angels with him. Then I heard a loud voice in heaven say: "Now have come the salvation and the power and the kingdom of our God, and the authority of his Messiah. For the accuser of our brothers and sisters, who accuses them before our God day and night, has been hurled down. They triumphed over him by the blood of the Lamb and by the word of their testimony; they did not love their lives so much as to shrink from death.

⬭ Read Colossians 3:13-15 NLT

You were dead because of your sins and because your sinful nature was not yet cut away. Then God made you alive with Christ, for he forgave all our sins. He canceled the record of the charges against us and took it away by nailing it to the cross. In this way, he disarmed the spiritual rulers and authorities. He shamed them publicly by his victory over them on the cross.

Engage:

3. ⬭ What is the basis for victory in spiritual warfare? How does the tension between the eternal victory in Christ and the temporal struggle with the forces of evil affect you?

≈ Read Ephesians 6:12-13 NLT

For we are not fighting against flesh-and-blood enemies, but against evil rulers and authorities of the unseen world, against mighty powers in this dark world, and against evil spirits in the heavenly places. Therefore, put on every piece of God's armor so you will be able to resist the enemy in the time of evil. Then, after the battle, you will still be standing firm.

Engage:

4.   ≈ Share how you've personally experienced demonic affliction, oppression, possession, or attack - or have you seen it in someone else?

≈ Read James 4:7 NLT

So humble yourselves before God. Resist the devil, and he will flee from you.

Engage:

5. ≈ How would you rate your personal level of 'resistance' at this time?

≈ Read Matthew 16:18-20 NIV

And I tell you that you are Peter, and on this rock, I will build my church, and the gates of Hades will not overcome it. I will give you the keys of the kingdom of heaven; whatever you bind on earth will be bound in heaven, and whatever you loose on earth will be loosed in heaven." Then, he ordered his disciples not to tell anyone that he was the Messiah.

Engage:

6.   ▱ What would result from engaging in 'binding and loosing,' as Jesus imparted to Peter - and, by extension, to you?

7.   ≈ Have you ever engaged in the binding of an evil spirit - and what was the result?

≈ Read Matthew 10:1 NIV

Jesus called his twelve disciples together and gave them the authority to cast out evil spirits and to heal every kind of disease and illness.

Engage:

8.   ≈ How does Jesus expect His disciples (and us) to respond to the problem of evil and the problem of demons?

≈ Read Mark 1:23-26 NLT

Suddenly, a man in the synagogue who was possessed by an evil[h] spirit cried out, "Why are you interfering with us, Jesus of Nazareth? Have you come to destroy us? I know who you are—the Holy One of God!" But Jesus reprimanded him. "Be quiet! Come out of the man," he ordered. At that, the evil spirit screamed, threw the man into a convulsion, and then came out of him. Amazement gripped the audience, and they began to discuss what had happened. "What sort of new teaching is this?" they asked excitedly. "It has such authority! Even evil spirits obey his orders!"

Engage:

9.   ▱ What are the characteristics of how Jesus dealt with a demon?

10. ▱ How could you take similar steps when you see something demonic?

≈ Read 2 Corinthians 10:3-5 NIV

For though we live in the world, we do not wage war as the world does. The weapons we fight with are not the weapons of the world. On the contrary, they have divine power to demolish strongholds. We demolish arguments and every pretension that sets itself up against the knowledge of God, and we take captive every thought to make it obedient to Christ.

Engage:

11. ≈ Share your experience of breaking free from the enemy's strongholds in your life.

12. ≈ Share a time you have helped someone else tear down a demonic stronghold.

13. ▱ What about in the broader world - are there any demonic strongholds that you see that need *you* to step towards with Kingdom authority?

≈ Read Ephesians 6:13-17 NIV

Therefore, put on the full armor of God so that when the day of evil comes, you may be able to stand your ground and after you have done everything, to stand. Stand firm then, with the belt of truth buckled around your waist, with the breastplate of righteousness in place, and with your feet fitted with the readiness that comes from the gospel of peace. In addition to all this, take up the shield of faith, with which you can extinguish all the flaming arrows of the evil one. Take the helmet of salvation and the sword of the Spirit, which is the word of God.

Engage:

14. ≈ How does this spiritual armor help you?

15. ≈ Choose one armor item and describe how it could help you if you regularly use it.

Pray≈:

~ for confidence and fearlessness in dealing with demonic darkness
~ for courage to be willing to serve Jesus by flowing in deliverance ministry
~ for discernment about where there may be something demonic that needs to be shut down
~ for love and tact to approach the engagement of deliverance ministry
~ for whatever other needs the group may have

Extra:

Read the following scriptures to understand the four categories of devilish activity better:

AFFLICTION - 2 Cor. 4:17; 2 Cor 12:7-10; 1 Thess. 2:18

OPPRESSION -1 Peter 5:8; Matthew 4:24; Matthew 9:32-33

POSSESSION - Acts 16:16-18; Mark 5:1-3; Matthew 17:17-18

ATTACK - Ephesians 6:12; Luke 22:31; Ephesians 6:11

SEVEN

YOU'VE GOT IT; GO FOR IT!

You're filled to flow in the gifts of the Spirit!

The grace of God gets shown off through the gifts of the Spirit, and in this chapter, you'll learn more about each one. You'll be invited to walk with an openness into the move of God and to be part of how the move of God is manifest!

Push past passivity - this is the flow life!

Jesus envisioned a future where His disciples would do even greater things than He did; He said so in John 14:12. His greatest desire was to empower His people to rise and live out the filled to flow Kingdom life! When Jesus conquered the grave and said, 'Go and make disciples…!', He commanded his people never to settle for simply sitting in church services as spectators. He was initiating a worldwide revival that would depend on men and women who would say yes and recognize that they've got it - and it's time to go for it!

When you're living the filled to flow life, you enjoy resting in God's presence. But you also know His Spirit is alive in you in a way that calls for action. You know you are empowered to change the world, one life at a time, one atmosphere at a time, one moment at a time. And - you are aware that living out of the flow of the spirit doesn't always happen by autopilot. In a sense - you have to choose to engage in the filled to flow lifestyle; Holy Spirit will rarely force it on you.

In this chapter, you will be shown how to activate and reactivate the things of the Spirit proactively. The outcomes depend on the Spirit! But your choice to be active and not passive makes all the difference in the world. Embrace this truth, even now: "I've got it, so I'm gonna go for it!". Get up, get off the shore, get out there, and catch the wind!

Catching the wind and sailing the seas

Growing up, one of my best friends was Larry - and his mom and dad were like surrogate parents to me in some ways. Larry's dad was British and had served in the Royal Navy; being on the water was his home territory, no matter where those waters were. One summer, he told Larry and me he had rented a sailing yacht in the Chesapeake Bay for a two-week sailing adventure. The time came for the trip - and I was excited to learn how to sail and happy to be on an adventure with my surrogate family.

We drove from New Jersey down to Maryland and got situated in the forty-foot sailboat that would be our home for the next two weeks. We planned to sail the Chesapeake Bay each day and put in at a different port town each night. But before we could leave port, Mr. Murphy had to make sailors out of us. So, one day, he taught us all he could about the sport. He gave us a crash course about the mainsails and the jib and how to 'come about' when tacking across the bay. He brought us into the bay near the port and ensured we could carry out his basic commands. He instructed us on how to trim the sails, manage the lines, and even operate the captain's wheel.

He gave us lessons in knot-tying, deck swabbing, and galley functions. He also demonstrated how to chart a course. It was the '90s - a decade before GPS was commonly available, so he opened up the paper map and ensured we understood how to read the nautical charts. He showed us how the buoy markers corresponded to locations on the map and how we could navigate to the port we were aiming for, even though it would be a seven-hour sailing journey without any electronics. By the end of that first day, words like port, starboard, bow, and aft were part of a new language I was starting to enjoy.

The second day, as we headed out of the slip and through the harbor toward the bay, he let Larry and I take the boat's helm. At this point, the vessel was under motor power - the sails were not unfurled. It was my turn at the wheel, and I stood there, my face beaming! I was doing it! I was doing it! The boat was moving, and I had my hand on the wheel! Mr. Murphy caught a glimpse of the expression on my face and said, 'You think you're sailing?' He laughed with a gleam in his eye. 'Just you wait, mate!' he roared in his strong English brogue. After about 20 minutes, we entered the bay's open waters. The wind picked up to about 25 knots. I could feel the speed of the sailboat increase as I trimmed the main sail - and as the ocean spray hit my face, I knew I *loved sailing*!

Toward the end of the first week, it was time to embark on our daily sailing adventure. That day, we planned to sail to Galesville, a picturesque small port city across the bay from where we were. Mr. Murphy said it would take us eight hours, so we needed to get out early. There were no cell phones or weather apps, and it was ominously cloudy, but we had our plan, so we set sail for Galesville.

The weather didn't care too much about our plan. Once in open waters, the skies went from ominously cloudy to downright apocalyptic. Mr. Murphy threw yellow rain jackets to Larry and me, and we geared up. He made us tie ropes to ourselves and tie ourselves to the boat! We were the only sailboat out there - and for good reason. The rain was coming down in buckets, the winds were at 30 knots, and six to nine-foot seas sent our small boat on a roller coaster ride. Larry, his dad, and I were the only ones above decks. The rest of the group were below decks. I knew that I was going to die; this boat was going to sink, we were going to drown.

I was scared to death! Mr. Murphy cried out, 'Come about!' - and the mainsail boom whipped across the deck like a baseball bat swung by Shohei Otani! If I hadn't ducked just in time, I'd have been cracked in the head and over the rails! Somehow, Mr. Murphy captained us through that crazy storm and the gale to Galesville. Once we got to that port, I never wanted to get on the boat again; *I hated sailing*!

The first day, when the sun was shining, the winds were steady, and the seas were calm - that was sailing. But four days in, when the wind was howling, the rain was pouring, and the boat was rocking - that was sailing, too! Your experience living the filled to flow life will be like that, too. Some days, the experience is all joy and breakthrough; other days - it's stretching, challenging, and exhausting. But essentially - you are a sailor; you're hoisting your sails and catching the wind - and moving with the current of the Holy Spirit. Some days into the sun, and other days - through the storm. But this is the adventure you are made for - catching the winds of the Spirit of God and yielding to the work of the Spirit.

> *The wind blows wherever it pleases. You hear its sound,*
> *but you cannot tell where it comes from or where it is*
> *going. So it is with everyone born of the Spirit.*

JOHN 3:8 NIV

In filled to flow life, you'll get out of it as much as you put into it. Many Christians have minimal experience with the winds of the Holy Spirit. They are like sailors who spend time on their boats but only in the harbor. Mainly at the dock - sometimes tooling around the harbor under motor power only. There are sails on their boat - but they never get unfurled. The flow of the wind never even hits the sails - let alone move the ship anywhere.

Many Christians never open their sails to catch the winds of the spirit because of ignorance about it - or fear about what the wind could do. There could be storms, and they could be challenging to control. But - catching the flow of the wind of the Spirit is what you're made for! Choose to let out those sails - let the wind of the Spirit fill those sails and flow! You've got it, so go for it!

Make a declaration: "I've got it, so I'm gonna go for it!"

Activation - well, imagine that!

For this activation, take a moment and think about everything you've read in this book. Think of all of the spiritual gifts you have already learned about. Get into a place of prayer, and ask the Lord to help you imagine a moment where you get to flow in the Spirit in any Biblical way. Just let your imagination run wild for a moment, with a flow from the mind of Christ within you.

~ Which gift did you first imagine operating in?

~ Who was around either with you or that you were ministering to?

~ What does this say about the kind of flow life and spiritual gifts you'd like to pursue?

Stir it up...

Jesus made the connection between wind and the way the Holy Spirit works. Wind is essential for sailing - and wind or air movement is also crucial for fire. Without the movement of air - the fire goes out. Just as the sailor must choose to leave the harbor and hoist the sails, the fire stoker must ensure that air can move across embers and fuel wood so that flames can grow.

Think about this: on Pentecost, as recorded in Acts chapter two, the Holy Spirit came with both mighty rushing wind and tongues of fire upon each person. On that day, wind and fire were no longer metaphors - they were reality! Holy Spirit was seen, felt, and observed as wind and fire! And the presence of the Holy Spirit in spiritual gifts is like a fire in the life of a believer. That fire has to be tended to. The fire of the presence and gifts of the Spirit needs to be stoked. Take to heart the words of 2 Timothy 1:6-7.

This is why I remind you to fan into flames the spiritual gift God gave you when I laid my hands on you. For God has not given us a spirit of fear and timidity but of power, love, and self-discipline.

2 TIMOTHY 1:6-7 NLT

Many people celebrate verse seven; we have not been given a spirit of fear. Amen! But the context of that verse is about activating the gifts of the Holy Spirit! The revelation, in context, is that fear and timidity about the gifts of the Holy Spirit are not from God! So the Holy Spirit says, fan those gifts into flame!

Fires can get started, but they can also simply die out or be smothered. Your experience of the filled to flow life requires your active choice to engage with the winds of the Spirit. You have a responsibility - but you also have the power to choose to engage. Remember the verse above - He has given you a spirit of power, specifically, power for activating your engagement in the gifts of the Spirit. If you are passive - your passivity will likely keep you from the fullest experience of God's Spirit.

One way that flames are activated in a fire is through blowing air across the embers. Another way fires are increased is by stirring up the embers. This action causes the movement of air - and fuels the flames. For that reason, some translations use this language for the same verse. Consider 2 Timothy 1:6-7 again:

Therefore, I remind you to stir up the gift of God, which is in you through the laying on of my hands. For God has not given us a spirit of fear, but of power and of love and of a sound mind.

2 TIMOTHY 1:6-7 NKJV

The language here is related to physically moving embers to stoke a fire. But for me, what comes to mind when I read the NKJV is a spoon and a pot of stew. Imagine a chef in a kitchen making a pot of stew. He has all the chopped carrots, tomatoes, onions, and chuck roast in the pot. The pot is sitting on the stove, and it's cooking away. The chef just stands there, watching the pot. What will happen if he never puts his sizeable wooden spoon into that pot to move the ingredients around? The stew is going to burn from the bottom of the pot. The flavor will be tainted with burnt meat, and the stew will not be delicious. It would be a sad misuse of those ingredients. All that the chef had to do was to stir it.

Your life in the Spirit calls for you to grab hold of the spoon! Stir it up! If you stand in your spiritual life's kitchen and observe passively, you will miss out. You'll miss out on the fullness of what is available for you. So stir it up! Take the initiative! God says, "If you want it, you can get it! But you have to go for it!".

Let's actually use that camping gear!

I have ten sizeable black storage bins in my garage with bright yellow lids. Three of them are marked 'camping gear.' I have tents, sleeping pads, outdoor stoves, lanterns, sleeping bags, ropes, and more. It is so cool that I have all that gear! But you know what's sad? Those storage tubs all have a layer of dust on them. The gear is just buried right now. It's nice to know I have that gear - but - I have it to go out and enjoy the beauty and adventure of camping in the great outdoors.

I don't have tents, lanterns, or sleeping bags just to take up space in my garage. I don't have all that gear just to 'know that I have it.' I have those things so that I can use them! Some of my best memories with my kids were when we used that gear in the Cuyamaca wilderness in San Diego County. On those trips, we got dirty; it rained, got cold, and lost a couple of times. But you know what? We did some things we would never usually do - and the experience made us more alive.

It is as though your Heavenly Father is saying, "Come on! Let's do some camping - grab the gear from those bins, and let's go!" When you fan into flame the gifts of the Spirit and stir up the gifts of the Spirit, you will be more alive in God than ever. You will be refreshed and rejuvenated. You will bring blessings and breakthroughs to other people and be revived personally. Someone will be healed. Someone will receive a prophetic word that will fill their heart with hope. Someone else will be delivered from demonic oppression. Another person may finally receive salvation in Christ. Another person will experience a miracle. It will be worth it to stir it up - you've got it, so go for it!

Expect the supernatural - and engage to see it happen!

As a pastor, one of the ways I have begun to *go for it* is to take time after preaching the sermon to simply stand in God's presence in an open moment of prayer before God's people and say, 'Holy Spirit - what else? What else do you want to do?'. Then I wait - and pay attention. One Sunday recently, I did that - and I sensed the Holy Spirit showing me a silhouette of a body - and highlighting the jaw in pulsating red. As you've learned, sometimes, a word of knowledge comes as a visual cue. I opened my mouth and began to speak by faith. I said, 'I'm getting a word of knowledge for healing of TMJ.' I asked anyone who needed healing for TMJ to raise their hand. I asked prayer team members to lay their hands on those people, and we prayed for healing.

The following week, Sally waited to talk to me after service. She said, 'That thing last week about the TMJ, how did you do that?' I described how I received the word of knowledge. She then explained to me the pain with TMJ she'd struggled with for years. She shared that she didn't even raise her hand because she felt uncomfortable, but she privately agreed with my prayers for healing. She said that day, she tested it by eating a handful of nuts. Usually, that would not be possible for her because it would cause too many problems. But that day - there was no clicking, popping, or pain in her jaw. She had been TMJ problem-free for a week - after suffering with it for years! *That's* the kind of thing that can happen when you go for it.

As you read the gospels, you discover that most of the miracles, deliverance, and healing that Jesus did were *not* in the temple or the synagogue but out in the community. This indicates that you don't need to wait for your pastor or church to create the perfect program or service for the flow of the Spirit - although those times are excellent. You are a follower of Jesus - and He's modeled a life-style of going for it for you to follow. He said he expected you and I to do the kind of things he did and then some. Think about His words in John 14.

> *"I tell you the truth, anyone who believes in me will do the same works I have done, and even greater works because I am going to be with the Father. You can ask for anything in my name, and I will do it so that the Son can bring glory to the Father. Yes, ask me for anything in my name, and I will do it!*

JOHN 14:12-14 NLT

Jesus is clear about what he anticipates. He expects the supernatural and that you will engage to see it happen. Today, set that expectation! Take action! Pair your expectations with the vision Jesus had for His disciples. Even now, shout the words "Greater things!". Get around other people who have a desire for greater things. Cultivate relationships of love and support with like-minded, spirit-filled believers. At some point, you will have to take a step of faith. You've got to think of Peter in Matthew 14:29 - he stepped out of the boat and *walked on water.*

Take the risk!

There was no guarantee when he lifted his foot over the edge of that boat. It was a risk - but he took it. Faith is meant to be expressed when a risk is taken, come what may. Even if Peter had sunk immediately, it would still have been a victory of faith - because he had taken the step. What step would you be willing to take?

Activation - flowlife daydreaming!

When you daydream, sometimes you do so from your flesh. But you can also daydream from your spirit, the redeemed, regenerated spirit - where you have the mind of Christ. The goal is for you to live that flowlife in the Kingdom of God! Take a moment now, and daydream about the Kingdom flowlife.

~ Daydream about getting a word of knowledge about a person and walking up to them to share it and pray for them.
~ Daydream about laying hands on a person with a migraine headache and praying for healing
~ Pray and ask the Lord to allow the things you've imagined to become reality

Take note of what kinds of spiritual gifts you operated in as you daydreamed. It may indicate something about your overall Kingdom assignment!

Wait, this doesn't feel right...

Some things will get in the way of the free flow of the Holy Spirit and your ability to move with faith-filled expectations. Things that impede the free flow of the Spirit include unconfessed personal sin, relational dissonance, past disappointment with healing that didn't happen, confusion about spiritual gifts, experience with a bad example of flowing in the Spirit, and lack of love. However, cynicism is one of the greatest hindrances to the movement of the spirit. A cynical view of the move of the Spirit can lead to a calloused heart that chooses to stifle the Holy Spirit, disallow the flow of the Spirit, or respond snidely to the work of the Spirit. But the scripture commands a believer not to do this, in 1 Thessalonians 5:19-22.

> *Do not stifle the Holy Spirit. Do not scoff at prophecies,*
> *but test everything that is said. Hold on to what*
> *is good. Stay away from every kind of evil.*

I THESSALONIANS 5:19-22 NLT

There is room for testing - but first, there has to be room for 'everything that is said.' The injunction to hold on to what is good is a direct acknowledgment that some of it won't be good. And as believers, we need to understand that and make room for that. When there is a flow of the Spirit, a significant degree of it may be good, and some may not. That's okay! The New Testament's answer to that is *not* to shut down the prophetic flow, disallow words of knowledge, and stop faith-filled prayer for healing. The scripture just says to 'hold on to what is good' - and by inferral, let go of what wasn't good.

An environment of prophetic activation has to be marked by freedom and an acceptance that things may get a little messy. People need to know they are free to go for it - even if they don't get it right 100 percent of the time. There must be an atmosphere of trust that the leaders God has raised up in a movement or in a church will do some cleanup if things get too messy. However, the atmosphere must be maintained more like that of a research and development department than a sterile production center.

In a prophetic culture where people are free to be filled to flow, you should expect that people will do their best to press into their closeness with Holy Spirit and fan their gifts into flame so they can bring something prophetic. Their role is to offer up what they sense God is saying, to follow His leading in what they sense Holy Spirit is calling for. Your job is to test everything, discern what is or isn't good for you, and then hold on to the good. This kind of culture takes grace, trust, and love; those elements should be present in any healthy family, but they are especially important for a filled to flow community or a church.

As you begin to make more room for the movement of the Holy Spirit, you'll find that the sheer presence of God has astounding effects on people. On one hand, god is omnipresent; He's always there, everywhere. But at the same time, the scripture shows that there are moments where there is an increased measure of the effect of His presence at certain times. We sometimes use language like 'God really showed up' or 'He just walked into the room.' These casual expressions give voice to the perception that there is an increased measure of the effect of His presence. I'm okay with using more casual expressions if you are!

Various Biblical Manifestations of the Spirit

In the Bible, when God shows up, people get wrecked. Otherworldly things happen. People begin to weep, shout, dance wildly, and sing loudly. Sometimes, people fall down as though dead, places get shaken, people tremble and groan, and religious leaders lose their ability to do their orderly duties. Some people see visions and hear voices, while others in the same moment do not. Some people experience a sense of being uncomfortable, even to the point of being terrified.

Scriptures record moments when people cry out, sing in the Spirit, speak in tongues, see visions, hear voices, encounter angels, lift their hands, and clap. Noble men fall into trances, shout for joy, and sometimes even get supernaturally transported to other places. If you think this sounds crazy, you need to read your Bible. In fact - if you are resistant to these kinds of otherworldly expressions and wonder whether such things are 'legal,' I want you to take an hour and open the scriptures and meditate on the following scriptures - just for starters:

Acts 2:1-15; Revelation 1:17; Acts 9:4-8; John 18:6; Matthew 17:6; Ezekiel 1:28; Ezekiel 3:23; Daniel 8:7-10; 2 Chronicles 5:13-14; 2 Chronicles 7:1-2; Psalm 126:2-3; Daniel 10:7-11; Matthew 28:4; Daniel 8:17-18; Exodus 19:16-18; 2 Chronicles 34:27; Hosea 12:4; Acts 10:10; Acts 22:17; 1 Samuel 19; Acts 8:39-40; Acts 2:19; Exodus 13:21-22

All of these reflect varying degrees of manifestations of the flow of the Spirit or the presence of God. It is fair to experience concern over excessive sensationalism masquerading as a spiritual experience or revival. On the other hand, who gets to draw the line on what is or isn't excessive? It would be wise to make at least room for everything the scriptures make room for. And if specific manifestations of the spirit occur that there is no verse for (gold dust, appearance of oil, etc.), it just may be that God, who declares, 'Behold, I am doing a new thing!' is doing just that.

Nevertheless, a helpful lens exists for considering whether the Spirit of God is genuinely moving. In the 1700s, there was a great awakening in the United States, and Jonathan Edwards was one of the preachers at the forefront. He was one of the most highly regarded revivalists in the world in his day. He saw it all - and lived to tell the tale. He published a piece in 1741 regarding the Distinguishing Marks of a Work of the Spirit of God. It was republished in 1879 in The Works of President Edwards, Vol. 1. While his five categories are not neatly or succinctly stated, they can be summarized in the following way.

Jonathan Edwards - Five Distinguishing Marks of an Authentic Move of the Spirit

1. It brings honor to the person of Jesus Christ and increases peoples' esteem for Him
2. It produces a greater hatred for sin and a greater love for righteousness
3. It catalyzes a greater regard for Scripture
4. It leads people into truth
5. It establishes a greater love for God and man in the hearts of people

These five categories help us consider whether an authentic move of God is taking place - or whether there is a fabricated human frenzy. You should consider that church services, as you are accustomed to them, may or may not be the only format or context for a move of God. The moments of a move of God recorded in the Bible are vastly different than most church services I've seen. Nevertheless, regular Sunday services that are unsensational and relatively unremarkable can be the modalities through which God moves most mercifully. We as believers need to learn to accept the goodness of the Body of Christ and its gatherings, even when the experience is somewhat routine. The simplicity of the sacraments, centered around the preaching of God's Word, and the beauty of being together in God's presence for worship is, in and of itself, holy, beautiful, and necessary.

There may also be times when the Spirit of God is moving so powerful that people are deeply affected by God's presence. Sometimes, spiritual leaders proactively facilitate moments at the altar, inviting people to respond to a call to activate a particular spiritual gift. There are also moments when spiritual leaders create times of prayer and seeking God where there is freedom to cry out, to weep, to dance, to shout, and more. These expressions or responses might make you uncomfortable if you aren't used to it. But your discomfort is not the final barometer of whether the experience is genuine.

Times in the flow of the spirit often get a little messy. People succumb to the Spirit's power and fall down and even tremble. People enter into something like a trance state in which the Spirit of God works at a deep level to bring revelation. People do get baptized in the Holy Spirit and speak in tongues. New songs are sung in the Spirit, and prayer lines are called forward. The process is sometimes unpredictable - and the appearance of it all is unpolished.

There may even be some people who exaggerate their spiritual experience with demonstrative behaviors because the environment lends itself to that. But that does not mean the experience as a whole is unholy - or such an environment shouldn't be created. You may need to take a deep breath and pray: *"Lord, some of this is unconventional, some of this is unfamiliar to me, some of it makes me uncomfortable. But Lord, if you're at work through this glorious mess to display more of Your mercy, I'm going in, and I will stay!"*

The gifts of the Spirit are something that the believer chooses to engage with. I recall a woman in our fellowship saying, 'When the Spirit of God moves, I just have to say whatever He tells me right then and there! And I just open my mouth and start talking - and it's all God. It's all God!'. Thankfully, the Holy Spirit gave *me* the fruit of self-control, so I did *not* say what I thought about her statement. What I was thinking was - first of all - if it were 'all God,' it would have been *significantly* better! But I also felt concerned that this friend did not understand the nature of exercising the gifts of the Spirit. She did not understand that they are like tools that the operator chooses to use and is called on to use responsibly.

The overarching truth from scripture that reflects the right heart of moving in the gifts of the spirit is 1 Corinthians 14:32, which says: *The spirits of prophets are subject to the control of prophets.* This verse is specifically about the gift of prophecy - but it is a transferable concept we'd do well to heed. If we are going to exercise a gift of the Spirit, we do so as people who are in control. We can and should choose when to speak or pray and when not to.

Activation - take a walk on the wild side

Some ways the Spirit moves among a group of people are wild. You read about them above. If you already have an open disposition to some of the wild ways of the Holy Spirit, great! If you know you're a little resistant or hesitant about those things, it's time to open up. You can't force a move of the Holy Spirit in wild ways, but you can personally do some wild things to demonstrate you're openness to the Holy Spirit's wildness! In this activation, choose to do something a little crazy, just as a prophetic act to say, 'Holy Spirit, I'm open to anything!'

~ Pray: Lord, I believe that where the Spirit of the Lord is, there is freedom; so what I do now, I do as a prophetic act to invite more of the free flow of Your wild goodness into my life!

~ Stand up in your room, do a silly dance, and say, 'I'll be a silly fool for You if you need me to be!'

~ Strike a pose in a posture like a superman, a spy, or an athlete. Say, 'Holy Spirit, I'm open to any way you want to use me!'

~ Time for a twirl or two and a jump dance! Get up, do a twirl and a jump dance, and say, 'Holy Spirit, I'm ready for wild times with You!'

Varieties of spiritual gifts

Many of the gifts of the spirit are *all-access* gifts; they are open to anyone. Examples of these include administration, helps, and mercy. Some gifts are *generally* made available through the anointing of the Holy Spirit - such as the revelatory gifts. Certain gifts are conveyed through the laying on of hands - gifts like healing are released from one to another through impartation. Other gifts are assignment-oriented; interpretation of tongues and leadership are examples of these gifts available for a specific assignment. Finally, some gifts are given when one is appointed into one of the five Kingdom leadership offices: apostle, prophet, evangelist, pastor, and teacher.

Many attempts have been made to sort the gifts into precise categories. It is sometimes helpful as a way of thinking about the gifts. But the Bible itself doesn't draw hard lines around specific segments of the manifestations of the Spirit. The scripture declares that where the Spirit of the Lord is, there is freedom (2 Cor. 3:17). Rather than force the fluid and free wildness of the Spirit into a manufactured mold, I want you to embrace the full range of the varieties of the gifts of the Spirit. You should respect that some gifts require and are part of the governance of the Body of Christ and God's Kingdom - and those gifts are best not self-appointed.

The gifts of the Spirit listed in scripture... plus a few more!

This section will list the five key scriptures that mention spiritual gifts. As you consider the list of the gifts of the Spirit and the descriptions given, understand that the Bible itself doesn't provide definitions for the gifts of the Spirit. Based on my observations, I've written my working descriptions of these manifestations of the spirit. For clarity, I have repeated the definitions in each section if the gift is mentioned in more than one verse. You'll find these descriptions helpful - but they're not absolute. There is room for you to discover more of the nuance of each one as you experience or observe these manifestations of the Spirit in your own filled to flow journey.

Romans 12:6-8

Prophesying

Receiving and imparting inspired words for the edification of the Body - for encouragement, exhortation, warning, or consolation.

Serving

Using personal time and energy to cheerfully do what needs to be done so the church Body can function well

Teaching

Providing insight and instruction based on the Word of God and its principles so that people are informed of eternal truth in a compelling and empowering way.

Encouraging

Speaking words of life that show empathy, support, and affirmation creating a sense of empowerment and hope in the hearer.

Giving

Gladly releasing financial and material resources of one's own to further the work of the church and missions and doing so in abundantly generous ways.

Leadership

Giving inspiration, motivation, and direction to a group so that it can successfully move the mission of God forward together in a specific, measurable way

Showing mercy

Demonstrating empathy and care by shouldering someone's burden and taking care of them without condescending judgmental attitudes.

1 Corinthians 12:8-10, 27-28

Message of Wisdom

-supernatural ability to offer (or receive for yourself) pertinent spiritual counsel immediately when such guidance is needed.

Word of Knowledge

Spirit-inspired reception of a special word from God for events and happenings in people's lives or your own life. Words or phrases may appear in the mind, or an image may come to your mind.

Faith

Knowing when a situation is not hopeless or when God is doing a miracle. Ability to trust God to intervene in supernatural ways - even when things are seemingly impossible. Willingness to carry out God's will amid enormous difficulties and hindrances. Capacity to move out in deep belief in God when others are unwilling. Ability to trust God profoundly through challenges - and for a specific beneficial outcome

Healing

Effectively ministering by faith to those suffering from physical, emotional, or spiritual sickness so they are made well supernaturally. All believers should exercise this gift, but some will operate in this gift as a ministry of healing. These people are usually very sensitive to those who suffer.

Miracles

The demonstration of God's power in impossible situations.

Prophesying

Receiving and imparting inspired words for the edification of the Body - for encouragement, exhortation, warning, or consolation

Discernment of Spirits

The ability to know whether something is from God or Satan. An ability in the Spirit to detect the presence of demonic spirits. Ability to become attuned to a person's true motivations. Capacity to analyze people and situations for their spiritual 'pulse.' A profound sense of right and wrong in self and others. Skill in assisting others in identifying the root of their spiritual problems.

Tongues

Speaking forth a message in another language (earthly or angelic) from God to edify the Church or activation of a personal spiritual language for private communication with God.

Interpretation of Tongues

Ability to speak forth in intelligible language the message contained in another believer's message in tongues.

Apostle

Supernatural assignment to a governance leadership office in the Kingdom of God for strategic advancement, development, growth, and multiplication of the plans and purposes of God for His mission, Kingdom, and Church.

Prophet

Supernatural assignment to a governance leadership office in the Kingdom of God for declaring and decreeing the will of God, the hope of God, the living revelation word of God, and the flow of the Spirit for the will of God to be accomplished and the Spirit of God to be unleashed.

Teacher

Supernatural assignment to a governance leadership office in the Kingdom of God for Providing insight and instruction based on the Word of God and its principles so that people are informed of eternal truth in a compelling and empowering way.

Helping others

Spirit-born willingness and desire to come alongside others leading or carrying out ministry to give them the assistance, companionship, and support they need.

Administration

Spirit-born skill in giving strategic support for implementation and resourcing so that those leading or carrying out ministry have logistical and detailed assistance that helps them succeed.

Ephesians 4:7-11

Apostle

Supernatural assignment to a governance leadership office in the Kingdom of God for strategic advancement, development, growth, and multiplication of the plans and purposes of God for His mission, Kingdom, and Church.

Prophet

Supernatural assignment to a governance leadership office in the Kingdom of God for declaring and decreeing the will of God, the hope of God, the living revelation word of God, and the flow of the Spirit for the will of God to be accomplished and the Spirit of God to be unleashed.

Evangelist

Supernatural assignment to a governance leadership office in the Kingdom of God for developing, leading, and carrying out the work of evangelism in the world so that the gospel is carried forward to those who don't yet know Jesus.

Pastor

Supernatural assignment to a governance leadership office in the Kingdom of God for gathering the people of God as the church Body so that they may be cared for, tended to, developed individually and as the Body, protected, loved, and spiritually fed.

Teacher

Supernatural assignment to a governance leadership office in the Kingdom of God for Providing insight and instruction based on the Word of God and its principles so that people are informed of eternal truth in a compelling and empowering way.

1 Peter 4:8-11

Hospitality

Spirit-born willingness and skill in providing a warm welcome with an abundance of love while also including elements such as accommo-dation, decoration

Serving

Using personal time and energy to cheerfully do what needs to be done so the church Body can function well

Speaking

Ability to communicate orally with dynamic expression, passion, truth-ful insight, and in a compelling way to the listener for the sake of the apostolic movement of the Kingdom of God.

Joel 2:28-29

Dreams

Symbolic and story-based insight given by the Spirit of God while one is asleep. The revelation or insight may give birth to prophetic insight about one's life. The dream-birthed insight could also be for the church group or movement of God's people it addresses. Like prophetic words, they must be discerned and tested.

Visions

The Spirit-given perception of a scene or image that conveys a message of prophetic flow, subject to all parameters of the prophetic.

A few others?

While scripture does list specific gifts of the Spirit in the New Testament, the Spirit of God works in countless ways beyond what is listed in these verses. One great example would be the gift of artisan craftsmanship reflected in the artist Bezalel. In Exodus 31, God spoke to Moses about a man named Bezalel and said that He had filled him with the Spirit of God for the work of designing and crafting the holy temple, its decorative elements, and all of its accessories for worship. This moment is the first time scripture specifies the Holy Spirit filling a human being. Another example would be in the story of Samson. From Judges 14-16, time and time again, the Spirit of God came upon Samson for empowerment of super-human strength and supernatural courage. These manifestations of the Spirit could be added to our lists of gifts - or we can simply recognize that the manifestation of the Spirit covers an extensive range of expressions beyond the conventions 'lists of the gifts'!

Now that you know all of the differing manifestations of the Spirit, it's up to you to engage in the flow. You are filled to flow! You've got it - now go for it! Catch the wind! My prayer for you is that you are part of a community of believers where there's grace. Grace is needed because you will need room to try engaging with the gifts of the Spirit.

Sometimes, the full measure of the Spirit will be upon you, and you'll flow in full measure! You'll pray for healing, and it will happen! You'll speak in tongues or interpret tongues, and a powerful word will be shared! You'll declare a prophetic word over a person, and they will tremble with delight knowing they've heard the Father's heart! You'll receive and share a Word of Knowledge that will rock a person to their core so that they'll experience the reality that they are totally seen and known by God!

Other times, you'll attempt to speak in tongues, and no one will translate. You'll speak a prophetic word - but the person listening may say, 'Huh. That doesn't mean anything to me.' You'll extend your hands and pray for healing - and the person will still have the condition and the pain. You'll speak a word of knowledge which doesn't land with anyone. If and when this happens - don't lose heart. That's normal! That's how it tends to go when you're learning to engage in the flow! It's similar to when a child is learning to paint. At first, their brush marks are barely a semblance of anything recognizable. And yet, the more color they put on paper, the clearer their expression becomes. Your growth and discovery in using the spiritual gifts will happen like that.

Many believers in Christ have no tolerance for the gray area in the prophetic flow. Their desire to honor God's Word has led them to a place where each line of scripture must be viewed in black and white. Their intention may be good - but it violates the scripture itself - because it makes no room for the process where we 'test everything and hold to what is good.' Learning how to flow in the Spirit includes a process of trial and error. If you are in a church where there is no freedom to express the gifts of the Spirit - or the sometimes messy experimentation with the gifts, you may need to cultivate a small group of friends with whom you *can* experiment.

If you are a church leader and you're reading this book, I urge you to consider making room for the learning process with the gifts of the Spirit. Create space for learning and experimentation. Cultivate a time and place where people can be free to move forward with trial and error in the flow of the Spirit. Establish a team with leaders who can help people experience this freedom. It is like a spiritual 'research and development' unit - not everything that happens in

R&D is meant for public consumption - but it is a vital part of moving toward the very best in what will be brought forward for the general public in the Church Body and beyond.

The wind of the Spirit is blowing. Hoist your sails! Tighten that jib, trim the lines - and feel the thrill of moving in the power of the flow of the Spirit. You were made for this! You are filled to flow!

Group Activation - tell me what you see

Some of the best experiences in the flow of the Spirit come when we seek to help others. In this activation, you will pair up with at least one person and pray, saying, 'God, give me a word or vision for this person and the meaning of it!'

~~ say, 'What I see for you is XYZ.'
~~ say, 'What I think it means is ABC.'
~~ If there are enough people, switch to a new person several times and repeat the exercise.
~~ We don't always say what we see - but this is an activation; I want to get the gears in motion!

Group Activation - new tools!

In this activation, you will be handing out or helping to hone the edge of the tools of flowing in the Spirit. Another word for this is impartation. This is an activation exercise; I want you to get used to helping to activate other people with Spiritual gifts. Review the list of the 21 different gifts (plus a few more) mentioned in the pages above with reference to the scriptures. Pair up with a person, take turns, and impart spiritual gifts to each other. Even if the person already has a gift, give it anyway so you get the learning opportunity, and so they get whatever additional goodness of impartation may come through YOU!

~~Lay hands on the person and pray in the Spirit briefly.
~~say "Man of God, Woman of God - In the mighty name of Jesus Christ of Nazareth, I release to you right now the gift of the Spirit of XYZ! Use it boldly, starting NOW!'
~~The recipient should say, 'Amen, I receive it!'
~~If it is possible, immediately experiment with using that gift.

It's okay if this is a little messy and even a little weird. Remember, Filled to Flow group activations are like the R&D lab of Spirit-filled life. There's room for trial and error; This is a starting place!

Activation - I bless you!

You've read and heard that sometimes there are wild and incredible manifestations of the Holy Spirit in times of awakening and revival. What if God wants to light such a spark through you? Take turns now releasing the blessing of the fire and power of God to one another. Pair up, take turns, and see what the Holy Spirit may do!

~ Place your hand on the person's head, chest, or shoulder, as appropriate, and pray in the Spirit for a minute, then say, 'In the mighty name of Jesus, I bless you with the fire and power of the Holy Spirit!' Repeat this a few times.

~ If you are receiving, let your response be authentic. If you don't feel much, don't fabricate anything. If you feel a jolt or heat or weakness, say so.

~ If the Spirit of God overwhelms you and you fall down, talk about it afterward to understand why that happened and its value.

FILLED TO FLOW
BIBLE STUDY SMALL GROUP GUIDE

Chapter Seven:
Flow Life: You've Got It, So Go For It!

You're filled to flow in catalyzing the experience of God's Kingdom!

God designed His people to experience His Kingdom through partnership. In this session, you will learn how to proactively activate and reactivate the things of the Spirit. You are part of God's plan to catalyze this experience!

Bible study group guide how-to summary:

▱ Means it's a Bible study reflection question. It's okay if just 1-2 people answer. It's okay to move through it quickly or even to skip. It also means there may not be time to include the reading of this scripture or the discussion of the question with the whole group. But consider these sections in your own study!

≈ means this is a group interaction reflection question. It would be good to ask several people from the group to respond. It also means that the scripture associated with this question should be read aloud to the group.

1. ≈ Icebreaker: Hand out pieces of paper and tell everyone to fold a paper airplane - whatever design they want to. Ask people to share where they learned about the paper airplane design they made and why they like it or believe it is a good design. Then have a paper plane airshow - see whose plane stays aloft the longest or goes the farthest!

2. ≈ Discuss any highlights from this chapter. Share an example of when you've seen the Holy Spirit moving mightily through a person or in a moment.

≈ Read 2 Timothy 1:6-7 NKJV & NLT

Therefore, I remind you to stir up the gift of God, which is in you through the laying on of my hands. For God has not given us a spirit of fear, but of power and of love and of a sound mind. (NKJV)

This is why I remind you to fan into flames the spiritual gift God gave you when I laid my hands on you. For God has not given us a spirit of fear and timidity but of *power, love, and self-discipline. (NLT)*

Engage:

3. ⬜ What happens if you don't 'stir up' the gift of God which is in you?

4. ≈ From the list of Biblical gifts of the Spirit described in the pages above, which gift do you have in a primary way or want to have more of?

5. ≈ What are some of the blessings and benefits of the manifestations of the Spirit? What kinds of things can happen when you *do* fan into flame the gift of God that is in you?

6. ≈ What is the importance of fanning the gifts into flame, and how do you do it?

How, practically speaking, do you fan or stir up that flow?

≈ Read John 14:12-14 NLT

"I tell you the truth, anyone who believes in me will do the same works I have done, and even greater works because I am going to be with the Father. You can ask for anything in my name, and I will do it so that the Son can bring glory to the Father. Yes, ask me for anything in my name, and I will do it!

Engage:

7. ☐ What are some examples of 'greater things' you've seen done or greater things you sense God may want to have done?

8. ≈ How can you activate your expectation for what God may want to do through you?

≈ Read Matthew 14:29-31 NIV

Then Peter got down out of the boat, walked on the water, and came toward Jesus.

But when he saw the wind, he was afraid and, beginning to sink, cried out, "Lord, save me!" Immediately, Jesus reached out his hand and caught him. "You of little faith," he said, "why did you doubt?"

Engage:

9. ≈ What gets in the way of healthy spiritual expectancy for the supernatural, and what helps foster healthy expectancy for the supernatural?

10. ☐ How do you discern the right time to take a faith-filled risk?

11. ≈ Share about a time when you personally followed the flow of the Spirit into a faith-filled Kingdom risk with a gift of the Spirit.

⊐ Read Ephesians 5:15-16 NIV.

Be very careful, then, how you live—not as unwise but as wise, making the most of every opportunity because the days are evil.

≈ Read 1 Thessalonians 5:19-22 NLT

Do not stifle the Holy Spirit. Do not scoff at prophecies, but test everything that is said. Hold on to what is good. Stay away from every kind of evil.

Engage:

12. ⊐ Out of all of the gifts, which ones require greater accountability, and why?
13. ⊐ What are some examples of being unwise in interactions with people or circumstances regarding making the gospel or the flow of the Spirit known?
14. ≈ How have you seen the Holy Spirit stifled, and how have you ever contributed to that?
15. ≈ How have you experienced or carried out the process of discerning a prophetic word, testing it, and holding to what is good?

⊐ Read 1 Corinthians 1:27-28 NIV

But God chose the foolish things of the world to shame the wise; God chose the weak things of the world to shame the strong. God chose the lowly things of this world and the despised things—and the things that are not—to nullify the things that are

Engage:

16. ⊐ How have you seen the foolish things 'shame the wise' in terms of the experience of or flow of the Holy Spirit?

⧄ **Read 1 Corinthians 14:32 NIV**

The spirits of prophets are subject to the control of prophets.

17. ⧄ What are some manifestations of the spirit that make you uncomfortable? What should you do with that discomfort or tension?

18. ≈ How Share about how you have personally exercised restraint over the manifestation of the Spirit through you, according to 1 Cor. 14:32, and why?

Pray≈:

~ for openness and boldness to the flow of the Spirit for all group members
~ for awakening and impartation of any of the gifts of the Spirit discovered in this session
~ for a stirring up of and fanning into flame of gifts of the spirit for group members
~ for whatever other needs the group may have

End note:

http://www.onthewing.org/user/Edwards%20-%20 Distinguishing%20Marks%20of%20the%20Spirit.pdf

EIGHT

WHO ARE YOU WITH THAT FLOW?

You're filled to flow with the fruit of the Spirit!

If you're filled with the Spirit, the flesh gets defeated, and the fruit of the Spirit grows! This chapter will deepen your conviction about the importance of character and integrity. You'll learn to cultivate a holy life where the fruit of the Spirit grows and becomes more evident in and through the choices you make!

Who you are is how you'll flow - so grow

It's incredible to think about how much God wants to do through his kids- and how much He trusts us! When you're living the filled to flow life, you're living as a conduit of the blessings of God to a world in need. It is a beautiful adventure, a satisfying journey, an epic trip! And all the while - the Spirit of God is filling you, flowing through you. And who you are matters; who you are becoming matters.

In this chapter - you will take a look in the mirror. You will see an invitation to affirm certain things about who you are already. You will also see an opportunity to step up into the best that God has for you in your journey of becoming who He envisions you to be. Embrace this chapter as a calling to keep growing in Kingdom character.

You're filled to flow - so who are you?

We had our Christmas Eve services at Centerpoint Church a few years ago - and Christmas is a big deal. Many people in our congregation bring their friends, and we invite the community at large. There's a high degree of expectation that we represent ourselves well. During the most full service, we had a beautiful time of worship, and it was time for me to preach. I went out on the platform to share my message. There were hundreds of people in the service. I was just getting started with a welcome, and I saw that people were already laughing and smiling. I hadn't even said anything yet; I was thinking, 'This is gonna be great service!'

Just then, one of our pastors came out on the platform toward me just as I had begun my opening story. That never happens when I'm preaching. He put his arm around my shoulder, turned me aside, and said, 'Your fly is open!'. There was nowhere to hide! I walked toward the drum set, adjusted my wardrobe malfunction, and continued! HAHA! How embarrassing! Looking back, I wish I had dealt with that privately before being in front of people! At the same time, I'm grateful that my friend had the respect to let me know that something was showing that wasn't right!

In chapter five of the book of Galatians, the Holy Spirit speaks through Paul to let us know that it is possible for something to show that it shouldn't. He says, in a sense, 'your flesh is showing.' He doesn't use those exact words - but that is the idea. This chapter indicates that there are two ways of living. There is the way of the Spirit - and the way of the 'sinful nature,' sometimes translated as 'the flesh.' These words are written because, in our freedom, we have the liberty to respond to the impulses of the flesh or the leading of the Holy Spirit. And the way of the flesh or sinful nature - it gets ugly. The leading of the Holy Spirit leads to the most beautiful human expression possible. It's called the fruit of the Spirit. Consider the simplicity of what is described.

But the Holy Spirit produces this kind of fruit in our lives: love, joy, peace, patience, kindness, goodness, faithfulness, gentleness, and self-control.

GALATIANS 5:22-23 NIV

Some theologians will point out that the word fruit is singular, therefore, there are not nine 'fruits' of the spirit - but one fruit - love - and eight different facets of that love. At the same time, nine specific words are all used with differentiation to describe what it looks like when a person keeps in step with the Spirit. Each of these words conveys an aspect of the kind of character that the Holy Spirit wants to produce in and through our lives.

Fruit grows - but steps are chosen

On the one hand, these are things that naturally grow in and through your life when you are experiencing more of the Holy Spirit. On the other hand, these are also things that the scriptures command or call out for us to engage in as behavior choices elsewhere. Further, the context of Galatians 5:16-23 conveys another metaphor - walking - to describe the closeness with the Holy Spirit that leads to the fruit of the Spirit coming through our lives. Walking involves steps - and steps are chosen.

That means that these nine things can grow in and through our lives. However, we must also choose ways of living and interacting that reflect the Holy Spirit's leading in our daily interactions. These nine things don't tend to happen on autopilot. I have met enough grumpy Christians to know that, and you have, too!

Imagine life with these fruits!

Can you imagine how much better your relationships could be with more fruit of the Holy Spirit? To tease out the scriptural metaphor, fruit is usually the result of deliberate cultivation. A gardener takes pains to prepare the ground, to get rid of destructive pests, to protect the plants, to nourish and water them as they grow, and to harvest the fruit.

Imagine how much better the dynamics would be with friends, husband or wife, kids, parents, and people at work - if you could actively follow the Holy Spirit into intentionally cultivating these nine relational dynamics. Your marriage would be maximized. Your parenting would be more positive. Your friendships would flourish.

You must recognize that the first fruit of the Spirit is love. It does come first for a reason; it is the only word on the list that is also used in the Bible after the expression 'God is': *God is love (1 John 4:8)*. In your Christian faith - love is the core dynamic that sets you apart! In Christ, you have been deeply loved, and now, in Christ, you are called to love deeply!

You are a rifleman

A friend told me he was disappointed that his son, an engineer in the Marines, couldn't be home for a family reunion. He had to requalify on the rifle. I asked, "Wait - I thought you said he was an engineer, so why does he have to qualify on the rifle?". Pat explained the Marine philosophy to me, voiced by General Gray: "Every Marine is, first and foremost, a rifleman. All other conditions are secondary". My friend explained that every year, every marine has to re-qualify as a rifleman. Why? Because it's the core dynamic of who a marine is! A rifleman - ready to deploy into battle! Yes - that marine might be a commandant, cook, engineer, or enlisted man - all are riflemen!

Activation - this is who I am

This activation is one I suggest you put into your daily time with God each morning. I think this one is as important as coffee, and that's hard for me to say! :) Take three deep breaths, and exhale very slowly each time. Sit in God's presence, and imagine you are being held by God so closely you can hear His very heartbeat. As you do, walk through a simple expression of truth:

~ 'Heavenly Father, thank you for loving me. I am safe with You. You love me; Your Spirit empowers me. Thank you!'
~ Declare who you are: 'By faith, I am a Man/Woman of God!'
~ 'I have access to Spiritual gifts, and I am empowered with the gift of XYZ in particular, and I will fulfill my Kingdom assignment by using it.'

...you are a LOVER!

As a follower of Christ - love is the core dynamic of who you are! Yes, you may be a teacher, a construction worker, a sales manager, a business owner, a doctor, a nurse, or a ministry worker - but as a Christian, you are a lover! A lover of God and a lover of people! The Marines force the issue yearly by saying, 'This is the main thing!' each member has to requalify. In some ways, I wish we could do the same as Christians and say, 'I know you have your opinions and preferences about spiritual gifts and the end times, and whatever else, but beyond all that - you are a lover! Time to requalify!'

Maybe we should ask ourselves, "Is my flesh showing? Or is His fruit growing?" For the remainder of this chapter, I'd like to give you some core declarations to make. According to the Word of God, these statements are the truth about who you are. There may be a gap between the full extent of the statement - and how you're living. However, consider these phrases like chat GPT prompts; they can correct and cause what comes next. Say them out loud - almost as though you were informing your old nature that the jig is up - because you know who you *really* are.

These declarations are not magic. You will still need to work on making the choices that align with these sentences. But acknowledging out loud what you aspire to does have a way of recalibrating your trajectory. So read each one out loud, boldly, like a fighter getting up from their corner and back into the ring. 'I've got this! I'm a champion!' they might say to themselves. They're psyching themselves up a bit - because they need to. You and I need to psych ourselves up a bit too! These declarations can help.

I'm growing in the fruit of the Spirit

As I've already noted, the fruits of the Spirit reflect personal choices to live out of the new nature rather than out of the old, rotting flesh. The Holy Spirit has given you a new way to be human, and this approach to life creates a greater radiance of God's image in your life.

You align yourself to *love* and are joined with the One whose *joy* gives you strength. You are walking in and working toward *peace* with people by God's power. You are stepping up your *patience*, even when provoked. You are extending *kindness* and *goodness* instead of selfishness and bitterness. You follow through with *faithfulness,* and you genuinely move in *gentleness*. You keep yourself from foolishness through sober-minded *self-control*. This is true because you are *growing in the fruit of the Spirit*!

I'm keeping in step with the Spirit

In every moment, the Holy Spirit is moving in a direction —and as a filled-to-flow believer, you are paying attention. You know that you choose the direction you move in with actions, reactions, attitudes, consumption, meditation, tone of voice, and even the expression on your face. You are determined to go in the direction the Holy Spirit is moving.

When you choose something out of step with the Spirit, you experience a loss of peace. It is subtle - but it is noticeable. If you've missed the way of the Spirit, ask yourself where you began to lose peace. Go back to that moment and repent. If you need to, make amends with whomever you've hurt - and you'll sync back up with the Spirit for whatever is next. The Spirit of God will never lead you into sin or give in to the flesh, which leads to death and chaos. The leading of the Spirit is so beneficial because - as Romans 8:8 (NIV) says, "The mind governed by the flesh is death, but the mind governed by the Spirit is life and peace"!

So I say, walk by the Spirit, and you will
not gratify the desires of the flesh.

GALATIANS 5:16 NIV

I'm living a holy life

There was a time when the idea of being holy meant becoming a monk or a nun, living in a cloistered community where the temptations of the world were disallowed. And yet, the invitation to be holy is given to every believer, not just those who join a monastery: "But just as he who called you is holy, so be holy in all you do; for it is written: "Be holy because I am holy." (1 Peter 1:15-16, NIV).

The essence of the word 'holy' is to be pure and set apart exclusively for God. The question is, how can this be true about you - without you needing to go and live in a Christian commune? The answer is to respond to the leading of the Holy Spirit so that you have the fruit of self-control. This will empower you to make choices that align with the righteous goodness of God wherever you are. There are some environments where the level of temptation is excessive - and you *should* remove yourself from such places if possible.

When you consider the utter perfection of God, summed up in the word 'holy,' you should tremble. The biblical phrase *the fear of the Lord* expresses the overwhelming awe that results when you consider our Heavenly Father's power, purity, and absolute otherness. His life-giving holiness starkly contrasts this world's messiness, deathliness, and sinfulness. He hates sin because of the damage it does to people. He responds fiercely to it - and awareness of that induces appropriate fear. And yet, the context of this fear is a relationship with God, who has revealed Himself as a good and loving Father. His furious response to sin will be tempered by His fatherly love and mercy for you as His child. The result is that the fear of God leaves you motivated to live a holy life.

Holiness. It's an adventure with God. His light is pouring through you. His power is flowing through you. His love is carrying you. You're advancing His Kingdom and overturning the devil's darkness. You're experiencing otherworldly satisfaction at the very deepest level. And yes - you're turning your back on sin because of both the friendship and the fear that mark your relationship with Jesus. As a filled to flow believer, you are living a holy life!

Now, may the God of peace make you holy in every way, and may your whole spirit, soul, and body be kept blameless until our Lord Jesus Christ comes again.

1 Thessalonians 5:23 NLT

I'm confessing sin and repenting whenever needed

When you've missed the mark of holiness, simply confess your sin, repent, and return to your righteous walk with the Lord. Depending on the severity of the sin, you may need to admit it to a spiritual leader who is over you so that any corrective process that may be required can be carried out. There may be practical consequences due to some sin - and you may not be given a pass on those. Keep the eternal perspective in view. Jesus is coming again - and He desires His Bride, the Church (which you are part of), to be pure and spotless. The only way to be pure and spotless is by either avoiding sin or confessing sin, followed by repentance. That's the pathway to holiness - part of the filled to flow life.

When there is sin in your life that has not been confessed - and there has been no repentance, the sin becomes a spiritual blockage.

The Spirit doesn't flow well through the foulness of rebellion to God's standard. The sin that is willfully, continually chosen creates something like spiritual constipation! That blockage gets dealt with through confession and repentance. Proverbs 28:13 states that when you confess and renounce your sin, you'll find mercy and prosper!

I'm living in integrity

As a child, you probably learned a nursery rhyme about the personified egg who experienced a horrible tragedy. Of course, you know I'm talking about this tragic tale: "Humpty Dumpty sat on a wall, Humpty Dumpty had a great fall," and you know the rest. In the children's book I read, he was portrayed as an egg, and it was over when he fell. A cracked egg couldn't be restored. Thanks be to God; our Heavenly Father *does* know how to restore us when we're broken. By the power of the Holy Spirit, we are far more resilient than an eggshell! However, it is better to avoid cracks in the shell if possible!

For a disciple of Jesus Christ, cracks show up when we make choices in private that are not in alignment with the values of the Kingdom of God as written in the scriptures. Those cracks reveal a lack of integrity. When something has integrity, it is complete and functionally sound for its purpose. As a filled to flow believer, your purpose is to be so alive to the Spirit of God that His presence and power can flow through you to display God's grace and goodness. For that to happen, you've got to be a person of integrity.

Remember that the Holy Spirit is a person. As a person, He can be pleased or displeased by the choices you make. This is why Ephesians 4:30 says, "And do not bring sorrow to God's Holy Spirit by the way you live." You can grieve the Holy Spirit through actions and choices that lack integrity. But you can walk in integrity by lining up your private life with your public life and doing what is right in God's eyes.

I have found that to stay on the path of integrity, I need multiple accountability partners. These are individuals with whom I meet every other week or so to confess any known sin or any current temptations. The practice of regular confession of sin and acknowledgment of the allurement of evil creates a flood of cleansing mercy and makes integrity possible. When you know there are people you will immediately give an account to for what you've chosen, you are more motivated to choose what is right. Get an accountability partner now! It'll help you stay in the flow!

> *Do not let me be disgraced, for in you I take refuge. May*
> *integrity and honesty protect me, for I put my hope in you.*
>
> Psalm 25:20-21 NLT

I'm carrying anointing that comes from intimacy with God

In Matthew 25, Jesus tells the parable of the Ten Bridesmaids. The groom was running late, and the women were waiting for him through the night. The foolish bridesmaids took their lamps out in the dark with no oil. The wise bridesmaids made sure their lamps had plenty of oil. They told the foolish ladies, 'Get your own oil, girls!'. Okay, I'm paraphrasing here. But that is the essence of the story. It's a Kingdom parable. To be ready for the coming of Christ in the end times - and for His appearing at any time, you've got to have your own oil.

The oil symbolizes the presence of the Holy Spirit in a person's life. The anointing of the Spirit of God cannot be fabricated or manufactured. It cannot be copied. And you can't make it through the darkness on someone else's oil - you need your own. The anointing you carry comes from your own closeness with King Jesus.

You are the only one who can cultivate a lifestyle of intimacy with God. When you choose to spend time in God's presence, meditating on God's Word, and singing in the Spirit, your anointing increases.

When you devote yourself to ministering to the Lord through your adoration and praise, praying for an extended period just to be in His presence, and you are filled with awe, you get oily.

So do it! Get oily, my friend, get oily! Let the Word of 1 John 2:27 (NIV) be true of you: "As for you, the anointing you received from him remains in you…" The darkness of this world is severe. But the anointing you carry calls in the light of Jesus. The filled to flow life only works if you're filled - and in this case, filled with the oil of gladness that is Holy Spirit. Maybe the declaration should just be: "I'm oily!"

I'm loving God through my worship

There are so many opportunities in this world for expressing affection. There's the simple act of hitting 'heart' and 'like' on a post. Or you can go to the extremes of fandom, shrieking at the mere sight of a celebrity you obsess over. There is ample opportunity to show your devotion. As a filled to flow believer, you are a *worshipper*. You worship the King of Kings and the Lord of Lords. He's your Savior, Your Shield, your Defender, and the Lord your Shepherd. He is God Almighty, your Heavenly Father. He is Jesus Christ, God incarnate, Friend of sinners. He is the Holy Spirit, the Comforter. God is worthy of Your adoration and affection!

Your spirit within you is refreshed and strengthened by expressing love for God through worship. You can express worship through your financial giving to the ministry of your church and missionaries. You can worship God through your service in ministry. But there is something profound about singing out heartfelt affection directly to the Lord. John 4:24 (NLT) says, "For God is Spirit, so those who worship him must worship in spirit and truth." The word for worship carries the connotation of bowing and kissing the hand of the One you adore and reverence. The Biblical record calls for many forms of expression of this adoration - but the predominant one is in song. So, sing out your worship! When you do this alone, you can express yourself without caring about how your sounds affect or distract anyone else. You can shout, make up new melodies, and sing in tongues in total freedom.

You can worship in song with other believers and experience the mysterious healing wonder of the resonance of many voices coming into accord around the adoration of Christ. When you worship with others, it is generally loving to restrain your volume and sounds so that you don't interrupt the experience of others or cause confusion. But when the leaders call for singing in the Spirit and shouting praise, go for it! Move beyond routine expression - and give God extravagant worship!

I'm going forward with a humble heart

One of the most underrated qualities of beautiful character is *humility*. When you think about it, *pride* is the quality that marks Lucifer's demise. Humility is at the core of the majesty and excellence of Jesus Christ. People who are filled to flow must learn to go low. Flowing in the Spirit is an expression of greater authority; in the Kingdom of God, greater authority must be carried with even greater humility. This is what Jesus modeled, and Philippians 2 details it.

Aren't you grateful for Jesus' humility? Even though he is God - He set aside all His divine privilege just to be able to enter into this world so that you and I could be rescued. Aren't you grateful for the humility of Jesus, that He would leave the glory of eternity and heaven to condescend and stoop down into time and space with us? He came - not as an all-powerful genie of some kind, but as the humble king born in the manger, sent to the Cross, willing to serve you and me by taking all our sin and shame upon himself so we could receive the fullness of His grace.

Jesus is our model, and because we are not God in the flesh, it may require a bit of intentionality to get there. When you choose humility as your inner posture, you have that deep awareness of your room to grow. You have clarity of how dependent on God you are. You have a profound and earnest sense of value for other people. This humble posture creates a sense of hunger inside of you to keep going and growing rather than 'resting on your laurels.' It creates within you a desire to help other people, give value to other people, and do well for other people. It stirs a tenacious desire to grab hold of God and His strength and power because you know you need it. The result is that rather than setting goals and plans and doing them with your own strength, you are attached to the one who created the universe, and *His* strength and power are flowing into and through you!

You're teachable, curious, and open to correction and new discoveries when you go forward with a humble heart. You avoid boasting and welcome feedback about how you're coming across and doing. You value others, and you communicate it, and you resist disparagement. You're quick to serve in whatever capacity the situation requires. Your posture is thankful - and you're actively sharing your authority with others through empowerment. You release offense and forgive easily - because you know how Jesus's mercy has flooded your life.

Humility is having a deep awareness of how much room to grow you have, clarity about how dependant on God you are, a keen sense of value for other people, and a default towards throwing arrogance and pride aside and doing whatever you can to serve others with a glad heart. Humility is the key that unlocks the door to a leveled-up experience of the flow of the Holy Spirit.

> *And he gives grace generously. As the Scriptures say, "God opposes the proud but gives grace to the humble."*
>
> JAMES 4:6 NLT

I'm making peace with people

Imagine two different people coming into a room where a few people are calmly having a nice dinner that includes Brussels sprouts and broccoli. The first person comes in and smells the broccoli and Brussels sprouts. She pulls out an aerosol bullhorn and blasts it, deafening everyone's ears. At the same time, she dramatically pinches her nose and shouts, 'Oh my gaaaawwwd! It smells like absolute garbage in here!'. She walks rapidly around the room with a look of horror, waving her hand in front of her face as if she's warding off a demonic swarm of flies. She then pulls out an aerosol can of air freshener and sprays it in every direction around the room. Finally, she shrieks profanities and slams the door on the way out, on her way to the midweek service at church.

I know what you're thinking. Who walks around with an aerosol can of air freshener in one pocket and a bullhorn can in the other? The person in my story does, that's who! But another person walks into the same room - and he also smells the strong scent in the air. He smiles and gently says, 'What a wonderful dinner, my compliments to the chef!'. He then walks over to the side table and pulls a lovely citrus-scented candle from his left pocket and a lighter from his right pocket. He lights the scented candle and says, 'I'm so glad to see my friends enjoying a healthy meal! Can I clear these plates for you?'. He was on his way to the midweek service at church, but he wanted to connect with these friends before leaving, even though he'd end up being a little late.

The second person was making peace with people. You need to be aware of how you're showing up. You can come on the scene with an attitude, insults, and caustic behaviors, resulting in chaos and strife. Or, you can arrive with a gentle tone, a helpful disposition, and affirmation of what is good; the result will likely be peace. Take my silly 'candles and cans in pockets' story to heart - and be like the second person. Move toward peacemaking in a proactive way!

You've already embraced the revelation that the Fruit of the Holy Spirit is required for the purest flow of the Holy Spirit. Peace is one of the fruits of the Spirit that calls for determined action on your part. Jesus said peacemakers are blessed, and He indicated that peacemaking reveals who you are as a child of God (Matthew 5:9). Conflict and chaos occur in relationships due to wrongs that have been done. Reconciliation can happen when wrong is acknowledged, when apologies are made, and when grace is extended.

If you want to experience more of the flow of the Spirit - go low. If there is a relationship that is broken, consider whether there is something you've done that has created the disconnect. For some of us, our first thought about a relational problem centers on 'what they did.' If that's happening for you, press past that. Reframe the disharmony with a question about how you contributed to the problem or did wrong by the other person. Release your desire for vindication or their acceptance of fault. Go in the Spirit, and offer a sincere apology if the context makes it safe and reasonable to do so. You may find that your attempt to make peace brings peace to you - whether they receive it well or not. You'll know you did what the Word of God calls for. This is who you are - you are a filled to flow believer who is making peace with people!

If it is possible, as far as it depends on you, live at peace with everyone.

ROMANS 12:18 NIV

I'm seeing with childlike wonder

You've heard the expression, 'Everything I need to know, I learned in Kindergarten!' I can't vouch for the veracity of that statement. But I *can* attest that we begin to think in concrete operational terms soon after kindergarten, and after that, we learn to think analytically. It's an excellent and necessary skill - we often grow so much in this area that it almost extinguishes the fire of imagination.

As a child, you had a God-given ability to daydream. You thought of what was possible and fantasized about unknown realms and superhuman experiences - and it was easy. You stood on a coffee table with an outstretched arm and were the captain of a ship being tossed on the seas! (wasn't that fun? Don't you miss those days?) As you age, you learn how unreasonable that was and stop doing it. After all, it wasn't productive or useful. In a way, the color left your inner vision. It's time to rescue it back!

You'll need to exercise faith to live this filled to flow life. Your faith is the ability to perceive the possibilities and believe in God's power to bring it about. You may need to undo some default patterns of thought that indicate why something cannot happen. You may need to put on some new lenses - the lenses of childlike wonder.

As obstacles and challenges emerge, allow yourself to ask this question: "I wonder how God will come through?" and "I wonder whether God will come through this way or another way altogether!" Consider this question: "I wonder whether I could imagine five or six different ways forward, no matter how unreasonable they are?" If you begin to look at things with this thought process, *you may start seeing things.* Yes - you may start seeing things! You may start seeing the things that are supernaturally possible, that are available in the realm of God's kingdom, and that there is potential simply because the power of God is at hand and the Spirit of God is flowing!

But Jesus said, "Let the children come to me. Don't stop them! For the Kingdom of Heaven belongs to those who are like these children."

MATTHEW 19:14 NLT

I'm running bold for God's glory!

Fear can serve a purpose; it's an alert that danger could occur. Fear is meant to be metabolized and converted into awareness or action. Fear becomes a problem when we allow ourselves to be paralyzed by it. That happens for some of us because of the past pain we've lived through. The horrible experiences we've been through have left a mark. We equate movement toward the difficult thing with pain, and something inside us resists movement. We're stuck - and unfortunately, our companion where we are stuck is the threatening, menacing, condescending, and constricting spirit of fear.

By now, you know that such a spirit is not from God. You know the truth: "For God has not given us a spirit of fear and timidity, but of power, love, and self-discipline" (2 Timothy 1:7 NLT). You might have gotten used to being timid, but that doesn't mean it's right for you. You may be familiar with feeling afraid and paralyzed - but that doesn't mean you have to stay that way. God designed you to move with Godspeed in this life! There is a uniqueness to the design of God over your life that is intended to display the momentum of the Kingdom of God. So run! Run boldly in this life for God's glory!

When I called, you answered me; you greatly emboldened me.

PSALM 138:3 NIV

The grace of the Lord Jesus Christ, and the love of God, and the fellowship of the Holy Spirit, be with you all.

2 CORINTHIANS 13:14 NIV

I'm filled and flowing in the Spirit! I am filled to flow!

God established the Church of Jesus Christ to make disciples. As a disciple of Jesus, you are ultimately commissioned to carry the good news of the Kingdom of God to others however you can. But here's the thing. Sometimes, the church can function like some kind of spiritual holding tank. With honor for the bride of Christ, don't let that happen to you! Serve within the Body of Christ in the flow.

Stagnation is real. Life can sometimes become brutal and challenging. Our congregation's leaders do not always support spiritual development as they should. The environment can sometimes be so stifling that stepping back and watching other people's TikTok and Instagram reels about flowing in the Spirit is easier than stepping into the flow yourself.

Remember the Disneyland analogy. No one would make all the effort and spend all the money to get inside Disneyland just to hang out by the gate. There could indeed be some risks - but that was the point of going to Disneyland! Stepping fully into this filled to flow life is risky. You could pray for healing, and it might not happen, and that could be disappointing. Yes, people might have to wait for some supernatural breakthrough; yes, people could begin to exercise spiritual gifts and mess it up. Yes, people might experience the Spirit of God moving in a way that is beyond the ordinary, and it might shake them up.

But, like going to Disneyland, the point is to experience the Kingdom, not to stand around and admire the flowers just inside the gate! The purpose of coming to Disneyland is to go on Space Mountain or ride the Big Thunder Mountain Railroad - or at least walk around the whole park beyond the wanna-be-paid paparazzi by the gate taking pictures! To fully enjoy the Filled To Flow life, you cannot wait for someone to create the opportunity to flow for you. You need to pay attention to the leading of the Holy Spirit, remember all that you have learned in this book, and take a risk!

You are filled with the Spirit so the Spirit can flow through you to a waiting world. Don't settle for being filled to dam capacity. I mean the structure that stops the flow of water, of course. And you have the living water of Jesus Christ Himself rising up within you! Don't settle for being filled to stagnate. Don't settle for being filled to puddle up. So break open the dam, and let the river flow! Someone needs the touch of Jesus today - and it might just need to come through you - so go for it! You are filled to flow!

Activation - Declaration of Flowdependence

Read through the declarations above. Say each one out loud as a reminder of the truth about who you are in and through Jesus Christ!

1- I'm growing in the fruit of the Spirit
2- I'm keeping in step with the Spirit
3- I'm living a holy life
4- I'm confessing sin and repenting whenever needed
5- I'm living in integrity
6- I'm carrying anointing that comes from intimacy with God
7- I'm loving God through my worship
8- I'm going forward with a humble heart
9- I'm making peace with people
10- I'm seeing with childlike wonder
11- I'm running bold for God's glory
12- I'm filled and flowing in the Spirit- I am filled to flow!

FILLED TO FLOW
BIBLE STUDY SMALL GROUP GUIDE

Chapter Eight:
Kingdom Character:
Who Are You With All That Flow?

You're filled to flow in the fruit of the Holy Spirit!

If you're filled with the Spirit, the flesh gets drowned out, and the fruit of the Spirit grows! This message is about cultivating a life where the fruit of the Spirit grows and becomes more evident in and through your choices!

Bible study group guide how-to summary:

▱ Means it's a Bible study reflection question. It's okay if just 1-2 people answer. It's okay to move through it quickly or even to skip. It also means there may not be time to include the reading of this scripture or the discussion of the question with the whole group. But consider these sections in your own study!

≈ means this is a group interaction reflection question. It would be good to ask several people from the group to respond. It also means that the scripture associated with this question should be read aloud with the group.

Engage:

1. ≈ Icebreaker: Share a simple high note from your personal life from the last week.
2. ≈ Discuss any highlights from the chapter. Share an example of a person you know who has great godly character.

≈ Read Galatians 5:22-23 NIV

But the Holy Spirit produces this kind of fruit in our lives: love, joy, peace, patience, kindness, goodness, faithfulness, gentleness, and self-control.

Engage:

3. ▱ Which fruit of the Spirit comes most easily to you?

4. ▱ Which fruit of the Spirit is more challenging for you?

5. ≈ Pick one of the Kingdom character traits (fruits of the Spirit) you feel you're doing well with; describe how it shows up in your life.

▱ Read Galatians 5:16 NIV

So I say, walk by the Spirit, and you will not gratify the desires of the flesh.

Engage:

6. What things help you continue walking by the Spirit?

7. What things tend to throw you out of step with the Holy Spirit?

≈ Read Romans 8:13-14 NIV

For if you live according to the flesh, you will die; but if by the Spirit you put to death the misdeeds of the body, you will live. Those who are led by the Spirit of God are the children of God.

8. ☐ What are some examples of misdeeds of the body that need to be put to death?

9. ≈ Share about an element of the flesh you have put to death in your life - and why that victory is essential for your Kingdom calling.

≈ Read Ephesians 4:30 NLT

And do not bring sorrow to God's Holy Spirit by the way you live. Remember, he has identified you as his own, guaranteeing that you will be saved on the day of redemption.

Engage:

10. ☐ Why would the Holy Spirit experience sorrow about your life choices?

11. ≈ Share about any in which you have made choices in your life that brought sorrow to the Holy Spirit

☐ Read 1 Thessalonians 5:23 NLT

Now may the God of peace make you holy in every way, and may your whole spirit and soul and body be kept blameless until our Lord Jesus Christ comes again.

≈ Read Psalm 29:20-21 NLT

Do not let me be disgraced, for in you I take refuge. May integrity and honesty protect me, for I put my hope in you.

Engage:

12. ≈. What has helped you to live the life of integrity God desires?

≈ Read Psalm 51:10-12 NLT

Create in me a clean heart, O God. Renew a loyal spirit within me.
Do not banish me from your presence, and don't take your Holy
Spirit[a] from me. Restore to me the joy of your salvation, and
make me willing to obey you.

Engage:

13. ⊐ What is the value of the purity of the Spirit of God?

14. ⊐ How does the holiness of God's Spirit affect us?

15. ≈ What heart changes do you need so that your character is
    more aligned with the character of Holy Spirit?

⊐ Read 1 Peter 1:13-16 NLT

So prepare your minds for action and exercise self-control. Put all
your hope in the gracious salvation that will come to you when
Jesus Christ is revealed to the world. So, you must live as God's
obedient children. Don't slip back into your old ways of living to
satisfy your own desires. You didn't know any better then. But now
you must be holy in everything you do, just as God who chose you
is holy. For the Scriptures say, "You must be holy because I am
holy."

Engage:

16. ⊐ What kinds of things come to mind when you think of
    holiness? What does holy actually mean?
17. ⊐ What does the revelation of God's holiness call you to?
18. ⊐ How could holiness be a life-giving adventure for your life?

⊐ Read Proverbs 28:13 NIV

Whoever conceals their sins does not prosper, but the one who confesses and renounces them finds mercy.

≈ Read Acts 3:19-20 NLT

Now repent of your sins and turn to God so that your sins may be wiped away. Then, times of refreshment will come from the presence of the Lord, and he will again send you Jesus, your appointed Messiah.

⊐ Read Revelation 3:19

Those whom I love, I rebuke and discipline. So be earnest and repent.

Engage:

19.≈. How does repentance help you cultivate Kingdom character
   - and is there anything you need to repent?

⊐ Read John 4:24 NLT

For God is Spirit, so those who worship him must worship in spirit and in truth."

≈ Read Ephesians 5:18-20 NLT

Don't be drunk with wine, because that will ruin your life. Instead, be filled with the Holy Spirit, singing psalms and hymns and spiritual songs among yourselves and making music to the Lord in your hearts. And give thanks for everything to God the Father in the name of our Lord Jesus Christ.

Engage:

20.≈ Share your favorite worship song and how it helps you keep in step with or experience more filling of the Spirit.

Pray≈:

~ for more significant growth of the fruits of the Spirit in each other's lives
~ for increased quality of one specific fruit where there's been a challenge
~ for more integrity and holiness in the group members
~ for whatever other needs there may be

Epilogue

Wow, what a journey! You've completed the FILLED TO FLOW book experience. What now? Now, continue growing in your filled to flow life!

I invite you to join my community by following me on Instagram and other locations:

@john.v.hansen

@filledtoflow

Find my latest teaching messages at Centerpoint Church:

www.mycenterpoint.tv

https://www.youtube.com/@CenterpointChurchMurrieta

Find my personal updates here:

www.johnhansen.tv

Find FILLED TO FLOW merch and updates here:

www.filledtoflow.com

Find out more about upcoming books here:

www.growflowsow.com

Please leave me a review.

One more thing: I would greatly appreciate it if you would leave a review for my book on Amazon. Your input will help others determine whether this book could help them and help me as I write other books in the future.

https://www.amazon.com/author/johnvhansen

Thank you for joining me on this journey and trusting me to guide you. I hope we can encourage each other to live boldly in this life with the Holy Spirit… We are FILLED TO FLOW!

FILLED TO FLOW

NOW, GO LIVE OUT THE SPIRIT-FILLED LIFE!

Made in the USA
Monee, IL
30 March 2025

14650736R00167